NEVER PASS THIS WAY AGAIN

NEVER PASS THIS WAY AGAIN

Gene LePere

ADLER&ADLER

Published in the United States in 1987 by
Adler & Adler, Publishers, Inc.
4550 Montgomery Avenue
Bethesda, Maryland 20814

Library of Congress Cataloging-in-Publication Data
LePere, Gene, 1926-
    Never pass this way again.
    1. LePere, Gene, 1926-   . 2. Women prisoners—
Turkey—Biography. 3. Americans—Turkey—Biography.
4. Smuggling—Turkey. I. Title.
HV9776.7.A34L42 1987   365'.43'0924 [B]   86-28713
ISBN 0-917561-38-4

Printed in the United States of America
First Edition

PROLOGUE

The events in this book are real. They happened to me. I have tried to report them with as much honesty as I can summon and to relate them in a way that makes the reader feel the shocks and fears, insofar as possible, as I, myself, experienced them.

Although incarceration in a Middle-Eastern prison is fraught with physical peril, the apparent threats and dangers that give drama to these events were for me not so much physical as they were emotional: shock, bewilderment, fear of the unknown, isolation, alienation, and the anxiety of defying the imposed will of a repressive government.

Luck plays a great part in all our lives. In this drama I reaped my share of bad as well as good luck. But in the final analysis, I believe I was more the beneficiary of good luck than bad. I had the good fortune to find a Turkish attorney who was trustworthy, competent, caring, and kind, and to receive the assistance of compassionate strangers—Turks, Americans, and British—people who came forward with generous support, sometimes at personal risk, demonstrating what I have always hoped was true: that humanity knows no national boundaries or political ties.

A significant feature of this experience, one that gave it drama and added to my trauma, was "culture clash." This incident could not have happened in the United States to a U.S. citizen, nor in Turkey to a Turk. I was shocked by the events related in this book because nothing in my life had prepared me for them. But although Turkey, as a result of its unique history, has evolved a value system, laws, customs, and traditions dif-

v

ferent from the United States, one cannot judge the country and its people harshly.

The American way is familiar, comfortable, predictable to its citizens. The Turkish way, to a foreigner, is strange and full of both pleasant and ugly surprises. The moral of the story is the need to recognize the real differences that exist and for any traveler to acquaint himself with the laws and customs of the country he is about to enter.

Only after my return home did I begin to appreciate fully the difficulties faced by my family in attempting to secure my freedom. There is no recipe for the rescue of American citizens from legal entanglements abroad, and thousands of traveling Americans every year experience minor or serious confrontations with foreign laws. Their families struggle in anguish, as mine did, with little direction from the U.S. State Department, who must limit its assistance to the monitoring of human rights issues and the courteous two-way transmittal of information. For this reason I offer the name of an organization called the International Legal Defense Counsel. Based in Philadelphia, this small and experienced group of attorneys provides legal assistance to Americans abroad. It is an important resource for families confronted with problems like mine. I wish we had known of it before I left for Turkey.

Last, nothing in this book should be perceived as an indictment against Turkey or the Turkish people. Within the context of their laws, I was treated fairly and with respect. Within the context of their culture, I was given every chance to be myself. Among my own sex I found true compassion and friendship. I am deeply indebted to these women, especially the Turks, whom I will never forget.

PART I

I awakened in the night, anxious and uncertain of where I was. Four exposed bulbs, each a miniature noose hanging from a twelve-foot ceiling at the end of an eight-inch bare wire, bathed the room in a dull, eerie light. From the cot in the corner where I lay, I could hear the pulsing hush hush of night breathing and, raising myself to an elbow, saw the rounded shapes that could only be women, women asleep in the room around me.

Was it night? Where was I? Why were the lights burning?

Instantly alert, as only the very anxious can be, I glanced at my watch. Two-thirty, it read, and told me little. A long wall in front of me, lined by great oversized windows that framed the black sky beyond, confirmed the hour. It was night.

Who sleeps with the lights on? Where was I?

Then, in a rush of memory I recalled the events of the past three days. In horror I knew where I was.

I was in prison. In a prison somewhere in Izmir. Or outside Izmir. A prison, in any case, in Turkey.

I, in a Turkish prison? How was such a thing possible? How could it have come about? How could being here be real?

It couldn't be real. It was a hallucination. The product of a vivid imagination.

But it was real. I was here. And I could barely comprehend the fact of it.

Burrowing back under the covers of my strange bed, in an agony of frustration, fear, and bewilderment, in utter disbelief,

I allowed memory to take me back, allowed myself to relive the unbelievable from the beginning.

The beginning. Was the beginning in Turkey? Or in New York?

It was Thursday, August 25, 1983, when my ex-husband, Jim LePere, drove me and five pieces of luggage to Kennedy Airport where I boarded a TWA flight to London, arriving the next morning at eight. Some thirty hours hence I would embark on a six-week Mediterranean cruise.

After a fast check-in at a convenient hotel, unwilling to miss a single adventerous hour in that marvelous city, without sleep I walked around London by myself, getting blisters on my feet, seeing the sights, investigating small shops, and, after making the first of my Christmas purchases, lunching at Harrods.

Saturday I boarded the ship, the *Sea Princess*, at Southampton. I'd never been on so ambitious a cruise before.

Twice in the past, each time for two weeks, I'd gone to the Caribbean—traveling alone. Cruising was a method of travel I reserved for times when I was very tired. In this instance, I'd been working very hard and hadn't taken a real vacation in twelve years. What could be better, I thought, than to visit a dozen countries without catching a single plane or checking in and out of rooms?

The convenience of my floating hotel far outweighed, for me, any restrictions of travel. I had been content being cossetted by the personable, efficient staff of the Peninsular and Orient Line aboard their beautifully appointed and well-managed luxury liner.

And now, Wednesday, September 28, nearly a week into the third of three two-week Mediterranean cruises, we were lying off the small Anatolian port of Alanya, where I and a small group of passengers were soon to board a bus for a three-day overland tour of archeological sites and museums.

I was very excited about going in spite of the additional cost of £135 ($202 American), the inconvenience of bus travel and the anticipation of questionable accommodations. It surprised me that this unusual opportunity had attracted only 22 of the 750 passengers aboard.

I hurried through my morning dressing to rush topside to

the open deck of the promenade. I wanted a panorama preview of the tantalizing shore.

What country in the world evokes images as exotic as Turkey?

Sultans and harems, Topkapi and fabulous jewels, the Golden Horn and the Bosporus by moonlight. The minarets of Santa Sophia silhouetted against a darkening Istanbul sky. Fierce, olive-skinned men with glittering eyes and bushy, bristling mustaches. Scimitars and sloe-eyed women, whose veils and voluminous clothing cloak them in mystery, shapeless yet more seductive than their fully revealed European sisters.

I believed I had a closer acquaintance with Turkey than most of the passengers on board, since I'd been there twice in the past. Once in 1955, on a wedding trip with my first husband, again in 1972 with my second, Jim. Each time I had flown in, staying about three days, and flown out baffled by the language and customs, charmed by the exotic sights, sounds, and smells of this uniquely alien land.

On deck, I stood silently near the stern of the ship, staring at the landfall more than a mile away. Shielding my eyes from the bright, early morning sun that danced off the undulating waters of the Mediterranean, I squinted at the city beyond, strangely medieval and inviting, rust-red, and, in the dim distance, cloaked in a patina of romance.

So, this is Alanya, I thought, this colorful stone fortress against the blue-green water's edge, rising from the twelfth century like a movie set. Why not? This is Turkey. It's supposed to be make-believe.

The sea was calm.

Lifting my small disk camera to eye level, I snapped three contiguous shots of the shoreline.

The ship glided closer to shore. Leaning against the teakwood rail, I felt the heat rising from the polished wood, warmed by the morning sun.

I glanced at my watch. Seven fifteen. The captain is right on time, I noted, anchors will probably drop precisely at 7:30, as the schedule advertised. I'd better get below if I'm to have breakfast and be ready for an 8:30 launch.

Reluctantly I turned away, walked swiftly across the wooden, outside deck, down an outside staircase, and ducked into the rear door of the veranda deck a few steps from my cabin. Into the fifth week aboard, I now knew every shortcut of the *Sea Princess*.

Before publication of Billy Hayes's *Midnight Express*, most Americans, I suggest, viewed a trip to Turkey as an opportunity to step into a living fairy tale: Aladdin's Lamp was lurking deep inside the Grand Bazaar. All you had to do was locate it and the genie was yours.

Despite Billy Hayes's horrible experience in a Turkish prison, publicized in book and film, middle-class traveling Americans continue to view Turkey in the same storybook way. Only drug-seeking youngsters encounter trouble with Turkish authorities. We, the hard-working, middle-aged, respectable tourists, feel no identification with these hapless souls. Our attitude has ever been, "It's their own fault."

Yes, a trip into Turkey still held an illusion of adventure, a hint of danger, the promise of romance—all under the protection of an American passport.

Not wanting to carry my camera to the table, as I was passing the door anyway, I dashed momentarily into my cabin.

My one suitcase for the overland tour, following instructions, had been left outside the cabin last evening and removed sometime during the night, since the corridor was clear this morning. However, overnight items—toiletries and makeup—were to be carried in hand luggage. For this purpose I had selected a cloth tote, a gift from my sister Robin. It was partially packed and lying on the daybed. In a hurry, I laid the camera beside it and checked my hair in the mirror over the desk/dresser as I headed for the door. Every frosted hair in place, I hastily left for a quick breakfast.

The *Sea Princess*, under British registry, was actually the old *Kungsholm*. When P&O bought it from the Swedes, they wisely left most of the elegant, tasteful decoration and furnishings intact. It was a beautiful ship, well-built, comfortable, and maintained in exquisite condition.

There was only one dining room. In the midsection of the main deck, its location maximized comfort even in rough weather, and it was sufficiently large to be able to serve eight hundred diners in two sittings.

Because I was the only passenger aboard booked for three consecutive cruises, the officers knew me and my dining room assignment had been the captain's table since the start of the third week. It was an oval table, which seated eight people and dominated the center of the room. Neither the captain, who appeared only for dinner at the second seating, nor his steward, was present when I hustled in that morning. The waiter who greeted me took care of passengers assigned to this table at the first seating. I thought he was not nearly as good as our waiter.

"Good morning, Madam," he greeted me, politely, pulling out a chair.

Good morning," I replied, nodding to the three people already seated at the table. Since I didn't know any of them, I assumed they, like the steward, belonged to an earlier shipboard life than the one to which I was accustomed. One, a withered woman with gnarled fingers, was knifing hot kippers onto the back of her fork. The smell of the fish carried unpleasantly across the table.

I'm a good eater. Too good. I come by it honestly. No member of my family seems to have fully mastered the art of weight control. I'd come aboard with a wardrobe of sixes and eights. After four and a half weeks, size tens would have felt more comfortable. Determined at this point to take myself in hand lest I be forced to walk naked off the ship when the cruise ended in Venice, I held back as I gave my order to the waiter.

"Melon, one boiled egg, coffee," I said firmly.

"Yes, madam. Rolls?" He worked against me, rolling the "r" as his Goan accent dictated.

"No rolls. No bread. Thank you."

When he was gone, I looked to the others at the table: the over-dressed couple at my left, whom I judged to be married because they were sitting together and too old to be living in sin, and across from me the single lady eating kippers.

I hadn't expected to see anyone this morning with whom I'd become friendly. I had made my farewells last night. How many people, after all, could anyone say she was close to, four days into a new cruise? There were Hugh and Robby Dundas, a genteel, British couple whom I'd met as my new dining companions at this very table the first night out of Athens, and Connie Cooke, also British, who also had been on the second cruise. Last night after dinner, the Dundases expressed their regret that I would be away for two nights, and I promised to rejoin them on Friday.

My connection to Connie Cooke was something different. We had met about ten days before, and since both of us were traveling alone, we'd adopted the habit of meeting in the bar before dinner. I don't enjoy alcohol, so I had low-cal sodas while Connie sipped gin and tonics and we made "women talk." Given any other situation, we would not have become friends; our nationalities, backgrounds, education, and interests gave us little in common. It was a shipboard friendship of convenience.

Connie and I had said our good-byes last night, and I guessed she was still asleep while I was with the uncommunicative trio. I preferred not to eat in silence.

"Are any of you going on a tour of Alanya today?" I asked. The husband looked up from spreading marmalade on a piece of dry-looking toast.

"Morning tour," he nodded to his left, "The missus and me."

Kippers placed her knife and fork neatly on the side of the plate, wiped the corners of her mouth with a linen napkin, and addressed the waiter in a deep, gin-mellowed voice as he bent forward pouring coffee into my cup.

"I'll have my tea now," she said, imperiously. And to me, "I wouldn't set foot into that barbarian countryside at any price. I don't know why anyone else would either. I shall probably go ashore in Izmir, a reasonably civilized town, mainly to see Ephesus. After all, one cannot come all this way and not take advantage of the chance to have a look at the most impressive Greco-Roman ruin anywhere on earth." She paused, as the waiter set a cup and teapot before her.

"These Turks are positively Byzantine," she continued, "Take Istanbul, cosmopolitan even under the sultans, with its Hilton Hotel and modern plumbing. Don't let that façade fool you. It's only skin deep. They are still living in the seventh century." She poured tea, added sugar and cream, and stirred.

"Down here in southeastern Turkey, it's only half civilized. Of course, one can't compare it to eastern Turkey, which hasn't changed in a thousand years. No, Atatürk's dream of a modern, Western democracy hasn't quite been fulfilled. Perhaps it never will be."

I was not as astonished as once I would have been, by the length, quality, and force of Kippers' speech. I'd come to understand the educated English are not only better informed than Americans, they are also more biased.

"I'm impressed with your knowledge of Turkey," I told her sincerely. "I wish we'd met before. I'm leaving on the overland bus tour in a little while. I'm not really well prepared."

"That's what the guide's for," Husband volunteered.

"Guides'll never tell you what you need to know," Kippers said. "Guides, no matter the country, will tell you what they want you to know and want you to believe. That's hardly the same thing as the truth, you know."

As the waiter brought my egg, Husband stood.

"We'll be goin' now, folks." He nodded, without making eye contact, in the general direction of Kippers and me and addressed his timid wife. "Let's go, Gladys, if you want to get a seat in the front of the bus." With that, he turned and left.

Obediently, Gladys placed her napkin on the table, stood, hesitated, gave a tentative smile, and followed her husband from the room.

With them gone, I wanted to get Kippers back on the subject of Turkey. But, looking at my watch, I realized there was no more time.

"It was really nice meeting you," I said. "I shall keep in mind everything you said." She smiled.

"I said very little that will be useful, I'm afraid, and you mustn't let me spoil your trip. Enjoy every moment. Actually, I envy your going. It's too arduous a journey for me, I'm afraid. Do look me up when you return. I'll be interested to hear about it."

There were the gracious, good manners of the British, I thought. First the opinions, boldly expressed. Then, humble self-effacement.

"Thank you. I'll do that," I promised. "And have a marvelous time at Ephesus. I'll be there Friday, too. Maybe we'll run into each other."

So saying, I left the table. As I swiftly made for the exit, I heard Kippers call after me, "Don't drink the water and no raw fruit." Smiling and nodding, I passed through the doors of the dining room into the hallway.

At that point I was on A deck: two decks below the veranda and my cabin, three below the promenade where I was to meet the overland party.

I turned toward the stairway only to find the area filled with uniformed soldiers—Turkish soldiers, I presumed. It gave me quite a start to see them milling about.

There were a lot of them, heavily armed with automatic rifles and black, long-nozzled, evil-looking hand guns strapped into polished brown leather holsters.

I looked at the faces of the soldiers. They were kids. About high school age, I thought.

Bewildered, I searched for a crisp white uniform to tell me a ship's officer was on duty and in charge, but the mass of milling khaki bodies formed a formidable screen.

The scene seemed ominous. So large a presence of heavily armed, unsmiling soldiers gave one the feeling the ship had been taken over. The mood of happy tourism was, for the moment, spoiled. I was offended. Was I, a tourist, unwanted in this country? Instead of being welcomed as a guest who would benefit the Turks' economy, I had the strong sense the ship and its passengers were under some unknown suspicion and that thought raised doubts about the journey ahead.

But I brushed the notion aside, remembering I was traveling under the aegis of a British company, protected by its tour guides, my American passport, and my own innocence. I had no hidden agenda.

Back in my room, I made last minute repairs to my makeup and took care of some other necessities. After making sure I had taken everything I'd need for three days, I said a silent and sad good-bye to the tiny space that had been my home for more than thirty days. With sudden clarity I became aware that when I got back, the cabin and I would be facing our final week together.

Part of me was more than ready to go home, to get back into the rhythm of satisfying work. Five years before, I had left corporate employment for private consulting. My MBA was in management and I had work experience in marketing, so I was able to use both disciplines. The first few years were a struggle. More than once I thought I'd have to go back to paid employment, but 1983 was a good year. The business was taking hold.

My future work seemed assured. A week after I got home, I would start a four-day-a-week consultation for a small New York City personnel-management firm that was experiencing the typical growing pains of success. My assignment was virtually to restructure every aspect of the company. I was excited and challenged to begin working with the principals, whom I knew and liked.

My work week would be filled with an assignment to complete a project already begun for a publisher whose offices were driving distance from my home in Westchester, New York, where I'd been living for the past ten years.

I realized there was probably more work than I could do in a five-day week, but I had no objection to working Saturdays, Sundays, or evenings, when I got infected with the excitement of solving problems.

This was what urged me home. But would I be less than human if I admitted I was experiencing some conflict? By this time I was pretty well spoiled by what was a truly delightful, very luxurious, and marvelously irresponsible shipboard life. The truth is, I like seven-course meals, eternal sunshine, and being waited on. God, it was nice. Nothing like home, where I carried out the garbage and paid bills. Aboard the ship it was easy to forget I had paid for all this attention and to feel very privileged.

I was very privileged. And I knew it.

With hand luggage and purse in hand, I joined a waiting group of passengers in the designated public room on the promenade deck, looking about, hoping to see someone I'd met before. But I didn't recognize a single face and wondered how it was possible to be locked aboard with only 750 people and, in four days, never have seen any of these 22: not in the dining room, not on either the Haifa to Jerusalem tour or the morning in Alexandria, not at the evening entertainment, nor in the casino or sunning on deck. Amazing!

It was obvious as we all stood waiting that everyone felt awkward, but I sensed that, given a bit of luck, by the time we reached Izmir, we would become a cohesive group with a shared history.

The wait was longer than expected. Instead of bussing off at 9:00 A.M. as was expected, it was nearly 9:00 before we were called to leave the lounge after Mr. Jackson showed up.

Jackson, a quiet, conservative, sixtyish Englishman, was the ship's shore excursion lecturer. He and his wife had been traveling on P&O ships for twenty years, amassing a huge collection of color slides of every conceivable port and every imaginable tourist site on every possible P&O route. The Jacksons, the day before the ship arrived in each port, conjointly put on a smoothly performed dog and pony show.

Mrs. Jackson showed slides to the accompaniment of Mr. Jackson's highly articulate narrative. He offered facts as impressively detailed as the number and location of the buses in Piraeus, in which you could make your way into Athens like a native. That he was reliably accurate, I can attest, since I did exactly as he said, paid the ten drachmas as he'd instructed, and a half hour later found myself in Constitution Square, as he'd promised.

Jackson, for the next three days, was the advance scout for P&O, accompanying the passengers to assure an objective, yet experienced, opinion of the tour.

Once he showed up things got cracking. After delivering an apology for the unfortunate delay, Jackson and a ship's officer led us from the lounge (carrying the hand luggage and cameras) down the stairs to the main deck where the portside door was open and the gangway to the launch in place. The soldiers were still in evidence, only their numbers had thinned.

As we neared the exit portal, the soldiers agressively blocked our way. They would not permit us to leave. Already tired and frustrated, there was some grumbling among the passengers, who were, most certainly, not accustomed to being treated this way. The ship's officers asked us to step back a moment, complying with the Turks' wishes. It seemed odd to have the P&O authorities submit to what appeared to be merely a whim of schoolboys. But after another five-minute wait, all crowded together in the narrow hallway, we were finally allowed to leave the ship.

There were no further delays or unpleasantness. The launch ride to shore was swift and only slightly choppy. At the dock there were seamen waiting to help us ashore. Everything seemed entirely normal.

No explanation was asked or given for the blockade on A deck.

Our luggage was already stowed in the compartment beneath the modern, air-conditioned tour coach that was parked and waiting on the quay with its motor running. Mr. Jackson helped us board—the step from the ground to the bus was abnormally high—then took a seat in the rear. When at last the doors closed and the driver shifted gears, I joined in the collective and audible sigh of relief. We were off, at last.

Only then, with the bus in motion, did the guide step forward, take a mike, and introduce herself. First impressions count. She was dressed in a gray cotton, A-line skirt that was a bit too tight and a white, Dacron short-sleeved blouse.

I remember precisely her opening remarks.

"At last, we are on our way. It is too bad we make a late start, for there is much for us to see today. My name is Sylvia Franco. I am a Turk and I am your guide for the next three days."

I liked her immediately and admired her accented but excellent English. She was a take-charge lady, and had anyone asked, I'd have said she was Jewish: interchangeable in appearance and manner with any number of forty-five-year-old American Jewish women, she seemed familiar to me.

In time Sylvia confirmed my guess as to her heritage. A descendant of Jews who fled Spain during the thirteenth-century Inquisition, Sylvia's family, together with hundreds of other outcasts, found sanctuary in Turkey. Her family, even now, practiced a form of Judaism hardly different from that of her thirteenth-century forebears. But in matters of education, these Jews were less traditional. Their children were sent off to Israel and to the United States for college and advanced degrees.

After introducing Mehmet, the Turkish driver, she assured us the roads were safe, the bus reliable, and Mehmet a paragon of artful experience. No one believed a word, certainly not I. It would have been better to have said nothing. All she had managed was to introduce doubt where none had been before. This gave me my first insight into the enormity of the Turks' inferiority complex, as well as their standard technique for covering it up.

Kippers had been right about this area of Turkey. It was southeastern and called Anatolia. (You may be sure Sylvia didn't say they were only half-civilized.) Our route was arduous, although that bit of intelligence was kept from us the same way the doctor doesn't tell you that the prescribed treatment is going to hurt like hell. It was chosen for two major reasons: there was a predominance of ruined ancient cities here and there were roads that led to them.

Before noon, we had traveled no more than thirty miles after stops for walking tours of three major sites: Seedeh (Side),* with its Roman aqueduct and agora marked by fallen columns; Aspendos, a ruined theater and coliseum; and Antalya, where Sylvia literally ran us through a modern museum housing salvaged Roman and Greek statues. This first day was proving to be a marathon.

The sheer volume and numbers of antiquities began to dull the sense of wonder. I couldn't keep the sites sorted out in my mind. The next stop, not too soon for me, was for "comfort."

The bus pulled onto a wide, paved area in front of a good-sized, modern building that proved to be a well-appointed diner-type restaurant. Under Sylvia's leadership, and with no urging, twenty-two English-speaking tourists tumbled out of that bus into the blazing, dry, midday heat.

We entered a small lobby, wide but shallow. Inside, the temperature was comfortable, and in front of a counter was set a tray of glasses containing a pale, cloudy fluid. Sylvia invited us to quench our thirst, but only a few brave (or very thirsty) souls accepted. I thought it safer first to use the restrooms; then, if no one died from drinking the stuff, I'd try some. It didn't look very refreshing: the plain glass was full of smudges and empty of ice.

Restrooms was correct. There were two.

I followed several women into the tiny anteroom where others already waited. Both stalls were in use. When one of the two doors opened and one of the Englishwomen came out, someone moved quickly to take her place.

"I should warn you," the Englishwoman said to the waiting

---

*For the convenience of the reader, difficult Turkish names are spelled phonetically. The correct Turkish spelling is given in parentheses.

crowd, "it's rather less than we're used to and you want to be sure you've brought your own tissue."

That put us on notice. The next stall that was vacated, as by agreement, we took turns examining the room.

I quickly saw the problem. There was little about the "toilets" that looked familiar, with the possible exception of the wooden overhead tank with rusted accessories and a missing chain. There was no seat, no bowl, nothing.

Instead, on the floor, was a flat, marble plate with a hole in it and a stench from which I shrank in dismay.

I generously allowed others with less sensitive stomachs or more urgent needs to go ahead of me while thoughtfully considering alternatives, and when my turn came, I did what I had to do. I wasn't placing bets on how soon we'd see better; indeed, I assumed it could be worse. I saw a number of women leave the room in the same condition as they'd arrived—women of principle. So much for my character. I am a pragmatist above all things. By the time I returned to the front room, most people had gone outside and Sylvia was shooing the rest of us back to the bus.

Twenty minutes farther along the road we came to Per'ghe (Perge). Sylvia, apologizing for the shortness of time, rushed us, in twenty minutes, through an impressive ruin that required several hours to be fully appreciated. Partly because time was so limited, partly because the printed materials for sale were scarce and of poor quality, I was using disks like crazy, shooting pictures of everything. I seemed to be lagging behind the group at every turn, catching up on the run.

I was overwhelmed by the quality and number of significant things to see and knew I'd never be able to absorb or retain a fraction of them. A tour is the worst possible time to "see" things. While I find I am able to retain a true sense of the character of towns, landscapes, sites, I lose detail. I cannot "see" so quickly. A photo helps me remember. And to me, everything was well worth remembering.

It was 2:00 when we finally arrived in a little seaside town where Sylvia promised us a good lunch. The bus came to a stop on what was decidedly a street, unpaved, but the first real street in a real town we'd seen all day. Lining it were a few tourist shops, selling the obligatory Turkish *kilim* (rugs) and useful or decorative articles made of the alabaster and onyx for which Turkey is noted.

There was no time for shopping. Sylvia rushed us toward the restaurant, which turned out to be an attractive and inviting place, largely due to the setting. Under a tin roof, it was open to the air and located at the edge of the sea. The seating arrangement reminded me of a country dinner put on by farmers' wives to raise money for the volunteer fire department. There were rows of long narrow tables with straight-backed wooden chairs on either side. Every diner was provided with European utensils, a napkin, and, at convenient intervals to be shared by several people, tall, graceful bottles of what turned out to be a somewhat acidic Turkish wine.

It was obvious from the preparation and the speed with which the meal was served, that the owners had been waiting for us. We ate small hors d'oeuvres made of cheese imbedded and fried in a flaky pastry; breaded and sautéed fresh local fish with rice and a finely chopped salad of tomato, onion, and greens; and for dessert, a too-sweet pastry soaked in honey. The waiters hovered, pressing wine upon us. Finally, Sylvia urged us to try a Turkish liquor called *raki*. It proved to have a licorice flavor. Clear in the bottle, becoming milky when mixed with water, it seemed indistinguishable from the Greek liquor, ouzo. But most of us were too polite to offer this comment aloud.

Our discretion was, to me, something like whispering about sex in front of three-year-olds and teenagers. In the former instance they couldn't understand a word you said and in the latter they already knew everything you were trying to hide from them. Thus far, other than Sylvia, we hadn't met a Turk who spoke or understood a word of English. And Sylvia obviously knew more about the virulent antagonism between Turks and Greeks than we.

After we left the restaurant that afternoon, on the interminable bus ride that made up the remainder of our long day (excepting two brief refreshment stops), Sylvia recounted the history and development of Turkey, touched on its culture and religion, and brought us up to date on modern conditions. She interrupted her monologue for questions and, occasionally, to point out something of interest as the bus made its slow ascent toward the mountain resort of Pamukkale, where we were to have dinner and spend the night.

"The known history of Turkey," she said, "begins in the Bronze Age with the Cappadocians and the people known as Hittites. This civilization is the most characteristically Anatolian culture that has ever grown up in the plateau of Asia minor. The Turks have encouraged archeological study of these vigorous people, who flourished from circa 1750 to 1200 B.C. At this time, there are several very important sites under excavation."

Just before taking the cruise, I'd accidentally come upon a thin but fascinating volume on the Hittites, which stimulated my curiosity.

"Sylvia," I interrupted, "will we have a chance to see things from the Hittite civilization?"

"No," she answered, without explanation, but with what seemed to me a flicker of discomfort, "we will not."*

That was a real disappointment. But I was utterly fascinated by the sights beyond the window as the bus lumbered along the narrow road. Looking sometimes interfered with catching all of Sylvia's recitation.

"The fall of Troy and the Hittite Empire opened the coast to European enterprise, and by 700 B.C., Greeks from the nearby islands came pouring in. . . ."

I became distracted as I watched two young children, dressed in white and navy uniforms and carrying books, walk slowly at the edge of the road. The passing bus lifted the dry road bed, obscuring the children in a swirling cloud of dust. When I found myself again listening to Sylvia, I'd missed the events of nearly a thousand years.

---

*I hesitate, after the fact, to interpret this exchange, but in the light of future events, I think Sylvia missed an opportunity to tell us what I later learned: that no tourist is allowed on or near sites in the process of excavation or restoration. I believe, had she offered that perfectly reasonable explanation, the next question would have been, "Why not?" and she'd have had to answer, "The Turks are fanatics about preserving their archeological treasures and will go to any lengths to do so." Or words to that effect.

But she didn't and we didn't. The opportunity passed unnoticed.

". . . . Justin made Constantinople the seat of the Holy Roman Empire, the Byzantine era began . . . now Istanbul, the Santa Sofia Mosque. . . ."

Outside, not a cloud in the sky. We passed a crew of laborers widening the two-lane macadam road. The bus had begun a low-grade climb, and to the right lay a broad deep plain extending as far as I could see. In the foreground, beside the road, lay miles and miles of withered crops.

"What's that in the fields out there?" someone called out.

"The last of the cotton crop," Sylvia said. "Cotton is one of the three main crops for Turkey. The others are tobacco and sesame seeds. Look, you will see women are in the fields, picking." She pointed. "Little remains on the branches; the first picking was made a few weeks ago. But Turkey is a very poor country. Our farmers cannot afford to leave even a few bits of cotton."

I looked for the pickers. Yes, there was a woman. She was almost reclining on the ground under the burning sun. Over her shoulder was looped a long, white bag. I understood that she dragged it as she moved between the rows.

There was a rhythm to the way she stripped the almost bare branches and stowed the cotton bits in the sack. It was so hot, even in the bus; it must have been intolerable out there.

The scene had shifted, the bus carried us on, but I still saw the woman in my mind. Young, overdressed for so much heat, a bleak life . . . how could I judge?

"Look, people," Sylvia interrupted her history again, "to the right we are passing a few farm houses and you will notice something unusual on the roof."

I did look and saw what appeared to be stacks of wheat, triangulated into little tepees.

"This you will see only in Turkey. It is the sesame. After it is harvested, it must be dried. So, it is placed on the roof to dry in the sun."

I stared at the sesame-adorned houses as the bus sped by. Poor shacks, humble . . . A woman, carrying a heavy bundle, walked from her house. I couldn't see what it was that burdened her and felt, sharply, the sense that there was something wrong about this: stealing glances from a moving bus into other people's personal lives. It was a kind of voyeurism that made me feel like a Peeping Tom. It seemed as if what lay beyond the window wasn't real life, but a movie set; that the people were two-dimensional actors and I was the audience; that when the bus passed and I was gone, the projector shut down, the movie was over, the people and their setting no longer existed.

Did her home have electricity, I wondered? Had she ever seen a phone? A TV? Did she love her husband? Was he good to her? Were they happy? What were her dreams, the aspirations of these women laboring in the fields?

It is good to be an American. I have always been a patriot, but moments like these highlighted my latent feelings.

The bus slowed. The road was under construction. Sylvia instructed us, but I was distracted by what I observed on a rather flat plain to my left. Periodically I noticed hill-like mounds with outcroppings of rocks surrounded by dirt. Something told me these were uninvestigated ancient ruins just aching to be dug out, and I was overcome with a sense of wonder at the rich archeological heritage of this surprising country.

Sylvia continued, ". . . when the discovery of Troy at what was known as Hisarlik, in the late nineteenth century, opened up to the world the richness of Turkey's archeological past and led to the discovery, excavation, and reconstruction of many, many ancient cities, such as we have already seen today."*

The business woman in me was curious.

"How can Turkey, which you've already said is a poor country, fund so many archeological projects?" I asked, "It must be very costly."

"You are right," Sylvia replied honestly. "Although Turkey has trained the finest archeologists in the world in our outstand-

---

*It also, indirectly, led to the Turks' fanaticism about the preservation of their ancient treasures. I've read about Heinrich Shliemann, who found Troy. Without regard to the Turkish sensibilities or pre-agreed terms, he exported, wholesale, chunks of the treasures uncovered both at Troy and other sites of major importance. The Turks, no longer a world power as before, seemed impotent either to stop him or to prosecute successfully for the return of their property.

The Turks have long memories and the humiliation still rankles. Sylvia didn't even give Schliemann credit for what was, at that time, a world-shaking discovery. Up to then, the world believed Homer's Troy to be mere fantasy.

ing universities, we are absolutely unable to do everything ourselves. But we have requests from universities all over the world
to send their students and professors to study here.

"Right now, we have teams working at a number of these
excavations, for example, from Belgium, from Germany, and
there is one from Harvard University, of the United States."

"What kind of contracts does Turkey make with these foreign teams? Do they get to keep some percentage of their finds?"

"Not at all. They are happy to have the chance to work on
such important archeological excavations." Abruptly, she
changed the subject.

"I think I must tell you, now, about modern Turkey. Modern Turkey's story begins with Mustafa Kemal Atatürk. To us
he is like the American George Washington, the father of our
country, as it is today.

"After a long and bloody war that caused much suffering to
the people of Turkey, the peasants who live from the land, the
Turkish army, under Atatürk, drove the Greeks back to the
Mediterranean and out of our land, freeing Turkey from their
domination. Atatürk was a great general and a great leader. He
was a man of vision and personal charisma. On October 29, 1923,
he declared Turkey a republic and soon after began his revolutionary programs to change it into a modern Western democracy.

"His task was ambitious. Only a man of his strength of
character, brillance, and abilities could have conceived of the
dream of a modern Turkey. Only a most unusual man would
have had the energy and determination to carry it out."

By then the bus had entered what appeared to be a fair-sized
town. Sylvia paused, leaned toward Mehmet, conferred briefly
in Turkish. Then she said, "Now, we are nearly to the spot
where we may go down from the bus, stretch our legs, and have
refreshments. You will see a beautiful place, overlooking the
Aegean. When we return to the coach, I will continue the story
of Turkey's modernization under Kemal Atatürk."

I watched with interest as the bus wound its way into town.
It was nearly a city. I found it a pleasant change, after driving
on a straightaway for so many hours, to watch and feel the bus
follow a zigzag route through a checkerboard of blocks. There

were two- and three-story buildings, and people on the streets dressed in modern garb. There was even an outdoor café.

We paused before it as the bus slowed to make a right-hand turn, giving me time for a good look. At five small round tables were seated clumps of patrons drinking tea, coffee, and what looked to be something "refreshing." There was a strange uniformity to their appearance: similar height, coal black hair, olive skin dressed in white shirts with the sleeves rolled above the elbows, dark somber ties, black or very dark brown trousers, and relaxed, comradely smiles.

All were men. Only men. Where were the women?

In the fields picking cotton.

The refreshment stop turned out to be an open-air (again, a tin roof) aerie. From the approach to the town, a slow grade, and the town itself, which was flat, I hadn't realized we had climbed so high above sea level. A rusted metal railing, cemented into the cracked and broken cement beneath our feet, prevented spectators from falling into the sea a thousand feet below. If one could overlook the dismal, rusted tables and stiff, unyielding, wobbly wood chairs, the grime and indifference with which the place was maintained, it presented a spectacular view. Far below, bathed in late sunlight, was a small fleet of white boats—cabin cruiser-size—gently swelling on a restless azure and marine sea. I stood a long time, held by the hypnotic play of white-capped waves lapping against the vaulting cliff, transfixed, until Sylvia called me to select a drink.

The options were limited. I chose an acceptable-tasting "Coke" in an unfamiliar bottle, debating whether I should pour it into the glass that came with it or risk putting the mouth of the bottle into mine. Decisions, decisions. The dirt on the glass was visible. The bottle won. What I didn't see wouldn't hurt me.

Other than the view, this stop was forgettable.

Back on the bus I looked at my watch. It was only five but it had been a long day. I hoped we'd be at the hotel soon.

Sylvia huddled with Mehmet until we were out of town, where the road began to climb more sharply and the first imposing, bald mountains could be seen in the distance. Then she went back to her theme: modern Turkey.

"Until Atatürk's revolution, 98 percent of the people were illiterate. The Turkish language was written in the Arabic script and was very difficult to teach or learn. Women were, under Muslim law and teachings, the chattel of men. It was prohibited to show one's face to any man except one's husband, and a wife could be divorced by a man at his whim. He simply said, three times, 'I divorce you.' So easy, 'I divorce you,' 'I divorce you,' 'I divorce you,' and she was cast out from the house. These women had no other hope to stay alive than to sell themselves."

The bus strained, climbing more steeply into the mountains. It had grown unbearably warm; people began to remove scarves, light jackets; men opened the collars of their colorful, casual shirts a bit more and I could hear the irritable remarks of some of the passengers. Someone must have spoken to Sylvia, for after breaking off and consulting with Mehmet, she announced that the air conditioner had been shut down to relieve the engine as it pulled up the mountain.

There was nothing to do but suffer in silence. I had visions of this "modern, Turkish tour coach" breaking down right here in the middle of absolutely Nowhere, the World. By all means, turn off the air conditioning. It wasn't very efficient in any case.

Sylvia was back on mike and pointing again. The topography of the region was entirely new. We were passing through rugged, rocky crags, and where the road had been blasted through the mountainside, the geological strata showed multicolored: marble, alabaster, and onyx. Between the many pinnacles lay triangular sloping plains: some looked to me like the moon; they even had moon rocks. Others were not so bare. It was one of the less bare slopes to which Sylvia called our attention, pointing out, in the far distance, a shepherd and his flock of black and brown goats.

"In Turkey, we still have some nomadic people who live today as they have lived for hundreds of years. How long we shall have them, who knows? But you are lucky to see them, for soon they will be leaving the mountains for the winter."

I watched the shepherd and saw his tent, made of the skins of the brown and black goats. There wasn't much grass to sustain the goats, and I wondered what this man's wife found to feed her husband and children besides goat meat. Did nomads

plant vegetable gardens? I doubted it but was too tired to ask
Sylvia, who was taking a break.

I was hot. I heard the steady sound of a snorer and wished
I, too, could sleep. But, I felt I must keep watch outside the
window. Nary a goat, a nomad, or a moon rock, I told myself,
will escape my eye today. I may never pass this way again.

It was a few minutes after seven when the bus stopped again,
this time in a wooded glade in front of a modest house. The
passengers awoke when, bouncing on the uneven ground, the
bus pulled off the road. We had all slowed down considerably.
The older people were stiff.

We were led into a charming *lanai* under a grape arbor. The
grapes were nearly gone, but the leaves made a cool bower
under which we were seated at a long table covered with oilcloth and presented with cool glasses of very good lemonade.
Close by, out of sight, ran a mountain stream whose babbling
waters played a soothing accompaniment to the chatter of the
passengers as we relaxed in this fine, inviting atmosphere. We
lingered as long as we could, restored by the shade, the delicious
drink, and the kindness of our husband and wife hosts.

Sylvia had to coax us back to our mobile torture chamber.
The wife walked us to her "front door" where, on a small table,
were displayed a sampling of fine embroidered and crocheted
cloths. I stopped to examine the beautiful work, and Sylvia
explained it was the artistry of our hostess and for sale.

I much admire native arts, especially women's domestic arts,
and, in particular, fine needlework. It is women's universal
mode of creative self-expression and it binds us together. I don't
know if whittling and carving do as much for men.

In this, as in many things, I am influenced by my maternal
grandmother, a significant member of the household in which
I was raised. She was a role model and an important figure in
my life. I had another grandmother whom I didn't know well;
when I speak of Grandma, I mean Rose Berman.

I cannot remember seeing Grandma without a piece of work
in her hands: blind hemming a silk dress; knitting a warm cardigan; molding a handful of raw fish into a gefilte fish pattie;
wrapping a cheese blintz; hemstitching a batiste handkerchief;
plaiting a smooth braid; packing grapes, sugar, and alcohol into

a crock to become wine; or crocheting a fine lace bedspread. It seemed to me then, there was love in her moving fingers, and so much pleasure for her in the work, I was compelled to learn to do everything, too.

She was a patient teacher. I learned much from Rose. And through doing, I learned enough to respect women's craftsmanship.

The Turkish woman's work was worthy of respect. It was exquisite. I thought to buy and hesitated. It was late, I was tired, it was my first day in Turkey and I had nothing Turkish to compare it with, it was expensive. . . . I let the moment pass.

The bus journey resumed. Although late, it was still daylight as we climbed deep into mountains, whose dark, masculine shapes loomed ahead, outlined against a still cloudless sky. They held me hypnotized as the bus slowly crawled its way upward, always straining, around hairpin turns. The roads were good, Mehmet competent, Sylvia silent. The sun would soon set; the heat had abated.

For the moment, the passengers were content to loosen clothing and remove shoes, struggle for a comfortable position and catch some sleep.

Somewhere out there is Ararat, the mountain resting place where Noah, with God's help, gently brought the paired wanderers to safe haven. Perhaps, I thought, that is also a true fable. As the mountains rose to meet the sun, the sky turned a glowing orange. I watched, fascinated, as the color deepened imperceptibly to a pale, then rich, salmon, and went from deep salmon to crimson and from crimson to blood red. Never had I seen so stunning a sunset. It did not take place in one shallow spot close to the horizon. It surrounded the planet and everything on it.

For an hour I was held spellbound. When it was over and the sky dark, I was crestfallen. I hoped it would never end.

The bus strained in darkness. We *were* on the moon. I looked into the blackness beyond the window and had the sense of what it must be to be blind. I had no field of vision. Without a moon, there was no light anywhere in the wilderness by which to get a bearing.

Above, in the equally black heavens, slowly the starlight bled through, and before long, the sky was ablaze with constellations. I recognized the Big Dipper, the Little Dipper, and Orion and so exhausted my tiny fund of astronomical knowledge. What a waste. The city-suburbanite who seldom has such an opportunity comes to it unprepared.

I was alert to find even a single light on the horizon, something to tell me the traveling cargo of the bus was not the only humanity on earth. And I saw one, then another and a third. Not close together, not terribly far apart. I remember thinking I could not live in such isolation. I needed more people than "they-out-there" had.

I felt very tired, weak, short of breath. What I needed, desperately, was sleep. I could not find a comfortable place for my body. It had had it with the seat. When, for God's sake, would we get there? What damned fool planned this overland trip? What could he, she, they have been thinking of? We paid good money to be tortured. The ancient ruins are fine, but Turkey isn't ready for middle-class, middle-aged tourists.

I decided. This is a four-day tour, not three.

It was 9:45 when we arrived in Pamukkale.

The hotel was on one floor, making it more like a motel. In the dark I couldn't see that it fronted on an unpaved road, from which it was only a few steps to the marble-floored lobby. The desk was on the right side of the small room, perpendicular to the street, and across from it was the entrance to a shop. The shop's lights were on. One was spotlighting a small, finely made, silk prayer rug next to which, in the open door, stood a smiling salesman.

Splendidly dressed in a three-piece Western suit of good cut, it seemed he, too, had been awaiting our arrival, unaware that *this* group of "rich Americans" had brought with them only a flickering interest in food, and none at all in spending money. At least not tonight.

Rooms were assigned and keys distributed. Sylvia was quick to request that we take no more than fifteen minutes to refresh ourselves since dinner was ready and waiting in the open-to-the-air dining room. I was dismayed to learn that special entertainment had been hired in our honor.

In no way did I want to make an evening of it. I was way past hunger, almost to dead. All I wanted was to be alone and horizontal—even a board would do.

Access to the rooms was from an exterior walk that lay along the left side of a very large, very shallow, natural-spring, warm-water swimming pool. My room was close to the lobby and my first impression of it was early 1940s Alabama tourist cabin. It was not first class by my standards. That went for the bathroom, as well. I'd been praying for a long soak in a bath, but was grateful to see it had a shower—of a sort.

I was beginning to get a handle on Turkey's standard in tourist accommodations. It required its own scale.

Dinner was an experience. Maybe it was just that I was tired.

Again, the twenty-two people of our party plus Jackson and Sylvia were seated on both sides of one long table. In the busy, noisy room there were at least five more tables of equal length, parallel to ours. They were half full of local diners.

The courses were many, the service acceptable, the food strange but very good. Sylvia bounced up and down assisting, interpreting, making sure we had everything we needed. Everyone was working hard at pleasing.

Soon after we were seated, the entertainment went on. Twelve skinny, costumed teenagers, six of each sex, stood up from the floor where they had been sitting like statues and started the rhythmic movements of the traditional Turkish dance. Still seated on the floor, providing suitable accompaniment, was a four-piece "drum and whine" band.

The din in the room was unbelievable.

I love music. I love dance. Any kind of each. But, the amateur dancers were awkward and ungraceful instead of sensuous and the music too exotic, insistent, too loud for the hour and my mood. I stared, fork raised and forgotten before my mouth, fascinated, embarrassed, wanting to approve, unable. Egged on by visions of making an irresistible name for themselves with the P&O passengers and finally getting in on some real tourist money, the town of Pamukkale had turned itself out to score a "triumph." Unfortunately, their best efforts, to me, stank.

It was time to go to bed. I was not the only one who had come to that conclusion. It was well after midnight, the end of one hell of a day, and Sylvia, observing the signs of an immediate departure by a number of her charges, shouted last minute instructions.

"Please, people, I know you are tired, it has been a strenuous day. I promise you from tomorrow we will not be so many hours in the coach. Let us meet at 9:30 in the morning for a tour of the Roman necropolis, after which we will see the White Terraces for which Pamukkale is famous. Breakfast will be served here, in the dining room, from 7:30 onward. You may come in when you like.

"For those of you who are early risers, you may see some of the White Terraces on your own. There are some located just at the area at the far end of the hotel swimming pool." She smiled, wearily. "Now, good night. And sleep well."

We who were departing thanked her, said good night, and quickly left. As I went past the dance floor to the exit, tired as I was, I was drawn to watch one of the local patrons who had left her table by popular request and was moving, Turkish style, to the undulating rhythms of the same band.

The woman was thirty-five years old and twenty-five pounds overweight; she was wearing a nondescript street-length dress of modern vintage. But her soul was in her eyes, in her belly, in her hips. She was Selma Sensuous! The real thing. She was great!

And, she knew it.

I went to bed feeling a lot better about Turkish dancing—and Turkish women.

I had asked for a board, anything on which to lie horizontal. I got it. I believe I also got a block of wood for a pillow. It made no difference at all.

I fell asleep instantly and awakened with the sun, refreshed.

Another perfect day. It seemed there were nothing but perfect days this time of year in the mideast.

After a shower, I put on what I call "my-coat-of-many-colors" dress. It's a sundress with an A-line skirt of two-inch diagonal, rainbow-colored stripes, cut on the bias. It sounds awful; actually, it's very nice. I chose it because it was comfortable . . . and cool.

Showered, dressed, combed, and made up, it was still only 7:45. I decided to look for the White Terraces I'd been hearing so much about and stepped outside into the bright day. The night before, I'd seen nothing. The Turks didn't waste electricity. But this morning I was delighted by the fresh, clean look of the area. There was a cement path from my door to another that circled the rectangular pool. Low subtropical plants and bushes (I recognized a scrawny oleander) softened the angular lines of the flat-roofed buildings.

I walked to the pool edge. The interior of it was painted a strong blue and, although the water seemed clean, there was a white flaky substance covering the bottom. In the center was a rock-covered cement island, also painted. The overall effect was somewhat shabby, but not uninviting. It was the white dust that put me off. I soon realized it was the calcium from the natural springs.

Looking up I saw no horizon except the end of the pool where the land abruptly ended, as if gardens and pool floated in space. I walked the length of the rectangle as far as the paving allowed and looked over the edge. There, just below me, were the White Terraces, looking exactly like large free-form basins of snow filled nearly to the top with water. They were unexpected and very beautiful.

Far below and beyond, fifty miles or more, the entire valley stretched before me; mountains beyond hills beyond hills; rollicking, rolling, reaching; soft mountain greens, shadowy lavender, graying purple; shaded blues in the early morning light.

I stood a long moment, transfixed. I was powerfully moved by a sense of the vast mysteriousness of the earth and how small I was, how limited my understanding. It was peaceful here at the top of the world.

Sylvia was alone at a table in the dining room when I arrived a short time later. I was glad for the chance to have her to myself —a rare opportunity—and took a seat across the table from her.

"You're up early," she said. "Did you sleep well?"

"I was very tired last night. I went right to sleep. And this morning I am refreshed. I've just come from seeing the terraces. They're very beautiful."

"They are unique to Pamukkale. For centuries, calcium has been deposited by natural springs to form them. It is something tourists come from all over the world to see. We shall see some, even more beautiful, later this morning. Now, help yourself to the bread and butter." She signaled a waiter and ordered tea, honey, and little flaky cakes, and pointed out a white cheese and olives that looked, smelled, and tasted suspiciously, to me, like feta and Greek olives.

My soul was full of peace, here. Everything was so . . . was the word, natural? I wanted Sylvia to know how enriched I felt by the trip thus far. It was in large part due to her talent and effort. She was full of knowledge, a thorough professional.

"Sylvia, there's too much to see in only a few days. I am so stimulated by just the one day. I like Turkey so much. There's so much to learn, to absorb. There's no way I can take it all in in so short a time. Even the needlework on the last stop yesterday. I'm sorry I didn't buy it. It was beautifully made. It's all overwhelming."

She smiled, pleased. "Then you must come back."

"Oh, yes. I shall. For three months at least. Then I'll have time for everything!"

"Three months?" The odd discomfort I'd seen before swept across her face. Certain questions seemed to evoke it. I had the sense of a struggle between her natural tendency to be outspokenly frank and an imposed, controlled reserve.

"No," she said, "three months is too long."

"Why too long? It may not be long enough. I'd rent a house or apartment and a car. I'd drive all over and take the time to see everything slowly and carefully. I'd call on you to go with me to new places."

"Three months, you will not be happy." She was sure.

"Can you tell me why?" I asked, spreading butter on the flaky, triangular cakes and dripping honey over both.

"Ah," she struggled, "as a woman, living here, your actions will be more . . . restricted than they are as a tourist. It would not be so comfortable."

"So, women have not been fully liberated from the Byzantine era in modern Turkey." I smiled, reminding her of yesterday's incomplete lecture. She acknowledged my barb with a smile. Her answer deflected the issue with a neat promise.

"I shall say more about that this afternoon when we are on the bus. For now, let me repeat that you have more freedom as a woman tourist than you would as a woman living here." She stood. "And now forgive me, I must make arrangements for lunch. Will I see you at 9:30?"

"I wouldn't miss it," I said, truthfully. She waved and strode from the room as I finished my tea. Coffee is my preferred drink, but I've tasted Turkish coffee. It's not something one carelessly puts into an empty stomach.

Like good sports, the whole group gathered for the morning tour and followed an ebullient Sylvia away from the hotel, taking a left turn down the dusty, unpaved street. It looked like we were going nowhere; the area seemed deserted, more like a wide place in the road than a village or town. The climate, flora, and painted plaster buildings reminded me, as does much of the Middle East, of Florida. Only the palm trees were missing.

Fifty yards down the road we passed through some ancient markers and abruptly were in the Roman necropolis surrounded by tombs of various design: round, square, peaked; little marble houses elevated on granite supports, others rooted in the ground.

Sylvia vividly described the function of the original Greek city of Hierapolis over which Pamukkale is built. It was thought that the water of the mineral springs there had significant curative powers. As its reputation spread over the known world, people of nobility and wealth came to be healed and built a city of marble on the spot, dedicated to health, complete with a hospital, mineral bath, and attendant physicians. And having the taste and means for more, they at the same time provided theaters, shops, and everything considered conducive to the good life.

In anticipation of death, they also constructed their personal tombs in a variety of styles that reflected the country or district of origin of the owner.

As Sylvia was concluding the lecture, two men entered the necropolis, one wearing civilian clothes, the other a soldier's uniform. There was no urgency in their movements. They strolled past our gathering, exchanged pleasantries with Sylvia in Turkish, and moved on.

When we were released to explore on our own I paused for a cigarette before going on. As I was removing one from my open pack, I looked up to see the soldier approaching me. In sign language, he asked for one also. Of course I quickly offered it, together with a light. The exchange was superficially benign, but it left me agitated.

Perhaps it was the holstered gun on his hip. Perhaps some scent of fear in the dry mountain air of Pamukkale. And, perhaps it was only that in every adult there is the remnant of a guilty child who is ready to cower before the real or imagined power of the authority figure.

Soon after, we retraced our steps past the hotel, where some of the passengers left the tour, then crossed the road to another one-story hotel, previously hidden from view by a soft barrier of wild sycamore and acacia.

Inside I was delighted by the sight of a natural-spring pool that lay immediately between us and the hotel proper. More beautiful and far more intriguing than the pool at our hotel, it was built over and around a Roman ruin. Shimmering beneath the clear, warm waters were fallen columns, capitols, and granite building stones. With envy I watched two swimmers trace graceful patterns through the exotic obstacles.

I wanted to know why we weren't staying at this hotel instead of across the road. Sylvia claimed the room accommodations were not as good but said she'd apply for permission to let us swim here. Several passengers, including me, wanted the chance.

But like biting into a luscious, golden fruit only to discover a bitter core, Sylvia related the story of a German tourist who had died here the year before. After catching a limb in a crevice, he drowned beneath these soft, inviting waters. Taking us to the exact spot of the drowning, she painted a vivid picture of the anguish of his final fate. The notion of swimming in this pool was quickly allowed to drop.

After refreshments under the cooling shade of the full-foliaged trees, we pushed on, out again into a burning sun climbing toward its zenith. A few more passengers deserted for our hotel. I remained with Sylvia and the tour.

She led us now along a newly tarred and oiled road, glistening in the heat of day. Although the roadbed was firm, my shoes were picking up a film of black oil that I knew would never clean off.

I fell behind the group as it trailed the road past a barbed wire enclosure that Sylvia said contained the Roman baths:

"Not open to tourists." No one objected to my habit of hanging back. It was now expected.

I observed Sylvia, ten yards ahead, drop off the road onto a wide, flat, sandy ledge and did likewise when I reached the same spot. The White Terraces lay not far beyond, I sensed.

Entering the dusty level I was forced to concentrate on the ground: the surface was uneven with half-buried stones. But, when I did lift my eyes, to my left I saw an old peasant woman, wearing a shapeless sweater and long brown dirndl skirt, standing next to a cloth-covered table on which were displayed stacks of needlework.

I was too far away to tell their quality but leaped at what I saw as a chance to recover from yesterday's mistake. How I regretted not having bought the elegant work. In spite of all the things I'd picked up at earlier ports of call, I needed a few more Christmas gifts. And, God knows, these poor Turkish country people could use the money.

A quick glance assured me where Sylvia was heading, so there seemed no risk of getting lost. I knew how to find the hotel in any case. In that same glance, I noted several men—maybe four—of various ages, dressed in the standard white shirt and dark pants I'd already come to know. They stood well apart in different areas of the level. I didn't associate them as being together and walked quickly to the old woman's table.

Oh, what a disappointment when I fingered the cloths and held them up for inspection. The work was amateurish, the fabric insubstantial, like gauze. The woman had neither talent nor taste, or perhaps she just didn't care.

She intruded herself into the examination, handing me cloths, chattering in what I guessed to be a mixture of Turkish and pidgin-German, for I understood only the word "shena," pretty. But it wasn't. Not even out of the pity of my heart could I bring myself to buy. I thanked her, said, "no," and moved away.

Or tried to. I found my path blocked by a young Turk who approached me boldly, holding out a carved stone head that I took from his hand and examined. It wasn't beautiful or well-made either, and I wondered if the cloths and carvings represented fairly the quality of local handiwork. Fleetingly I considered the question, does this odd setting and approach mean he hopes I'll think it's ancient?

The piece was crudely carved from stone. About two inches long and one and a half wide, it was a poor rendition of an oval head with features incised without art or style, all on a very long neck. If one dressed it from the neck down, it might have made a good puppet—Punch.

"Ten dollar," the young man said.

"Oh, no," I smiled, handing the head back to him. I didn't want it.

Again I tried to leave the area. Looking for Sylvia, I saw at a distance the upper part of her body only, her arms gesticulating as she made a point, but she was too far away to hear. The young Turk's eyes followed mine, but he refused to remove the head from my hand. Since he was speaking the same gibberish as the old woman, I could only understand the number "ten," said over and over, and tagged with the word "dollar" as he repeated his price.

"No," I said firmly, stretching my hand to return the head. Instead, I found I was now in possession of a second one nearly identical to the first.

Perhaps he thought I might like that one better. I hated the damned pushiness of the salesmen in this part of the world.

The week before it had been a kid in Jerusalem. He had made me crazy, *crazy* with his "Roman coin," and was insistent and obnoxious, crowding close, not letting me speak or get away. I bought my freedom with a twenty-dollar bill. I have the coin; what will I do with it?

Alexandria, that filthy city where you shrink from touching or being touched by anyone on the streets, had more than its share of overachievers. Of course I was approached. It's partly my fault, I realize. If only I didn't like to go off on my own. Yes, but I did it everywhere in Europe and no one bothered me. In Alexandria I was rescued by a male passenger from the ship. Score one for the tourists.

But, I can understand why they use the technique. It's effective. Money is what they want, not friends. Well, money is what they get. The hostage buys her freedom.

I felt like an utter fool to have been caught again, and argued with myself, looking for some excuse to sanction the folly of paying good money for these oddly made, ugly, stone heads. What were they supposed to depict? Could I offer them as gifts? "Here is a sample of modern carvings made by the natives of Pamukkale." I didn't even know if that was true.

I bought my first piece of "modern" art at fifteen, under the direction of my father. I supposed a representation of Turkish native art was not inappropriate. And at the same time, I would assuage the time-honored guilt of the haves over the have-nots by circulating some dollars through the Turkish underground economy.

I held up two fingers.

"Ten dollars for both," I said. Let him kill the sale. That's all they're worth to me.

He looked at my fingers and seemed to understand. "Ten dollar," he repeated, nodding. Okay.

I dropped the two heads into the tote in which I was carrying my camera. Burdened and unable to move easily, I reached into my purse, struggling to extract a ten-dollar bill without letting him see how much more money was in my wallet. But when I looked up holding the ten, I found him placing a third head in my hand.

"Oh, no, you don't," I said, trying to return it, "No more."

I could have saved my breath. He stepped back instead of taking it.

I looked quickly at the new head. It was different than the others, slightly larger, the work of another artist, certainly. Less deeply carved, it was also cracked, damaged, and dirty. I thought it was probably marble, where the others were—granite? I wasn't at all sure. This is not an area in which I am knowledgeable. Again I had the thought that if it was his aim to sell imitations of ancient art, the second artist has done a better job than the first. I could imagine this piece having fallen off some tomb in the necropolis nearby.

I wanted no part of it, in any case. I'd already been a good sport and taken two heads I didn't want. I wasn't going to buy a third. There is such a thing as overdoing it, fella.

"No," I said again, my attitude changed from the cooperative, pleasant tourist to annoyance.

But he wasn't taking no for an answer.

Hot, angry, and feeling abused, I looked around for help. The three other men, still at a distance, had been watching the exchange. I caught them staring; they quickly looked away. Even the old woman would not meet my eye. I would find no help here.

I looked to the place where I last had seen Sylvia. But now it was empty. The group was gone, and I wanted out.

"Okay," I offered in an angry voice, "ten dollars more and not another cent."

Having come to a decision, I moved abruptly. Taking out another ten, I stuffed it in his hand, snatched the head, and walked swiftly away.

This time I didn't try to go toward the spot where I'd last seen the tour, but away from the people—the old woman and the four uncaring men who wanted only to get money from tourists. Away from the dusty level, back onto the oily road. With swift determined strides I made for the hotel. Angry, feeling foolish, I was done with tours of Pamukkale. I'd go for a swim in the safety of the hotel pool just outside the room.

During the brief walk, I stewed, unaccountably upset, trying to understand the true source of my angry feelings. In all fairness, I couldn't blame these people for making money any way they could. They had to live, too. So who was there to be angry with?

Myself. I was angry with myself.

Why couldn't I just have walked away—*before* I spent the money—instead of after. I didn't even know these people; I cared nothing for their approval. What was it, then?

Was it my fault I had more security, more money, more freedom, more opportunities? I could not make it up to the whole world. Was it for this I allowed myself to be pushed around?

Well, I told myself sharply, if it was, I had damn well better get over that!

Inside my room I dropped the tote on the bed and tossed the third head beside it. Pulling the bathing suit I really hadn't expected to wear from the suitcase, I changed quickly and went outside for hydrotherapy. The day was too glorious to pout and fester, the water deliciously warm and soothing. Within minutes, I was back in a good mood.

After lunch we were back on the bus. The confinement seemed odd after so many hours of freedom. My still-damp swimsuit was in the tote beside me on the seat. The three heads were in my suitcase in the luggage compartment.

"The drive to Aphrodisias, our next stop, will take an hour," Sylvia began over the mike. "This gives me plenty of time to tell you more about modern-day Turkey since Atatürk's social revolution." The subject interested me.

One of the first things Atatürk did was liberate women, declaring them fully equal to men. He outlawed hiding the face in public—off with the veils!—and set an example by marrying a modern, educated woman who dressed in figure-hugging European clothes.

Determined to raise his people from ignorance, he embarked on an aggressive program of universal education, not only building schools and declaring attendance mandatory, but bringing European scholars to transliterate the Turkish language from Arabic symbols to Roman letters, advancing his dream to raise Turkey to equal status among Western democracies.

"I think of Turkey today," Sylvia said, "as a land of contradictions and contrasts. You must remember, the new Turkey is only sixty years old this year and it takes time for the old ways to pass and the new to take hold.

"In the country, on the farms and small villages, many people live much as they did before. The women still fulfill the same obligations to home, husband, and children, while, as you saw yesterday, at the café, the men take their freedoms as before. However, today more and more of our young women are attending schools of higher education and are taking their place as doctors, lawyers, dentists, and in other professions.

"On a single street in any of our larger cities, you will see the contrasts: women dressed in the most modern and fashionable clothing, women in peasant costumes. This is the best illustration I can give you of the old and the new living side by side in Turkey today. It is changing all the time. Women are attaining their place of equality," she looked to the rear of the bus,

caught my eye, and gave a conspiratorial smile, "but not everything we aspire to has been fully realized."

Brava, Sylvia. Spoken like an educated realist.

Foot tours of the ruins of two Greco-Roman cities in the afternoon completed the day's sight-seeing. The lights were coming
on as we reached Kush a dasi (Kuşadasi), a lovely seaside resort
community, where we were to spend the night at the Caravan-
sari Hotel. Here, we were only twenty miles from Ephesus,
where we would spend all afternoon the next day, Friday, before returning to the ship.

The hotel presented a fortresslike façade. It had an ancient
and honorable history, having served as a caravan stop on this
important trade route for hundreds of years before it was con-
verted to a hotel within modern times. The rooms lay off a hall
that circled a large, rectangular atrium on two levels. The
atrium contained a large public seating area, where later we
were served hors d'oeuvres and wine, and a mammoth dining
room, furnished with twenty-foot-long parallel tables in the
Turkish style.

Naturally, my room did not escape a quality rating. It represented a more sophisticated, if somewhat earlier period—Roar-
ing Twenties, suburban New York. But there were some ar-
chitectural difficulties.

The only window faced the atrium, where the party went
on unabated until midnight and the cracks in the door, combined with an inability to lock the window, forced more participation and less security than I thought desirable.

I did my best to ignore these drawbacks. The room had its
own tub. That, for a tub aficionado who'd been without one for
five weeks, was worth everything.

The tub was different from an American tub—more square
than rectangular, giving no room to stretch one's legs, and
twice as deep. That, together with a porcelain seat, led me to
suppose one is to sit, not lie, in a Turkish tub. I longed to fill
it and have a good soak but nowhere could I find a plug for the
drain.

After two frustrating trips to the desk, I finally got a plug
but now it was too late. Dinner was being served in the dining
room.

The evening meal was a repeat of Pamukkale. Only the entertainment differed. Turkey's version of Frank Sinatra with studied casualness belted a few ballads, after which his British wife "spontaneously" joined him at the mike. I suggest it was her fair skin and golden hair rather than talent that explained her popularity with the dark-haired, olive-skinned audience.

I was dragging when, after the meal was over, I finally filled the tub with lukewarm water. The kitchen must have used up all the hot water. And it's not easy to soak sitting up. Afterward, waiting for the noise to abate, I tried to read, but Turks, as I've said, are frugal with electricity. Two fifteen-watt light bulbs didn't shed much light. In the dark, listening to alien noises, conversation in languages I didn't understand, longing for silence, I rested until it grew quiet, then I slept.

It was morning when I discovered how careless I'd been. Tossing yesterday's purchases, unprotected, into the suitcase with my clothes, had damaged my favorite silk blouse. It didn't take a minute to see that all three heads had exposed jagged edges; one of them had caught some threads.

Another reason to regret yesterday's weakness.

Before I left the room, I wrapped each of the smaller heads in a pair of "used" cotton briefs and placed them in the rear, elastic pocket of the suitcase, out of the way. The larger posed a problem. I had nothing else to wrap it in. I'd have to work that out before I packed and left the hotel.

After breakfast I planned to hear a lecture on Turkish rugs. We were to meet Sylvia at 9:15 in front of the hotel. With speed and a bit of luck, I thought I could run out and buy an onyx chess set, get something to wrap the head in, and still make the lecture in good time.

Outside the fortress walls the weather held in spite of the light mist that had fallen before dawn. It was early, the mist was burning off, and few stores were open.

Luck led me from the door to an arcade a few yards away, where a pleasant-faced, gray-haired Turkish shopkeeper was opening his stall. Inside was a generous display of souvenir articles made of onyx, among which were two sizes of neatly fashioned chess sets. Perfect. I bought two of the small, one for me, one as a gift. Each was packaged cleverly in its own box.

The proprietor wrapped both sets together in a sheet of strong paper, then glued a tape across to hold the package closed. He placed the package in a plastic shopping bag, together with a small onyx egg he said was a gift for being his first customer of the day.

Such a gracious gentleman. He saw me to the door and, with a warm smile, wished me a pleasant stay in Turkey.

Back in my room I unwrapped the chess sets. It took only a minute to cover the last head with the brown paper and a bit of water from the bathroom tap to reseal part of the tape. I was packed and ready at the front door when Sylvia and seven others left for the rug store a block away.

I felt very pleased with myself.

Appalled as I was to learn that because only little girls had fingers small enough to tie the tiny knots, female child labor was the foundation of silk rug manufacture, I bought one anyway. It gleamed ivory and beige under the spotlight on the display floor, tracing a fine, insinuating pattern of red, salmon, gold, and blue. It measured only thirty-four by sixteen inches and cost twelve hundred dollars. Assuaging my conscience wasn't easy.

The remainder of the day passed quickly. I accompanied Sylvia when she took a few passengers to the local covered bazaar and from there to a jewelry shop, where her friendship with the Sephardic Jewish owner was supposed to grant me favorable treatment (read, price) on an Alexandrite ring.

Lunch was served on the quay at a charming outdoor café. We collected our luggage, reboarded the bus, and were off to Ephesus, the acme of the area's ancient offerings, the *pièce de résistance*, our farewell to Anatolia.

It might have been better if we'd seen Ephesus before exposure to all those other ruins. On a twenty-acre site lay everything we'd seen before, only bigger, better, more, and more impressive, all of it in one gigantic place.

Instead of heightened awareness, I arrived at Ephesus with a diminished capacity for awe. I was jaded.

Only one-eighth of this major site was open for inspection, the remainder being either under excavation or reconstruction, but what we saw had the impact of stepping back into an earlier, grander, infinitely more gracious and elegant time. The best way I can put it: the streets of Ephesus are avenues. The avenues are paved in marble. Even the horses walked on it.

Entering the grounds, which were enclosed in a ten-foot-tall cyclone wire fence, I noticed a huge sign. I don't remember seeing another like it at any of the previous historic sites. The message was written large and repeated in five languages: Russian, German, English, French, and Turkish. It said, more or less, "It is forbidden for anyone to touch or remove anything from this site: from the grounds, statues or buildings. Anyone who does so will be severely prosecuted under Article 68."

The sun was low on the horizon when the bus finally dragged into the backwaters of Izmir. I cannot speak for Sylvia, but I feel safe in saying that twenty-two passengers from the *Sea Princess*, Jackson, and an ass-weary Mehmet were awfully glad to be heading for the corral. The pioneer tour needed a bit of fine tuning but had been a huge success.

Without consulting us, Sylvia instructed the driver to head toward the highest point of Izmir, to a park that marks the ruins of Alexander the Great's citadel. It is a spot from which the entire crescent bay of Izmir can be viewed, arching widely below. In one glance I quickly grasped what, for centuries, has drawn people to this old city once known as Smyrna. A natural cove, it signals a place of safe harbor.

Three dogged tourists left the bus for a final photo. The *Sea Princess* could be seen far below at her berth at the dock. Then we wearily crawled our way back down the hills, through the narrow, turning, crowded streets, onto the wide *kordon* (boulevard) that follows a bold shoreline north through Izmir's business district, the Konak, and on to the peninsula that is the Izmir docks.

There, the bus pulled up alongside a cavernous building to discharge its tired tourists. Mehmet began unloading luggage from the belly of the bus, while Sylvia stood near the door saying good-bye to the individual passengers.

I waited until nearly the last, and when it was my turn, hugged, thanked, and asked her for her address so that I could write before my next trip to Turkey. She offered me the name and address of her employer.

Inside the customhouse we were directed to a seating area in a large, high-ceilinged room. I thought most of the customs' business took place within view although, toward the rear, behind glass partitions, I could see some shadowy movement in what appeared to be offices.

And directly ahead, through a great open portal, the white expanse of the *Sea Princess* cut off my view of the bay. I was acutely aware that just beyond sight the gangplank was laid, and I imagined, above decks, my little cabin waiting with a shower and fresh clothes. I thought after dinner I'd just crawl into that comfortable bed instead of seeking other entertainment.

The seating area lay left of the open dock door. Some distance from there, across a wide marble floor but directly in front of me, stood three low, parallel counters. Our luggage, carried in by porters, was slid into a rack nearby.

There were only a few officials in sight, and because the area was so spacious, I was hardly aware of them. Navy uniforms so dark as to look black; silent ebony-eyed, unsmiling men; standing, waiting, unobtrusive.

I saw no one from the ship, but there was one civilian: a slight, quiet man in a gray suit. He seemed to be waiting, too.

The seating was comfortable, although insufficient to accommodate all the passengers, and I felt lucky to find a place on a low sofa. Most of the women found seats; the men stood. On a large, square coffee table in front of me, I laid the hand luggage I'd carried all day: the cloth tote, the plastic bag with the chess sets, my purse. Trying not to give in to impatience, I sat back in the low sofa to wait.

I wondered how long the official procedures would take. Remembering the delays getting off the ship Wednesday morning, I prayed the Turks would be less rigid about tourists leaving their country than entering it.

About an hour out of Izmir, Jackson, who until then had left everything to Sylvia, had passed out green cards, with instructions to complete and return them to him with our passports. It was easy to do. Questions to answer like: When did you enter Turkey? How long will you stay? Why are you here? Business or pleasure? Traveling alone? Family members? The usual immigration stuff. Nothing more. And, when we got off at the dock, he'd taken them from us.

Now I saw, in a corner near the dock, at a beat-up walnut desk manned by a serious-looking official in uniform, Jackson hand over the small stack of documents. I watched as, with a curt nod of dismissal, the Turk began slowly, systematically going through them.

Good. It had started.

We waited ten minutes and I could sense a restlessness as the chatter died, started up, and people shifted positions. Mentally, I shifted the focus of my concerns to that night and tomorrow, and started thinking to myself: My hair's a mess. Thank God I have an appointment at the beauty parlor in the morning. Beauty parlor? You give away your age every time you open your mouth! Hair salon. What time is it? Ten, ten-thirty? I'll have to check my book.

Fifteen minutes passed. Twenty. The passengers began to complain aloud. "Why is it taking so long?" "What a grueling trip this has been . . . excellent, but I'm worn out." "I can't wait to have a shower," "a bath," "change of clothes," "decent dinner."

I think all of us enjoyed the Turkish meals. I did. But then I love any sort of exotic food. Anyone who elects to take a three-day jaunt in a Turkish bus has to be flexible; finicky eaters need not apply. I, myself, have always been proud of a garbage-pail stomach, but an unrelenting diet of ethnic food palls quickly and I was more than ready for a European-style meal.

With growing impatience I looked at my watch. Twenty-five minutes had elapsed since we sat down.

I was tired of waiting.

A woman sitting nearby tapped my arm. "I think he wants you," she said, pointing.

I looked up and saw the white-haired European in the gray suit standing a few yards away. He was looking in our direction. In a soft, timid voice, he called my name.

"Gene LePere?" I jumped to my feet and went to him.

"I'm Gene LePere," I said.

"Will you follow me, please," he asked and, as I fell into step at his side, "I am Charnaud, the agent for P&O Lines in Turkey. I will assist you through customs; you are first. Please," he pulled up at the luggage rack, "will you point out your bag?" I did and he took it from the rack.

Carrying it to the nearest counter, Charnaud laid it in front of a custom inspector standing on the opposite side. The Turk was a handsome, clean-shaven man, perhaps thirty-five years old, and as he motioned me to open the suitcase, I looked into his eyes. There was neither warmth nor personal curiosity in them. He had the unreadable face of a courteous professional.

Without hesitation, I worked the tiny padlock and unzipped the soft, canvas top, pulling it back to expose the articles inside.

I hadn't taken much with me; the suitcase was small. Atop everything was the silk rug, last to go in, rolled tightly, wrapped in strong brown paper, tied with white cord. Next to it nestled the largest of the heads in its makeshift covering, applied this morning. Beneath these was a plastic, zippered makeup case, a traveling mirror, and clothing for the three days.

Politely, the inspector ran his hand over the objects. Stopping at the head, perhaps reacting to its unexpected firmness, he pressed it slightly, lifted it, and indicated, without words, he wished me to unwrap it.

I leaned forward to comply and as I released the first bit of paper, Charnaud interjected.

"It is only onyx," he said in English, addressing the Turk, but I also understood the implication.

It's a souvenir, he was saying. Let's not delay my passengers with a lot of foolish, time-wasting examinations.

For a moment . . . I hesitated. The Turk also paused, as if weighing the judgment: proceed? let it go?

But I knew it wasn't onyx. What if he wanted the package opened anyway? Then it would seem as if I had something to hide. I was willing to expose the head.

"No," I said, looking at Charnaud and shaking my hand in a gesture of denial, "it's not onyx, it's marble." A souvenir in any case.

The Turk understood my gesture, if not the words, and quickly reasserted his request that I bare the piece, whatever it was. I complied.

When the head was exposed, the Turk seemed to tense. Using the manila paper as a tray, he removed it from the bag, placing both on the counter next to the suitcase. Then he systematically began to probe every corner of the luggage.

His fingers dug under the clothes, into each crevice, deep in the back pocket where, one by one, he brought out the little heads, one by one, removed the pastel-colored cotton briefs. One by one, he set the ugly objects on the wrapping paper next to the first, where they stared blindly at me like three lumps of gray fruit on a wrinkled napkin.

Through all of this Charnaud, at my side, was silent.

I was annoyed.

My God, I thought, he takes his petty authority seriously. I hope he's satisfied now he's messed everything in the bag.

But he wasn't. His deep-set eyes darkly serious, the Turk now gestured for me to remove the cord and wrapping from the silk rug. My irritation escaped control and I turned to Charneau.

"What's his problem? That is only a silk rug. It's wrapped so well. Why must I? . . ."

But with a strong gesture, the inspector intruded. The package was to be opened. Impatient, but resigned, I slipped the cords away and began to peel back the paper. Only when it was freed did the Turk reach out and take the rug into his own hands. He wasn't sinister or rude or rough. Only confident of his authority. And expert in his search.

He ran his hands into every crevice of the luxuriant silk while, I, watching, felt violated. My body tensed.

He found nothing and, satisfied, returned the rug to the bag. The search was over.

He had been looking for something, that was clear. But what or why, I couldn't imagine.

I waited to be released and looked to Charnaud, who excused himself, politely, and stood with the official, conferring softly in Turkish. In a few minutes he returned.

"I regret, Madam, there is a small delay. They will take the rest of the passengers through customs before completing your procedure."

"Why is that?" I asked. "What is the problem?" I was getting testy, tired of being pushed around.

"No problem, perhaps, only a misunderstanding, I am sure. However, we don't like to ask the others to wait any longer. When they have been cleared to go aboard . . ." He paused and, as if it were an afterthought, asked, "By the way, Mrs. LePere, where have you purchased these heads?"

The heads. Of course.

"In Pamukkale," I answered, "from a street vendor."

"Pamukkale?" He seemed puzzled and repeated, ". . . a street vendor? I see." Then, "Please excuse me, now. I will assist the others with the customs procedure. If you please, remain here. It won't take long, I am sure." His accent was British, but he had a funny, formal way of speaking English, as if it weren't his native tongue, and the timidity of his personality did little to instill confidence. But I was stuck with him; Charnaud was all I had.

At first I stood by the counter next to my open bag watching as the tour passengers were called up; couples or singles bent over the open luggage, faces drawn with fatigue, eager to be finished, to be free to go aboard. Was I as drawn, I wondered? Did my face show the effects of the past strenuous days as much as theirs?

Probably, I thought. I haven't applied fresh lipstick once today. That, by itself, makes me look sick.

My body seemed to grow heavier with every minute that passed. There was no reason to stand. Clearing a corner of the counter, I hopped up, glad for the moment to have lifted the load from my back and feet to a place that was, just then, more rested.

Forty minutes passed before I saw Jackson, who had positioned himself after the paid guests, close his leather suitcase. Before going to the dock, he stopped to say he would report my delay aboard and assured me help would come. I tried to reassure him. The problem could not be serious.

Now that everyone from the tour was gone, I'd soon be cleared. Thank God! I was increasingly aware of how tired I was. But many minutes went by before Charnaud returned, and when he did, he looked concerned. I almost snapped at him, "Will you please tell me what is holding everything up? I'm exhausted, dirty. I want a shower, dinner. It's been a very tiring three days. What is going on?"

He paused, trying to find the right words,

"I am sorry," he began. "The heads . . ."

"My God, what about the heads?" I cut him off, angrily,

"The customs believe they may be . . . ancient."

Ancient! So that's it.

I laughed. "Ancient, how is that possible?" I worked to control sarcasm. "I paid exactly twenty dollars for them, all three. It is not possible they are ancient."

It was Charnaud's turn to be surprised.

"Twenty dollars," he seemed astonished. And pleased. "I see. I will tell them that."

"Yes," I said, more patiently, now. "Tell them the heads cost twenty dollars from a street vendor. I don't understand why they are making such a fuss over them. Look at them. Do they look ancient?"

Charnaud's unexceptional features grew grave. "Mrs. LePere," he said, "this matter can be serious. It is not allowed to remove ancient artifacts from Turkey."

"I see," I said, remembering the sign at Ephesus. It didn't say exactly that. "I understand, but they are not ancient, so there's no conflict here."

"But the customs men are worried they may be."

I was frustrated.

"Look, I am trying to understand their point of view. But maybe they could try to understand mine. The heads are of no importance. Not to me, anyway. I never wanted to buy them, and there's no possible way they can be of value. But if that's what's bothering them, tell them they can keep the heads. I just want to go aboard."

Charnaud was silent a moment, then responded.

"Mrs. LePere, I shall tell them. You will please to wait. Make yourself comfortable. I am sorry for all this. I shall confer again with the officials."

And he went away again, leaving me sitting on the counter, swinging my legs, feeling foolish and frustrated.

Why were they making a federal case out of it?

I was keeping one eye on my watch, looking around to see where Charnaud was and when he'd return. This was getting ridiculous. I'd been held up well over an hour already.

But, when he came back, he still had no solution to the problem.

"We are in discussions. I have told them you have paid twenty dollars for the three heads . . . ."

"This is ridiculous!" I interrupted, losing all patience. "Tell them to keep the damned heads, who cares? I don't even want my twenty dollars back!"

Why was I stuck with this palid, ineffectual man to represent me? I wanted my words and my tone to galvanize Charnaud into action. I wished I could have delivered them myself to the Turks, but language was an insurmountable barrier between us. I had no choice but to rely on Charnaud. If I could only fire him with my indignation.

But the man had no timber to ignite. His reply when it came was spoken in the same, vapid voice. Perhaps that's why it took me so long to process the import of his words.

"It is not so simple as that," Charnaud said, pausing briefly. "They are speaking of keeping you here."

My heart lurched. Keep me here? I flushed, suddenly cold.

"What do you mean?" I asked, bewildered, gripped by fear.

"They want to keep you here . . . to have the ship leave without you."

Terror descended on me. It choked me and I could take only shallow little breaths, tight little gasps high in my lungs. I was frightened and didn't know why, seized by panic.

I withdrew from the room, deep inside, to counsel with myself. I must not give in to panic.

I don't know what Webster says about panic. I don't care. My operative definition of panic is incapacitating fear. Real or imagined, the key word is incapacitating. If you give in to panic you're lost.

I knew I must get hold of myself. It is my style not to give in to panic. I could not and would not allow my reason to be swept away by visceral fear. Why I was so afraid was something I could consider later. Right then, some instinct was telling me I was in mortal danger and if I lost my head I would die. I couldn't afford to lose my head.

At that moment I heard footsteps echoing across that huge, empty room and looked past Charnaud to see John Andrews, the ship's assistant purser, coming toward me. After the dark serious Turks in their dark serious uniforms, the sight of this open, smiling, familiar English face crowned with its thick thatch of sandy hair, this easy, confident man, tall and strong in a white, crisply starched uniform, was a sight that brought me back to my senses.

Charnaud, the Turks—none of this was real. The ship was real. John was real and he had never let me down.

Irrelevantly, I noticed he was sunburned, and grinning.

"Good Lord," he said, "Jackson reported one of the passengers having a bit of trouble. I should have known it was you."

"John," I blurted, unable to joke, "I'm terrified. They're talking about keeping me here."

"Not to worry," he replied, lightly, "not that we wouldn't be very glad to get rid of you."

"Please," I begged, "I just can't laugh about it. I'm too frightened."

Charnaud interrupted. "I shall go back to talk with these men. I am trying to make arrangements for Mrs. LePere to go aboard, together with her purchases."

I heard him and wanted to believe. Yet the fear hardly subsided. I looked at John. Only when I fixed on him, did the chilling fear diminish—not disappear. A cloud of unreality settled about me, formed of the mists of scattered impressions: a cold indifference, the impervious superiority of the Turkish male, the intractability of a rigid people, and something else I could not define that had to do with guns in the hands of soldiers. It gave me a kind of vertigo.

John was stationary, an anchor. I didn't want him to leave me.

But almost as soon as Charnaud left, John said he'd be getting back to the ship.

"Stop worrying, Gene," he said, reaching out to touch my clasped, clenched hands, "we're not going to let anything happen to our favorite passenger. I'll get on it right away."

I couldn't tell him how much I needed to have him in my sight. That was too babyish and I was too proud. I also believed the faster he returned to the ship, the sooner I'd be rescued from this nightmare. And when he left and I was alone, it wasn't impatience that occupied my thoughts. You have to feel very sure of yourself to be impatient. At the moment, I was far from self-assurance. I was shaken.

Now, as I sat waiting for my fate to be decided by a handful of Turks and a few Englishmen, I anguished over the improbabilities of chance and felt regret flush though my body, changing its essential softness into something dry and brittle. If only I hadn't stopped to look at the old woman's cloths.

If only, if only. If only I had bought the needlework the first afternoon, I wouldn't have stopped the next morning. If only I'd told the vendor to go to hell and if only I'd escaped to the hotel before buying. If only. . . . It didn't help.

At 8:15 Charnaud returned with the news that I was being allowed to go aboard for a shower and dinner. My initial relief evaporated when he continued by saying that as he had agreed to take responsibility for my reappearance on the dock at such time and for whatever reason I was summoned, he hoped I realized the difficult position he would be in, should I refuse to return.

I felt afraid to deny him; I needed Charnaud; I needed his goodwill. And I felt sorry for him, too. It wasn't his fault. I agreed to honor his word.

Before taking me aboard, he lifted my suitcase, leaving the heads exposed and vulnerable without it. But the inspector, who had returned when Charnaud did, picked them up and followed us across the room as we walked toward the dock.

Passing the seating area on the way, I was astonished to see the cloth tote and plastic bag still on the coffee table where they'd been left two hours before. I'd forgotten them and detoured my keeper past the table to pick them up.

Another "if only." Why hadn't I packed the chess sets in the suitcase and carried the heads in one of these bags? No one had shown the slightest interest in either. If only . . .

In a flash of anger, I turned back to the inspector, waving the two hand bags at him. "Don't you want to examine these, too?" I wanted to know. He came forward, gave the most cursory glance into each, and waved us out to the dock. What irony.

Charnaud left me at the door to the cabin, suggesting I freshen up and have dinner.

Alone inside, it was quiet. The air was gently, artificially cooled, and a soft light from the reading lamp cast a glow over the familiar objects, making the room seem cozy. I was so glad to be there. The bed had been made up for the night by the steward and I, weary beyond endurance, sat down on it where the blanket had been turned back to expose the clean white bottom sheet.

The suitcase lay on the day couch, forgotten. In this benign setting, familiar and comfortable, I had the illusion of safety.

But it lasted only a moment. Exhausted, shocked, and frightened, I anguished, my thoughts ranging wildly.

I wondered how Charnaud could be so callous as to think I could shower, dress, and sit down to a meal with 350 passengers who had nothing more serious on their minds than what to have for dinner. No one had told them they might be prevented from returning to their country, their work, their life. Had Charnaud been exaggerating? Had the Turks any real intention of keeping me here? What were the chances the heads were ancient? All of them? One? The two that looked alike? Why would someone have sold them if it's against the law to remove ancient objects from Turkey? Wasn't that against the law, too? And so cheap? Why hadn't someone told me it was risky to buy any carved objects? Sylvia? Jackson? How easy it would have been for someone to spell it out clearly.

Was Charnaud doing everything he could do? Could I trust him? What about the British? The captain? What could I expect in the way of defense? Protection?

The seemingly undisciplined, wildly ranging thoughts, darting like bees through my mind, were more than mental hand wringing. It was my way of assembling, processing, and analyzing data. From every recess and wrinkle of my mind, images and words were popping up; my brain was sifting, assessing, sorting, looking for every evidence to help me take charge of this crisis; to impact on it—or, failing that, to accept whatever was to come.

But everywhere the thoughts drew me, the channel ran out. Insufficient evidence. I just didn't know enough. And fear. I was stopped by fear. Again and again I saw the solemn, unsmiling, granite faces of the Turkish men, shut down and unreadable, unyielding and, I greatly feared, uncaring. The severe uniforms . . . the guns . . .

Much of the anguish I felt came from some deep knowledge that whatever it was the Turks decided, they would have their way. In part that was true because the captain, I knew from the experience of the past five weeks, was not a man with the confidence or strength to challenge their authority.

I had good reason to be anxious.

I couldn't remain alone in the cabin any longer. My churning thoughts drove me out and down to the bureau—the purser's offices. Along the way, through long, narrow antiseptic aisles, down staircases, I walked among other passengers, beautifully dressed, on their cheerful way about the ship. They were carefree and I was self-conscious, aware I was still dressed in the clothes I'd worn all day, that my face was unwashed, beet red from the hours in the sun, and devoid of makeup, that I looked haggard and drawn because my face shows plainly everything I feel.

But my need to see John Andrews was greater than my vanity. I could feel myself breaking loose. John, with his good humor, common sense, and take-charge manner, I believed, could anchor me firmly, again.

I doggedly followed the trail to the midship's office and, thank God, John was there. I waited for him on one of the upholstered benches in the lounge outside the cages.

"Stop worrying," he said, when he sat down beside me, "Let me tell you how these Turks operate. They like to make a cliff-hanger out of these things. They know we're sailing at midnight so, believe me, at five minutes before twelve, just like I'm sitting here with you, it'll be resolved. And you and I will go up and have a drink together. It'll all blow over like that."

"I hope you're right," I said, wanting him to be.

"I promise you I am," John replied, smiling as he stood. "I'm going to have my dinner now, but I'll be back at half-eight. You should have your dinner, too."

"I'm not hungry," I said, the anxiety still making me nauseated, "but if I could see the captain . . ."

"I'll arrange it. Can you return here to the bureau in about forty-five minutes? I'll see the captain and ask him to meet you then. Believe me, Gene, he's not going to sail without you."

On the hope Andrews instilled, that the captain would not leave Izmir without me, I returned to my cabin when John left for the Tasman Restaurant, the ship's dining room.

I arrived outside the bureau only minutes before the captain. John King was a tall, slender, nice-looking in a little-boy sort of fashion man, and young, I thought, to be in a position of so much responsibility. He was in absolute command of a luxury ship carrying 750 passengers and a crew of, I guessed, an equal number. That he was qualified in navigational skill I had no doubt. It was his judgment I questioned, whether he had the experience and seasoning. I thought him lacking a certain poise, a true self-assurance that generated confidence in others.

When he arrived he was in a hurry, smiling stiffly. He let me know he was working on the problem, that I was not to worry, and that he was now a half hour late to dinner.

"Charnaud," the young captain said, "is a worrier. The whole thing was badly handled from the start. A little bribe right off would have taken care of everything. But, in any case, Mrs. LePere, I will not sail from Izmir without you."

My relief was palpable. Hearing these words, I returned to my cabin and was able to unpack and put away the clothes and purchases of the last three days. Then, able at last to let go, I lay down on the bed and immediately fell asleep. Within minutes I was awakened by a knock on the cabin door. It was Connie, the one passenger I knew best.

She was shocked when I told her what was happening. Troubled and disbelieving, she dismissed any cause for concern on my part. "The captain would never go off without you," she said, again and again. "You didn't do anything wrong, Gene. Everyone knows you would never do anything wrong. Don't be silly, Captain King would never leave port without you."

She told me she had a date to go into Izmir with some of the crew but said she'd stop by when she got back. Meanwhile, she urged, "Get some rest. Everything will come out right." But spent as I was, sleep had fled, and after she left, a steward arrived from the dining room with a tray of sandwiches—little open-faced smoked salmon on slices of white bread with the crusts cut away—enough to feed four.

I sent a message of thanks to the maître d' for his thoughtfulness, but when the waiter had gone and I tried to eat, the food choked in my throat. Fear had stemmed the flow of saliva. I couldn't swalllow.

The tray sat, nearly untouched, on the desk/dresser. I rested, reclining on the bed; the room was quiet; time passed.

The phone rang in the dark room and I, nerves taut, over-reacting, jumped up to answer, my heart pounding. It was John Andrews.

"Gene," I heard him say from a long distance off, "A man

named Robert Ludan has come aboard to see you from the American consulate. Shall I send him to your cabin or do you prefer to come to the bureau?"

"The American consulate." I repeated, my heart lurching wildly as I found myself again panting and gasping shallow breaths. "If the American Consulate is here . . ." I articulated the terrifying thought aloud, "then this must be very serious."

John made no reply. Inside my body, deep in its innermost denseness, I felt something building on that initial brittleness, as if the soft, moist, life-giving tissue was slowly being replaced by some harder, less flexible material, as the once-living trees of Arizona's Petrified Forest had been turned into stone, or like some weird science-fiction transformation, I was being changed. From the core of my being, moving slowly, imperceptibly outward toward muscle and skin, I was turning into glass.

My sense of it was instinctive, visceral, not intellectual, for I blurted immediately, "I'll be right down," and left the cabin within seconds of hanging up the phone.

Bob Ludan was waiting inside the purser's office with Andrews, who left as soon as I arrived. A tall, slender man with straight dark hair and pleasant, even features, Ludan, looking very young in beige chinos, a plaid cotton shirt, no tie, and an Eisenhower jacket, offered his hand. I took it, voicing immediately, as we shook hands, my awful fear.

"If you're here," I repeated, my eyes boring into his, "this must be very serious, indeed."

"It is," he replied quickly, without trying to soften the blow or to apologize. "It is serious."

I stiffened, steadying myself for facts with which to assess and fight.

"The Turks are very sensitive about drugs, guns, and antiquities, about them being taken out of the country," he informed me. "When I came through customs just now, I took a look at the three heads. I'm not an expert, only an amateur archeologist, but in my opinion, two of the heads are fakes and one is very likely ancient."

He was detached, cool but not unkind, giving fact and opinion, a professional.

"What will happen?" I asked.

"The problem is they need to confirm the antiquity of these items and they don't have the expertise. It's a matter of getting some archeologists to say whether or not they are ancient and it's rather difficult to locate archeologists who will come to the dock at 10:00 on a Friday night. Therefore, they may keep you here over the weekend so that the heads can be evaluated Monday when the museum is open."

The nausea rose at "keep you here."

"Remaining here, having the ship leave without me," I said, looking at the floor, "is unacceptable. I cannot deal with the notion at all."

"I have tried to locate some archeologist friends of mine—Turks—and am hoping they will be able and willing to come. I understand the ship sails at midnight."

"Yes."

"Well, let's hope I can get them and hope the heads are not ancient."

"Yes," I affirmed; it was a prayer. Then Ludan, removing paper and pencil from a breast pocket of his jacket, asked, poised to write, "Are you an American citizen?"

"Yes," I replied, surprised at the question.

"Please give me your legal name, birth date, city, state, and country of birth."

"All of that's on my passport," I interrupted, puzzled that he wanted information readily available to him.

"The Turks have your passport," he said quietly.

And there it was. I knew it and didn't know it. Knew it and didn't want to know it. The Turks had my passport, and my country's representative had to go back to square one to help me. With each new reality driven home, the glassworks inside me enlarged and hardened.

"Yes. Of course," I said, and began to answer all his questions fully. "Gene Harriet LePere; October 16, 1926; New York City . . ."

I was with Ludan about twenty minutes. When he returned to the dock in pursuit of off-duty archeologists, there was nothing I could do but head back to my cabin to wait for a bunch of Englishmen, Turks, and now, an American—to determine my fate. Being unable to do anything for myself was killing. I am a person who needs to be in action, who needs to take charge of my own affairs. Sitting helplessly, while others—strangers, at that!—worked to protect my interests just increased my anxiety and frustration.

While I waited, I lay, fully dressed in semidarkness, on the bunk and considered Ludan, my American ally, the newest player on the stage and my best hope.

He was young. I visualized the smooth face with its high Slavic cheekbones. The eyes, I recalled, had a slight oriental cast to which his olive coloring and dark hair was suited. But I thought he was just an American, a mixture of who knows what international heritage.

There was a quietness about him and a gentleness, too. It was obvious from his attire I had interrupted him at leisure, yet he made no attempt to accuse me or to excuse himself for the informality of his dress. Unlike John King, who was probably ten years his senior, Ludan was self-possessed beyond his years. Perhaps it was his diplomatic training; perhaps I was prejudiced by chauvinism or desperation; to me he exuded a humble kind of good sense. This was my first experience with a foreign service professional and God knew I needed help, but I felt more comfortable with Ludan than with Charnaud or the captain. I was glad it was Ludan who came.

And now that I think of it, who sent for him, anyway?

Time advanced in minute, snail-crawling increments. Connie stopped in just past eleven, back from Izmir, but when she saw I was lying down, she insisted I get some sleep, saying she'd see me tomorrow. She gave me a warm hug and went off to meet other friends in the Lookout Bar at the stern of the ship.

But I couldn't sleep, and what I was getting, lying there, couldn't be called rest. My body tensed even in repose.

With a startling shrill, the phone rang again. It was eleven-thirty. "You are wanted at the dock to make a statement," John Andrews said when I answered, breathless.

A statement! At last! I, myself, will finally get to tell them what happened, to say I meant no harm . . . just to buy a souvenir . . . spend money . . . the poor people. . . .

I rushed down the corridor, almost running the thirty yards

to the stairs. I would tell them how the man forced himself on me, how I bought the heads just to get away, that I stopped only to see the old woman's embroidery.

I raced for the gangway, where John said he'd escort me to the dock. Why did I buy those damned heads? I hope they're all fakes. Ludan saw them . . . he's only an amateur, he admits. . . . John was waiting and we walked down the gangway to the dock together.

Inside the cavernous customs building, where four hours before I sat in hollow emptiness, a fair-sized crowd was gathered and the crush of their chattering voices covered the echoes of our steps as we crossed the cold marble floors to the customs counter and Bob Ludan. My senses were alive; I was going into battle.

In one acute glance my eyes swept and memorized the players and the scene. The handsome, black-uniformed inspector was there and three khaki-clad guards wearing Sam Brown belts with holstered hand guns over their tailored wool jackets. They stood, talking informally, at the perimeter of the crowd.

There were three other Turkish men in business suits moving about, and through the glass partitions behind the parallel inspection counters, under a bare light, I could see more people—three men in dark business suits, a stylishly dressed, dark-haired woman, and a stocky, gray-haired, swarthy-skinned man who, I was sure, was both important and a Turk. He was the only one with the confidence to have removed the jacket of his suit and conduct business, more comfortably, in shirtsleeves.

Entering the room, we had passed one of the ship's officers in knife-edged whites, carrying a walkie-talkie. I had seen him on the ship; his name was Robin, I remembered. He was connected to the purser's office.

Ludan, a head taller than everyone but John Andrews, was standing between the innermost counter and the glass-enclosed office, talking to a robust-looking Turkish civilian. He turned as John and I reached his elbow. Seeing us, the Turk receded, giving us privacy.

"Mrs. LePere," Ludan said, restraining a smile, "let me tell you what's going on."

"What do you mean, 'what's going on?' " I interrupted, agitated by anxiety and exhaustion. "I was told I would have the chance to make a statement. I want to make a statement."

"That appears to be unnecessary, at this time," Ludan continued, unruffled. "I was able to reach my friends and they were kind enough to come down. They've examined the heads . . ." my heart caught ". . . and, it's as I thought. The two smaller ones are modern, the larger one is of a late Roman period." My heart released and plunged. Ludan was frankly smiling now. "They say it is of no value." I was poised between despair and hope.

"They are making a statement." At that moment, the well-dressed woman, whom I watched exit the office a moment before, stopped in front of me at Ludan's side. He broke off to introduce us. She was slender and dark and almost beautiful, and her luminous, expressive eyes met mine with tender, female compassion. When she spoke, it was directly to me, in excellent English, colored by the accent and rhythms peculiar to Turks.

"I am glad to meet you, Mrs. LePere," she said, taking my hand, "and I want to tell you there is nothing to worry about anymore. We," she looked toward the office where her colleagues were waiting, "have made the examination. One of the heads is ancient but, I assure you, of no value and not important. We are just now waiting to have the typing of the report complete and we shall sign. I have told the chief to the customs, there are thousands of such unimportant objects in every museum warehouse in Turkey. It is absolutely possible you have purchased it from a seller in the streets. It is to be regretted what has happened to you, but you must not be afraid any more. I am quite certain you will have no more difficulties. You will sail with your ship."

Andrews, a foot away, listened to everything she said, his open, friendly face beaming when she finished.

"You see, Gene, what did I tell you," he grinned.

I wasn't so sure. I've got the collective superstition of thousands, maybe millions, of middle-European Jews in my genes, and that native wisdom says it doesn't pay to attract the attention of the *kahn aynhoreh*, the evil eye, with premature self-congratulation. I couldn't, no matter how much I wanted to, believe in victory at that moment. I wanted my news from the horse's mouth. But I replied to this lovely woman with a full heart and genuine tears trembling in my voice.

"Thank you," I said, squeezing the hand that held mine. "You are so kind to have spoiled your evening plans to come here and help a stranger. I'm very grateful, no matter how it comes out."

"Believe me," she soothed, "I am almost positive. It will be good for you."

After that Ludan and she fell into a lightweight, conversation, the kind you make when you're five minutes early to pick up your four-year-old from kindergarten and you sit in the car with the motor running, passing time with one of the other mothers you hardly know.

I fell silent, more anxious than ever as hope was raised and the moment of decision came inexorably closer. John kept up a chatter at my side. "I know you don't drink, Gene, but tonight, you're having a drink with me in the Pacific Bar. I won't take no for an answer. I told you it would be a cliff-hanger, but five minutes before we're due to sail they'll set it right. That's the Turks, alright, and here it is, five minutes before midnight and they're right on schedule."

"John," I gave him a quizzical grimace, "if this goes the way you say, I may have two drinks."

Around me everyone seemed to have forgotten why we were here. It was like a subdued party. John Andrews, still joking around, Bob Ludan, in his calm, controlled style, repeating again the favorable prognosis of his friends. Only I, the innocent, awaiting a verdict that, at that moment, seemed worse than a sentence of death, couldn't be distracted, couldn't make light of the situation, couldn't contain the anxiety of waiting.

Oh, God, does everything have to take so long in Turkey?

And just when my pulse slowed, when I began to feel the beginnings of belief, the gray-haired Turk, the man of the hour, now attired in a matching suit coat, strode from his office. All conversation ceased. The room fell into expectant silence.

He planted himself stolidly before the waiting throng, paused, and, in the incomprehensible language of Turkey, began his pronouncement.

I hung on his words, brief, delivered with a sober, expressionless, masculine voice, as if by giving them more than the usual attention, I would, by magic, understand Turkish. But it wasn't words that led me to enlightenment. I had only to watch the faces of those who did comprehend break and fall in dismay, to know the outcome of this dread, interminable watch.

I was to remain in Izmir. The ship would sail without me. From that moment all was chaos.

Everyone seemed to be in motion except me.

The chief engaged Ludan in an intense monologue. Andrews raced across the room to Robin's side, and together, via the hand-held radio, they tried to reach the captain. The lady archeologist was almost in tears, expressing bewilderment at an unimagined outcome, trying to comfort me and needing comfort herself. I, immobilized, stood and observed all the activity as if it had nothing to do with me. The players were distorted and distant as if seen through a long tunnel. Time was warped, slowed.

Though dazed, believing in the capriciousness of the *kahn aynhoreh*, I saw I was more prepared than they to absorb the shock. But the inner brittleness had taken a blow; I could feel pinpricks of pain—glass shards, no doubt—piercing the tender flesh deep inside my body and it made me straighten up and hold myself stiffly erect. Movements, now, had to be measured and careful, lest the fragile, newly formed, paper-thin glass structure of arteries and veins rupture and spill all the fluids of my body on the marble floor. I seemed calm, self-possessed. In truth, I was in a protective shell, ever so remote from the bustle around me.

But Robin and Andrews had my attention. I harnessed my pathetic, flickering store of energies, focusing it on their aside. Only the captain could still save me from the Turks. He could defy them, refuse them, use the power of his prestige, the economic power of the P&O against them. He could sail away with me. Hope flickered still.

I heard the captain over the hand-held intercom and instantly I became alert.

"You tell the chief of customs to come aboard to my cabin and tell me that to my face!" His voice was strong, firm.

Then Robin, looking about, demanded to speak to the chief, to pass on the captain's dictum.

"He has left the building," someone informed. And Robin spoke into the mike, to the captain safe aboard.

"He's gone, Sir, he's left the building. I'm afraid it's a *fait accompli*."

The excitement was over, the suspense, the last hope, all gone. The captain had entered the game much too late. He wished to play from the sidelines, not on the field, and even then, he entered carrying too little, only a boastful voice. His will was not committed. It was, indeed, a *fait accompli*.

Ludan told me I was to be allowed to reboard the *Sea Princess* one last time to pack a bag, that on his promise to have me appear at customs Monday morning, I was to stay in a hotel in Izmir over the weekend.

The hour for sailing had passed. It was well after midnight when he accompanied me aboard. At the captain's request, we went first to his cabin.

Making my way up the gangplank, every step was an effort. I suffered the debilitation of a long-distance runner after the race is over. When we arrived, I faced a somber company of ship's officers, looking as bewildered and embarrassed as I felt. John Andrews was there, and Robin, and their senior officer, the chief purser, a kind man with whom I'd developed a quiet friendship.

I stood, with what I hoped was dignity, before John King; Bob Ludan stood to one side. There was, I think, for most of us in that small room, an air of mourning. The others, their eyes fixed on my face, were silent as the captain, standing squarely, confronted me with a sharp face, asking,

"Did you really pay twenty dollars for those heads?"

"I did," I answered, meeting his eyes.

"And did you know they were antiques?"

"No," I said, "I did not."

He looked away, uncomfortably.

"Well, I'm sorry, Gene," was all he was able to say. There was an awkward silence. Then Ludan spoke,

"It's not my place," he said haltingly, deferential in his role as advisor to these men who were British and not his responsibility, "but I think it is important to advise your passengers of the laws of the countries they are about to enter."

"I didn't know," John King excused himself.

"I didn't know," the chief purser admitted sadly.

"I didn't know," poor John Andrews apologized.

Another awkward silence, again broken by the captain.

"Gene, if you'd like to take all of your belongings from the ship at this time, you may. If you'd prefer to take just enough for the few days, that's acceptable, also. I leave it entirely up to you."

A new decision. I wasn't up to it.

"I can't think," I said, knowing how late it was, embarrassed to have been the cause of the ship getting off schedule. "I have so many clothes . . . six weeks . . . gifts . . . ." So many gifts . . . tired . . . too tired, I think . . . "just one bag for the weekend, if you don't mind. I'm told I can rejoin the ship at . . ."

"Quite all right," King interrupted. He paused, seemed uncomfortable, then said,

"Before you leave tonight . . . er, there's a paper we've prepared for you to sign." And to Ludan, "Be sure Mrs. LePere stops at the purser's office, if you please."

The chief purser stepped forward to embrace me and place a kiss on my cheek. "I'm so sorry, Gene," he said.

John Andrews did the same. Knowing how sorry he had to be, I was unable to look him in the eye. How could I hide the accusation I felt. He had misled me. But as I was taking the hand King offered in parting, I felt that the captain had misled me more. Anger was just beneath the surface, but I pushed it from my mind. If I dwelt on betrayal I'd lose my composure. And composure was the only thing holding me together, a taut tissue covering a tidal wave of feelings. I was drowning.

Before going to the cabin, we stopped at the purser's office where I was handed the document to sign it. Old habits die hard: never put your name to anything you haven't read, I'd been taught. Apathetic and juiceless, I scanned the paper, knowing unless it was a confession of guilt, I would sign, discovering in the process how well-prepared the civilized English could be when protecting their own interests, though they seemed careless of mine.

The paper said, in effect, that Key Tours, Sylvia Franco's employers, would advance money for my out-of-pocket expenses in Izmir, for which I agreed to reimburse Peninsular & Orient within thirty days of my return home. The timing of the presentation for signature seemed overly calculating, but the arrangement was eminently fair—and helpful. This side trip was unexpected. I was low on funds and could run short.

Somewhere between the bureau and my cabin I lost Ludan and acquired a seaman, who followed me through the empty labyrinth of corridors, public rooms, and up the near-empty stairways into my starboard cubicle. He hovered as I got out the just-put-away suitcase and as I tried to concentrate on what to pack. His presence was inexplicable, annoying; it made me self-conscious and clumsy.

Was he a guard? Did they think I'd try to run? To hide? Didn't they realize I knew the odds against me were unbeatable, that it would be beneath my dignity to struggle or flee? I could never win against the ship's sellout or the Turks' determination. All I'd get for my defiance would be the embarrassment of a forced removal.

Or, was it that they were worried I would take my life? Did they fantasize this would be their response if were they in my place?

I sensed the captain believed me guilty and understood that assessment would make it easier for him to abandon me. The guard's very presence underscored the captain's need and I found it and King's attitude insulting. It was humiliating to be treated like a criminal.

I couldn't concentrate on what was to come, so I chose clothes at random, returning to the bag many articles that had just been removed. How many days would I be delayed? The weekend. Perhaps more? I found six pairs of clean underpants and took them all, and that seemed to decide it. I would take clothes for six days. Among those I chose were two "city" dresses, one for evenings, one for business, and three pairs of high-heeled leather sandals: random decisions made under pressure, the lateness of the hour, the guard's scrutiny. Sensing my tension, the guard stepped outside into the corridor, giving me an inch of breathing space for which I was grateful.

I opened every drawer, looking for whatever caught my eye; by seeing I hoped to remember and not to go off without things I couldn't do without, like vitamins and medication. In a drawer of the desk I found a small cache of instant coffee packets saved from the wake-up trays Eddie, the steward, brought to all his passengers. I put them in the bag, remembering how it had been to do without coffee on the overland. Hot water, I assumed, I could get.

When I'd finished and zipped the bag, I called the guard, who took the suitcase, while I locked the cabin door and pocketed the key. Poor little cabin. We weren't going to have a full week together but I would see it again Monday night—or Tuesday. No later than Wednesday, I was sure.

I thought of Connie, of my tablemates, of the appointment the next morning in the hair salon in the bowels of the ship on "D" deck. Hurrying behind the sailor, following my bag, I was afraid to look up, afraid of seeing someone I knew, afraid to say good-bye to the ship, afraid, embarrassed, humiliated at what was happening to me now and terrified of what was to come.

Ludan was waiting at the gangway and took my suitcase from the seaman. As we stepped across the threshold, I saw the raw, exposed, workings of the ship, now stripped of the cosmetics usually provided for the safety and psychological comfort of the passengers. As a liability soon to be discarded, I was no longer entitled to such niceties. For me the gangway was laid naked, and the instant I stepped from it to the dock, it would be pulled up, stowed away. The ship would then sail full speed for the next port, as if I'd never existed.

That walk down the slanted plank was torture. Four stories above, on the promenade deck, I could hear my former shipmates, in evening attire and a festive mood, lingering to watch the sailing. Wondering why the *Sea Princess* was so late departing, they would see me being escorted off the ship in disgrace. I felt utterly self-conscious and humiliated. I wanted to look up but hid my head instead.

On land, dazed, I followed Ludan the length of the customs building into a parking lot lit only by the moon and stars of a clear, Mediterranean night. There, a stocky man, tall for a Turk, remarked in English that he would follow us into town in his own car. Ludan told me he was a representative of Key Tours, that he would arrange payment for the hotel.

In the car, Ludan volunteered, "You know, an American citizen who requests a new passport is entitled to receive one."

I heard this as a definite signal. "Okay, then, I'm asking for a new passport and I'll fly out tomorrow."

"Oh, no," Ludan seemed taken aback. "That would put me in a very difficult position with the Turkish authorities. They've allowed you to stay in a hotel over the weekend only because I accepted responsibility for your appearance at customs Monday morning."

Deflated and confused, but wanting to cooperate, I assured him, "Okay, I won't ask. I don't want to do anything that would hurt my country."

Ludan and I talked as he drove. I couldn't understand the fuss being made by the Turks over the incident. None of the heads was rare or valuable. None was any longer in my possession. I had never attempted to hide them. Indeed, I'd been instrumental in seeing the first one exposed, in spite of Charnaud's attempt to gloss over it.

Ludan tried to explain the Turks' position. For more than a hundred years, their many Greek and Roman ruins had been plundered by archeologists from the Western nations. Untold numbers of priceless objects had been taken from Turkey; now on display in European museums, they had never been recovered. Deeply incensed, the Turks had enacted stringent laws to inhibit further removal of their ancient treasures.

What I heard made sense. I could understand how they felt.

In town, the streets of Izmir were dark and silent. It was about 1:00 A.M. on Saturday. In New York City on a Friday night at this hour, the streets would be alive with revelers.

We parked in front of the EFES hotel, preferred, I was told, because of its modern accommodations, but except for an expensive suite that I thought unduly extravagant, it was full. A block away, at the ETAP Oteli, I was checked into a room—the reservation made through Sunday night. I asked the Key Tours man to see that I rejoin the ship Monday, but he doubted there was air service from Izmir to Santorini, the ship's next stop. He thought I might fly into Dubrovnik or Venice and said he'd look into it. I agreed. I was agreeable to anything that put me back on the ship.

Before I went upstairs, I bought the European editions of *Newsweek* and *Time* for sale at the registration desk. By the dates on the covers, I knew they were two weeks old. But I'd been in the chrysalis of a luxury vacation for over five weeks; the contents would be news to me.

It was very late when Ludan saw me to my room.

"I hope you'll be comfortable here," he said. "I'll call you in the morning, about eleven. Is that alright?"

"Fine."

"Then I'll see you tomorrow. Get a good night's sleep, if you can."

"Yes."

He paused, turned. I watched him start back toward the waiting elevator. Now, I felt uncertain. I didn't want him to leave.

"Mr. Ludan," I called, my fears jumbled, unsorted. I chose one at random. "The water? Is it alright to drink from the tap?"

"The tap . . ." he repeated, pondering, "No. It would probably be better if you ordered the bottled."

I had to release him. "Thank you," I said.

"Good night," he answered, and stepped into the elevator.

The door closed, leaving me alone at 1:30 in the morning in a strange hotel room in a city halfway around the world from mine, with people who spoke a language I didn't understand, after a day that had turned my well-managed life into a plate of poisoned hash.

In bed, relieved to be prone, I thought about a new passport and wondered why, if he didn't want me to leave, Bob mentioned it at all. Then, exhausted, I slept.

I awoke, anxious and panicky, just after 7:00. Too early, but sleep had fled. I drew a bath—long awaited, not possible to enjoy—dressed, ordered a breakfast of scrambled eggs that, when they arrived, were watery and tastless. I couldn't force myself to eat them.

I tried, before Ludan was to call, to get my hair washed and set but discovered the hotel had no salon for women. Without a passport I was afraid to venture into the streets, so I went back to the room and read. A few minutes before 11:00, Ludan called, and at 11:30 we met in the small lobby of the hotel.

Seated in overstuffed brown leather chairs, waiting for the tea he ordered to be served, Ludan said, as he handed me several sheets of paper, that this was a list of attorneys.

"You think I need a lawyer?" I asked, surprised and somewhat shocked.

"I think it might be helpful," he replied in "diplomatese."

Tea was served; he poured. We were both smoking. The notion of needing a lawyer heightened the panic that was never far away.

"Why do I need a lawyer if I have you?"

"I'm not able to give legal advice."

"What am I being held for?"

"I thought I explained they have very tough laws against smuggling."

"Smuggling? They think I'm a smuggler?"

"They are holding you under the statutes against smuggling. I wanted to tell you, last night the customs chief asked me to say how sorry he is. He believes you had no intent to smuggle and are innocent. But recently they had some . . . problems. Several former customs employees are in prison. Because the heads were in the open a long time, everyone had a chance to see them. He was afraid to let you go even though . . . you are innocent. He's afraid of losing his own job . . . a pension . . . he has a family. He was afraid of going to jail, himself. He asked me to tell you how much he regretted having to detain you."

"A lot of good that does me," I said. "These people sound terrified for their own safety. What kind of a country is this?"

"It's a constitutional democracy . . . an important member of NATO, an ally of the United States. Turkey's in a strategic geographic and political position. It shares borders with the U.S.S.R., with Syria, Iran, Iraq, Bulgaria. Surrounded by countries who oppose the Western democratic ideal, it's the only democracy in the area and very important to the stability of the Mediterranean.

He leaned closer, lowering his voice. "In actual fact, since September 12, 1980, it has been under military rule."

"Ah, the guns . . . the soldiers . . ."

"Yes. It may seem unpleasant at first, but many people who lived here before the military takeover say they prefer having the soldiers. Before that, Turkey was chaotic, at the mercy of terrorists. Many innocent people were killed every day. Everyone was afraid to go into the streets, day or night. Under the generals, order was restored and people feel safe again."

"At a price, it seems," I commented. Ludan didn't answer.

When the tea was finished he proposed we leave the hotel and talk at his apartment. He'd arranged for a Turkish friend to join us. I believed Ludan was afraid to be overheard, or maybe feared being spied upon. The idea that an American diplomat could be fearful in Turkey added greatly to my own anxiety.

Outside, the beautiful weather held, but in the sparkling noon light, Izmir looked dirty. A fine dun-colored film covered everything: buildings, cars, the leaves on the trees that grew on the islands in the middle of the street.

On the road I asked Ludan how long he'd been in Izmir and if he'd ever had a case like mine before this.

He said he'd been assigned to Turkey a year before, after two years in the Far East, that this assignment would also be for two years, that he liked Turkey very much, especially Izmir, and, no, he'd never handled a case like mine. That was why he'd asked the Turk to join us and why he was trying to reach the Italian consular officer. An Italian had been arrested a month before under the same statute.

His apartment was large and comfortably furnished. I noted with particular interest a mammoth dining table and twelve chairs, deciding that entertainment must be a significant aspect of a diplomat's duties.

Here we were in Ludan's own home, but he still seemed stiff, to me. I don't know how I seemed to him. I knew I was going though the right moves, but the most important part of me wasn't there. It was focused elsewhere: worried, distracted, scared, I was much preoccupied with holding myself erect and walking carefully so as not to disturb the fragile structure growing inside. Careful, careful I had to be. Careful and holding in my feelings.

I thanked him for the tea he prepared, and waiting for his friend, Bob called the Italian consulate while I looked at the attorney's list still clutched in my hand.

Nejet GENCALP? M. Burhanettin KARAALIOGLU? Suha TANRIOIVER? Born in Denizli in 1953, speaks Turkish and English. No, too young and who could pronounce his name, anyway? Who could pronounce any of these names? Too harsh, too ugly; I shrank from making any selection. L. Atilla AKAT. Atilla? There's a name to curdle the blood. What's this written here in pencil? "Woman?"

That got my attention. Close to my age—seasoned but in her full powers—she was a graduate of the American University in Istanbul, fluent in English, and familiar with American customs. Best of all, I could pronounce her name. I worried that a woman in Turkey might not be treated with respect, but when

Ludan's Turk arrived I asked both of them what they thought. They said this was not a problem: professional women were treated as equals in Turkey.

I decided to interview her, and with the Turk's help, an appointment was set for 4:00 that afternoon.

Before he took me back to the hotel, Ludan reached the Italians, but if he learned anything important, he kept it from me. He wanted me to tell him the names of the persons in the States I'd like notified of my situation, but I thought it too soon to alarm them. "After all," I said, "this may blow over by Monday, and I'll rejoin my ship and come home on schedule. Why worry them for nothing?"

Ludan understood; he dropped the subject.

Atilla, as she asked to be called, arrived at my hotel early, and although she apologized that her English was rusty—"I've not used my English for two years," she said—I was delighted by her appearance and mastery of not only the language but American colloquialisms.

She was slender and had the Turkish coloring. Her narrow face was deeply lined by pain but made beautiful by courage. Stylishly dressed, she moved well. I found her graceful and poised. "Smart" was the word that came to mind, and in her I sensed energy and strength.

She listened carefully as I told my story in detail and, afterward, paid me the respect of spelling out some unvarnished truths about my predicament. That earned her my respect and trust. For as much as I didn't like what she said, I have always preferred the truth from which, up to now, I realized, too many people had been shielding me.

"The law is serious," she said, bluntly. "I hope the experts at the dock are wrong and the head is not ancient. Otherwise, you will be found guilty."

"But, doesn't the fact that I wasn't hiding them count for anything?" I pleaded, as if she could manufacture answers that pleased me.

"The law is not so important for motive. You have the heads on your person. That is most important for the law. What would really help you," she added, "is if you can direct them to the man who has sold you these artifacts." She sighed. "It is really too bad you have said to the customs the head is not onyx. Of course, I understand. You have been honest, but . . ."

I told her there was no way I could identify the man on the dusty level overlooking the terraces at Pamukkale. I'd hardly looked at him and certainly not into his face.

She said she understood, then told me the penalty for smuggling antiquities was three to five years, that a fine might be added but not substituted for prison time. With good behavior I would be out in one and a half years. This news was almost more than I could bear. I was ready to give way and cry, feeling terrified and helpless before the narrowness and rigidity of the Turkish law. I hadn't even begun to learn about or understand it.

Atilla wondered why I hadn't been brought before a judge last night, holding an argument, aloud, with herself, as to the meaning of this failure, "we have courts ready all night for this purpose." But when she saw how upset I had become, she repeated her hope that the archeologists who had come to the dock were wrong.

After she had told me what her fee would be—one price if I was set free on Monday, twice that amount "if things did not go as easily"—I hired her. Before she left we agreed to meet outside the hotel at 8:30 Monday morning and walk to the American consulate, two blocks away.

Alone, again, I was torn: secure in the honesty and competence of Atilla Akat, horrified at her assessment of my chances.

I spent the remainder of the weekend in the hotel room, ordering eggs from room service twice a day and reading every printed word of the magazines. When I'd read both once, I began *Newsweek* again followed by *Time*. They were all I had to keep me company, all I had to distract me from the panic that rose often and threatened to overwhelm me.

Sunday I had two phone calls. The first was from Bob Ludan, who seemed only to want to know I was there and alive. Atilla called soon after to say Turkey had gone off daylight savings time last night and it was an hour earlier than I'd thought. After I laid down the receiver I told myself, This lady is on the ball, she's looking out for me. I think I've lucked out. Then I reset my watch.

I hated that fate had chosen this weekend to be forty-nine hours long instead of the usual forty-eight. It already seemed interminable.

Sunday night I slept badly, up often, pacing the floor, wringing my hands, and praying to God to get me out of this nightmarish mess. Monday morning I was up early anyway.

After I dressed and had tea, believing one way or the other I'd be checking out of the hotel today, I packed my bag. With it zipped and ready, I left it near the door before I went to meet Atilla.

Ludan drove the three of us to customs. We arrived, as promised, at nine. Of course, the Turks weren't ready. Even in daylight, they were dark, mysterious, and forbidding. We were ushered into the chief's office, and although I remembered Bob said the gray-haired, important man behind the desk regretted the detention, and although he was courteous, none of it moved me.

Everyone and everything was far away, out of touch, and I was playing some part, moving from scene to scene, each with new actors; none of it was real.

The feeling of helplessness, of being caught in a swift current of events against which I could struggle but make no gain, stayed with me. Usually impatient, I sat quietly, left out of everything because of language. The others might have been discussing the weather, where they'd had dinner last night, or even my case. I had no idea. And these circumstances separated me from other people, carved into the day a sense of remoteness, of isolation.

I may have been an object of interest, something to be talked about, moved from place to place, even addressed on infrequent occasions, yes or no answers preferred. Unless I asked, translations weren't offered, as if it didn't concern me. On demand, only the sketchiest outline was given. Such treatment is depersonalizing, dehumanizing. The process that began Friday night, robbing me of dignity and self, of will and determination, continued all day Monday.

When the papers we'd been waiting for were ready, Atilla and I, under the aegis of a customs guard who carried the three heads, took a taxi—at my expense—to the Aegean Museum's newly completed, modern building ten minutes from the docks. Although it was not yet open to the public, the curators, conservators, and other personnel had moved from their old quarters in Izmir's museum of antiquities, and this was where the heads would receive "official" appraisal.

Ludan begged off coming with us; he had other work to do. We were to meet him back at the consulate when it was over.

The building sat on a rise, partway up a hill overlooking the Konak and the bay. I remembered the road. Sylvia had taken us all the way to the top before we went to the dock. How could I have known this building, which I had passed Friday afternoon, would become important to me?

Outside it was a pleasing amalgamation of modern architecture expressed in materials that did not clash with the nineteenth-century city. Inside, following the guard and Atilla through a maze of hallways and stairs, I saw the building was raw, unfinished, hollow, bare.

On the second floor we entered an office furnished with two old, battered walnut desks. Desks, I imagined, that had once been in use by New York Harlem bookies for fifty years before being shipped to Turkey in 1963 and sold at a profit to the Aegean Museum. Such thoughts were frivolous, I knew, but I was not needed here. They would handle everything without me.

Atilla made inquiries of a stranger passing in the hall. The guard and she exchanged words. A blond woman entered. She was short and stocky and had a bitter mouth in the center of her round face. Wearing a gray cotton "business suit" that pulled over her hips, she bustled, making abrupt movements that signaled, "I'm important, I'm busy. What do you want?" Real words were exchanged. I could only guess at what was said.

The heads, still nestled in the manila wrappings, were offered for her inspection by the guard. We all watched with interest as the woman cast a cursory, albeit experienced, eye over the three. She drew her conclusions with so much speed, I wondered at the authenticity of so hasty an opinion. In fewer than ten seconds—or so it seemed to me—she'd returned the two smaller heads to the guard with a disdainful gesture and, holding the larger in her hand, turned to Atilla, spouting rapid-fire Turkish. I, the invisible woman, waited.

"Blondie" (I know it was bleached) took a seat to my right and placed the head on the desk in front of her. A possessiveness told me it was hers now. Atilla sat in a chair in front of the same desk and across the room from me. I could see clearly the faces of the women as they spoke. The curator's was alive with anger, resentment, hostility, pride. Atilla's revealed no emotion; she seemed detached, a lawyer seeking information, assessing, perhaps, a witness.

Then, in an instant, without warning—as at the dock Friday night—in response to something the blond woman had said, Atilla's face broke. Her cheeks sagged, as if she had taken a staggering blow, and suddenly she looked old, old and defeated.

But she hadn't given up. I saw her arguing, questioning, saw her pull herself together. Soon after, the guard still with us, we left. I didn't know where we were going next and didn't really care. What I wanted to know and could hardly wait until we were outside to ask was, what had been said that was so awful?

"She said you must be tried under Article 68, 'they have stolen everything from us and are still not satisfied. They want more.' That is what she said."

There was more, I knew it, but Atilla wasn't willing—yet— to tell it to me.

There is a Yiddish word that best describes the next two hours. Shlep. I was given no sense of what lay ahead or why we went where we did. Mostly, I didn't ask. I was shlepped by Atilla. Pulled along, will-lessly taken.

Instead of returning immediately to the consulate, Atilla flagged a *taksi* (phonetically correct, easy to read, hard to get used to on a passing cab) and instructed him as to our destination. The guard sat in front with the driver.

In the back seat Atilla asked for an accounting of my funds. There wasn't much. Every gift had been bought, all shore excursions paid for, my room, meals, and transportation home prepaid. I was carrying about seventy-five dollars in American and English currency, and an American Express Gold Card. Atilla said I was going to need more money, for her fee and for my own requirements. We decided I'd have to arrange a transfer of funds from my account in the States to a local bank, for which Atilla would need power of attorney.

Instructing the driver again, we made an interim stop at an International Turkish Bank where, on the second floor, following a forty-five minute procedural struggle, my "foreign" money was turned into Turkish lira (at a rate of 250 to the dollar). The bank received my personal check for $1,000, and Atilla's right to draw on the cash—when it arrived at some unspecified time in the future—was secured by my signature.

The next stop was at the official, state-run notary office at the court building in the Konak. Faced with white marble, in the heart of the business life of Izmir where the streets were narrow and crowded with pedestrians, the court building was an imposing structure of seven stories. It towered above the adjacent buildings.

It was cold inside, or maybe it was me. For my important appearance today, I was wearing one of the two dresses I had taken into Izmir. Made of a wash-and-wear fabric in a pattern of irregular white dots over light gray (the colors were reversed in the trim: gray over white), it gave a modest appearance without being dowdy. It was cut in a princess line with a slit neck, self-belt that tied in front, and long sleeves.

On my feet I was wearing the only shoes that seemed to go with the dress—a pair of thin-strapped black, open, high-heeled sandals. My legs were sun-bronzed and bare.

In the sun I'd been warm, at the museum, comfortable, but here in the massive, cold court building, I felt chilled.

On one of the upper floors Atilla led me into a small, very crowded room lined with desks, counters, and filled with confusion. The only window was shut; the air inside was fog thick. To have lit a cigarette would have been an insult; breathing in that room was like chain-smoking. It was a very unpleasant place.

Nauseated, I asked Atilla why we were here. "To have a power of attorney so I may act to your lawyer," she said, confusing her prepositions. "In Turkey it is necessary for all lawyers to represent their client."

What should have been a routine matter, something handled

every day, became tedious because, in this room of expert smokers, sucking away on their strong Turkish cigarettes, not a soul spoke English.

With Atilla as interpreter, I swore to my name and that of my parents—Joseph and Jennie—to the date and place of my birth (Turkish typewriters have no "W" so New York was typed Nevv York); and Atilla, armed with her newly acquired authority, paid the fee from my hoard of lira. I couldn't get out of there soon enough.

We hadn't shaken the guard. He was waiting downstairs, where the three of us got into another *taksi* to be driven to the American consulate. After a morning of too much Turkey, I welcomed the sight and smell of my country's offices with their carpeted floors, American fabrics, light colors, new furniture, and modern equipment. The Americans smoked too, but there were no butts on the floor.

I had overdosed on Turkish delight and was overdue for apple pie; the consulate was an oasis of home in a desert of exotica.

Ludan invited us to take seats in a waiting room furnished with comfortable, stuffed leather couches and chairs. He sent out for sandwiches before he joined us. There I regained some advantage, and the guard, who appeared to be greatly enjoying what had to be an unusual day in an otherwise humdrum life, was odd man out. American consulate: English spoken here.

In front of Ludan, who was anxious to know all that had happened since he'd left us that morning, I was able to force Atilla to reveal what was to her the most damaging news of the day. Her belief that the sentence upon conviction for smuggling antiques was three to five years, was out of date. The museum curator had informed Atilla this morning the law was changed —effective July 1—three months past. The penalty now was five to ten years imprisonment plus fine.

In silence Ludan and I digested the news.

The sandwiches came, clearly Turkish and not American, but looking good. Bob, Atilla, and the guard began to eat and I forced myself to bite and chew; I'd had very little nourishment in the past three days. But anxiety and depression are not appetite stimulants. I returned three-quarters of the food to the plate untouched.

It was 2:20 when we arrived and an hour later when we left the consulate, now a group of five. Ludan introduced and brought along a tiny, sweet-faced Turkish employee of the consulate named Makbule Sevil. She was to act as interpreter, where one was required.

I knew I was to be presented, again in the court building, at the chief prosecutor's office, where he would examine the accusations against me by customs and supported by the hostile curator. He would then come to a decision about my future. As best as I could understand it, based on a youthful, but prolonged, experience as a probation officer in Los Angeles, this was roughly parallel to our presentation of evidence to a district attorney for evaluation of whether or not to proceed against a likely suspect.

All day Atilla had been carrying, in addition to her purse, a fat, two-handled briefcase. Now, she explained it was probable the prosecutor would move against me, and if he did, I'd go before a judge today. Inside the briefcase was her lawyer's robe, without which no "avocat" appeared in court. On the other hand, she had brought it only on the chance she would be allowed to defend me since, at the anticipated court, the accused is not allowed to be represented by a lawyer.

I was thoroughly confused.

There appeared to be no clear-cut procedural road map; the course was full of unexpected twists, turns, decisional forks, and detours. Ludan was an innocent; I, totally ignorant; Atilla, the only navigator with previous experience. Yet I had the definite feeling we were going into uncharted country studded with land mines. *Caveat*, Gene.

At the courthouse, it was back to shlep and be patient.

The papers were left with the prosecutor's clerk. The five of us—Ludan, Makbule, the guard, Atilla, and I—took seats on hard wooden benches in a hall filled with prisoners, guards, lawyers, families, witnesses, a fearful din of voices, and a haze of cigarette smoke. Under a sign that said "No Smoking" in Turkish, we settled down to wait. There was a carpet of dead, squashed butts on the floor to which Atilla, Ludan, and I added our share.

An hour passed. The level of my anxiety was unchanged. If anything, if it's possible, as the procedures closed the distance to final decision, I grew more tense, more physically protective, and more silent. The others chattered away in Turkish, relieving me of any obligation to participate.

The hallways slowly cleared until there was no one left but our small party, and after a time, because it seemed, even to Atilla, it was taking unduly long, she went to learn the reason for the delay.

She returned in a lighter, more optimistic mood and enthusiastically explained it was the clerk's opinion that the prosecutor wasn't going to see me because the case would be dismissed. I would be going home. This was translated for the guard's benefit, after which a certain levity found its way into the scene; smiles creased the faces of my four companions.

We waited another half hour. At last the clerk appeared from a doorway some yards down the hall. She walked to Atilla and delivered a document. Her face was unreadable, but Atilla's sharp intake of breath told the story. The case was not dismissed. The next stop was the courtroom.

I am not a pessimist. I never have been. I am always the one who believes there's got to be a pony underneath that pile of shit. Lucky in the past, luck was working against me now. Luck you can't fight. This time I wasn't going to be allowed to skip any stations of the cross. I wasn't surprised, but I seemed to be the only one who wasn't. Or maybe it was just that I was numb and the others could still feel.

In shock, the others were unable to act in that moment. So, I stood and they followed my lead.

Then I was shlepped to another hall, to sit on another bench outside a different door, under another no smoking sign, to wait and watch as a middle-aged Turk with a long-handled broom swept away a deluge of cigarette butts and burnt-out wooden matches, the miniature debris of a hundred personal hurricanes.

It was still light outside, perhaps 6:30, when four of us entered the courtroom. In the course of one assignment for probation, I'd been a court officer, spending several hours of every day in courtrooms. That early experience had little bearing on this Turkish legal arena. It was larger than a breadbox but smaller than a U.S. corporate flunky's office. In that approximately square room, the judge sat rear right at another of the Harlem bookie's desks, looking to my left as I stood with my back to the door. Facing him and looking toward my right, at a well-worn wooden table, sat a young woman who turned out to be the court stenographer. In front of her on the table was a metal typewriter, vintage 1935. It was similar to that used by the notary earlier that morning, a thousand years ago today.

The guard remained in the hall; Ludan and Atilla took seats behind me, against the corridor wall, to the left of the door. Makbule was at my side. Roughly centered in the the middle of the room, both of us stood holding our hands clasped before us, which Makbule had hastily advised just before entering the courtroom.

Tension, fatigue, and a lack of food were responsible for the vibrating tremors that broke, like waves, over my body. I wasn't afraid, only anxious to present myself so powerfully and so clearly in my first and only chance to "make a statement," that the judge would immediately recognize the whole episode as an embarrassing mistake, that a woman of my dignity and character was incapable of so heinous a crime as attempted smuggling.

What I'd forgotten to consider—given a favorable, caring, attentive attitude on the part of the judge, which I thought, now having seen him, unlikely—was the impossibility of impacting through the conduit of a soft-voiced, passive translator. My dream, urgent and desperate, for which I summoned every vestige of remaining energy, was impossible to realize.

The judge, in a black robe with red satin collar, looked unkind, tired, and bored. He spoke; Makbule translated. I was to identify myself: name, birth date, address, mother's and father's names. I spoke; Makbule translated. Everything I'd been through at the notary, everything had to be spelled—more than once. The stenographer typed direct from the translation. Finally I was asked to tell what had happened, how I'd come into possession of the heads.

All the pent-up words came pouring out. I made sure to speak slowly and articulate carefully, to organize the topic chronologically, to look at the judge's face, to hold his eye, to pause occasionally for translation. It seemed to me that each time, my lengthy discourse was followed by too brief a paragraph of Turkish. Makbule couldn't be repeating everything I'd said.

A third of the way through the story, the judge, whose

interest I thought I held, interrupted. Makbule reported he wanted me to be briefer. My heart sank, my hopes with it.

Swallowing, wringing my hands—still clasped, almost as in prayer—I tried to discipline my tongue, to sort the irrelevant from the crucial. Under fire, desperate not to alienate the judge on whom rode my absolutely last chance, I covered the story, leaving out the special pleadings, and prayed my personal presence—tired, middle-aged, dignified, honorable American lady whom you'd trust with your most precious possession—would make him believe me.

When I was finished and Makbule had repeated it in Turkish, the judge began speaking. The stenographer who, up to then, sat idly, began typing, a machine-gun staccato accompaniment to his words, using three fingers only. I couldn't believe it.

This was to be the official record? A summary in the judge's words, not mine, not even Makbule's. And I, not knowing if he was truly reporting the facts, worried that he hadn't said enough. I whispered to Makbule, and when the record was made, she asked the judge, on my behalf, if I might make a statement. He nodded his agreement.

"Your honor," I said, choosing my words carefully and pausing frequently, "I am a law-abiding citizen at home, respectful of the laws of my country and yours. I wished to be a good visitor to your country. I am innocent of intent or knowledge that any artifact in my possession was ancient, nor did I try to hide them. Please let me go home to my own country."

I was finished. The judge nodded and spoke again to the court reporter, who clacked away at the machine briefly. If a heart can truly be said to rise and hang in the throat, choking off breath, mine had. How long I waited to hear this man's verdict, I don't know. It didn't seem long. It didn't seem long enough.

Perfunctory was the word that came to mind. I could have phoned it in. In my deepest heart I felt the judgment was made before I entered the room, that everything that was played on this little stage between 6:30 and 7:15, Monday, October 3, 1983, had been a cruel farce.

Without so much as a "sorry," I was remanded, forthwith, to Buja (Buca) Prison.

My audience of spectator-rooters was appalled. Even little Makbule looked wounded.

My hardening, internal glassworks kept me from collapsing. In a state of shock, wanting but unable to comfort Atilla, I moved to allow them to escort me from the room. We would go first to the hotel to get my belongings and from there to the prison, in the outskirts of Izmir, east northeast of the city, in a suburb called Buja.

It is one thing to be ordered to prison. It is another to enter it.

The atmosphere in the taxi, driving to Buja, was oppressive, weighted with unexpressed feelings.

The customs guard, his work done, had left us outside the court building, and Makbule, after a sympathetic embrace, had departed at the hotel, where we picked up my bag. Ludan and Atilla, somber, protective sentinels, setting aside any personal plans, accompanied me in the taxi to prison.

There was little conversation. The cab plunged through the dark streets in a silence broken only when one of us, stunned but planning for the future, thought of something essential to voice.

The darkness of the Turkish night had descended, and my brain, unwilling to contemplate what lie ahead, focused only on the moment.

"The prison is not so bad as you may expect," Atilla volunteered. "You will not be able to bathe every day—I know Americans like to bathe very often—but Turkish women are very kind to helpless people. You will see."

I heard her. I sat motionless. I was resigned.

Looking into the black night, I saw unfamiliar sights move past; I saw and didn't process what I'd seen.

Ludan, who had been making notes on his yellow tablet, spoke. "I've been trying to write down a few words you'll need in prison. Water is *su,* food is *yemek,* bread is *ekmek* . . . yes is *evet.* What else?"

I tried to concentrate and was unable to think. I gave no reply. Neither did Atilla.

I remembered something. Reaching both hands to my ears, one at a time I removed the antique gold and diamond earings, a gift from Jimmy, my ex-husband, which I always wore. I took the star sapphire and diamond ring, given to me by my father, from the third finger of my left hand. If Turkish prisons were anything like those in America, I was unwilling to take these sentimental, valuable pieces with me.

"Please, Atilla," I said, my voice sounding flat and dead to my own ears, "keep these for me until I am out." I placed them into her hand. Without words, she accepted them.

Silence. The night seemed pitiless as we hurtled through blackness encased in a movable tomb.

Something prodded me. I could no longer help myself. Someone else would have to assume the burden for me. Two names came to mind. Jim LePere, my ex-husband, and Paul Attaguile, my attorney and friend. Key people, people who loved me, people to count on. Both had brains and courage, loyalty and determination, commitment.

"I have to tell you who to notify," I said to Bob. "It's time, now."

"Yes," Ludan agreed.

I spelled out their names and addresses and phone numbers, struggling to force my brain, numb and lifeless, to remember Paul's home number as well as that of his office. Haltingly, by sheer force of will, I produced them, surprising myself. When you're desperate, when you're up against a wall, when you *have* to remember numbers, see how well you can do it, I congratulated myself.

It seemed a long time had passed when the car finally slowed and turned off the main road, and I strained in the darkness, sensing the moment was near, to have a glimpse of the dread place to which I'd been banished. But all I saw in the still blackness beyond the window were looming shapes of full-leafed trees, outlined against a dark sky. And there, just there behind them, a great, grim wall. Nothing more.

The car came to a stop. Now, under a single bare light, I was able to see a uniformed soldier holding a rifle. He stood within an enclosure, near a gate.

There was a long moment during which nobody spoke; then Ludan, on the right, opened the door and got out. Atilla, in the middle, followed. Slowly, I slid the width of the back seat and, taking a deep breath, left the car to stand at Ludan's side. The soldier opened the gate.

"I can't go any further," Ludan said.

"I understand," I answered.

He held out his hand. I took it.

"I'll get in touch with Jim and Paul," he promised. "Is there anyone else?"

"No," I answered, "They will contact the others."

"Good-bye," Bob said, handing me his yellow sheet of paper with a pathetically small Turkish vocabulary, "I'll come to see you tomorrow."

"That will be good," I said.

"We must go," Atilla spoke, taking my suitcase.

"Of course," I answered, and turned to follow her.

Passing from one side of the gate to the other, through the open gap in a cold, chain-link fence, was the moment of passing from symbolic freedom into the black hell of eternal death.

I walked behind Atilla, forcing my footsteps, controlling my eyes to stay on her back, disciplining my mind not to think, along a short cement walk and into the prison.

The inside of the building was illuminated by electric light bulbs—bare, infrequently placed, of low wattage. The lighting served to heighten an already strong sense of unreality. It seemed as if I were moving through a dream, unable, as in a dream, to comprehend or to retain detail. Nothing in this dream fit into the context of my previous life's experiences.

We walked through corridors, making turns. The floors were raw cement, our footsteps loud. Along the way, like grim, moving shadows, we passed uniformed men who paused in their occupations to stare.

Atilla led me into a small office, an untidy nerve center that kept the prison running and smelled of stale smoke and dead cigarettes. There, presenting the court order to a middle-aged guard in a dark blue uniform, she began the admissions process of my incarceration. I, a passive ghost in her wake, stood motionless and silent. Around me, in increasing numbers, gathered a host of curious, uniformed, dark and mysterious Turks. All were men.

It is my belief that people cannot tolerate temper tantrums in adults. Such behavior is seen to be childish and inappropriate, and it serves only to embarrass the onlookers because they feel helpless in the face of uncontrolled terror and because it reminds them of their own unacknowledged fears. In the end it works against any hope of mutual respect.

I was pliable when Atilla, having received permission from the intake officer, led me to a table in the corner of the room and painstakingly recorded my fingerprints, for all time, on the prison's forms.

The next step was worse. Much, much worse.

Moved to the opposite wall, I was asked to stand while a guard hung a number around my neck. By nothing more than force of will, imposed self-discipline, I held myself tall and calm as a man in a white coat, using an ordinary tourist camera, snapped one full-face and one side-view photograph. The thickening glass structure inside, the walls of which were hard as a glass rod, held me erect. I would not break down. I would not.

The ultimate symbolization of the apprehended criminal—being photographed with a number on my chest, hanging from a string around my neck—was, for me, the single most humiliating experience of my life. I cannot conceive of anything that might happen to me in the future that could ever make me feel as bad.

Afterward I was led to an adjoining room, actually an intersecting hallway, where, in the center of the room on a wooden table, my suitcase was opened and the articles inside examined by the man in the white coat. Atilla stood at my side acting as interpreter. As we looked, I realized the bathing suit and silky, blue dress, packed at a time like this, when my brain was not functioning clearly, would be useless to me here. Atilla agreed to take them home.

It appeared the examiner was mostly interested in toilet articles and drugs. I later learned, because he told me, the examiner was a prisoner/doctor. He seemed familiar with the items I carried, commenting favorably on the vitamins and knowingly on the Synthroid .3 which, as a hypo-thyroid, I must have if I am to function. Then he took a 5 milligram tablet of Valium from the vial I had—clearly labled as a prescription—and, asking a guard for water, gave it to me, instructing Atilla to ask me to take it.

Valium is something I reserve for unusual occasions. I use fewer than twenty of that minimal strength a year and then, only to sleep. I was already exhausted. I didn't know why he was demanding I take it. I didn't want to.

The guard returned with what looked like a jelly glass filled with tap water. I hesitated. The doctor was kindly, nonthreatening but insistent. Atilla urged me to do as I was asked.

Water. Remembering Ludan's suggestion that I drink bottled only, I thought, What irony.

But that option was past. Gone, over. The realist acceded. Choking back a wave of nausea, I took the pill and drank, and to my surprise, found myself wildly thirsty. I drained the glass and wanted to ask for more, but did not.

The doctor allowed me to keep the solutions for my extended-wear contact lenses and a small bottle of Anacin. The remaining drugs he reserved, but Atilla told me they would be sent to the cell and held for me under lock and key. I nodded, hoping it was true.

At last the process seemed completed. The doctor closed the bag in which my clothing was tumbled and in disarray. I stood, passively waiting.

Atilla turned to me. "I must leave you now," she said, apologetically. "They will allow me to go no further."

I felt a certain panic rise and pushed it down. "Yes," I said.

She moved to embrace me in a strong hug, promising to come the following day. She reassured me I would be alright and told me not to be frightened. "Yes," I said, and watched her walk away.

Alone. I felt so alone. Surrounded by people, male soldiers, and guards, I'd never felt so alone before.

A youthful soldier approached and, taking the suitcase, motioned me to follow him. We left that room going into a corridor, then through a sliding barred gate into another area that was the intersection of two perpendicular corridors; the walls were actually bars. It was a key junction where two young soldiers stood talking.

There, my guide indicated I was to accompany one of the soldiers. I nodded and reached to take the suitcase from his hand. He resisted giving it up. Surprised, I pulled at the handle only to find him unwilling to release his hold.

"I have to have my suitcase," I said. "My clothes are in it. I need them."

He answered in Turkish and I understood nothing. I tugged, but he refused to relinquish the case, and we spoke at each other in our separate, useless languages.

Suddenly the full impact of my situation came clear. Hopeless. It was hopeless. Without language I couldn't survive here. Without my pitifully few personal possessions, which I needed unquestionably, I would be bereft of everything that was mine. Everything that was me.

At last, after so long a time under the most difficult circumstances of my life, my self-containment broke. I began to cry.

Hopeless. It was hopeless.

Instead of exercising his uncontestable rights, the soldier placed the suitcase on the floor between us in a gesture of temporary truce and tried to get me to stop crying. How could he know my tears belonged to shocks and fears sustained over three days time. The loss of the suitcase was only the newest threat. I was inconsolable and hardly noticed that he spoke with one of the other soldiers or when that soldier left the room.

We stood there, my soldier looking sympathetic, the other, bored; and I, feeling utterly vulnerable, was in tears and drawn inward. Therefore, I was astonished to hear a female voice behind me say, "What you crying? Soldier try help you." I looked up to see a pale, sharp-faced, young woman dressed in cotton pajamas burst into the room. She radiated so much energy she almost vibrated as she took charge, and in my relief to hear English spoken, I fell on her with renewed tears.

Shrugging me off, she reached for the suitcase. "No cry," she said, "Soldier want put suitcase in safe place. No get stolen. He try help you."

"But, I need my clothes," I said, "everything inside."

"Okay. We take."

Swiftly she stooped, and opening the case at the same time as she spoke to the soldier in Turkish, she began swooping up the mangled contents. I looked questioningly at the soldier, and when he smiled, I smiled back.

Dividing them between us, the woman and I carried my things from the room accompanied by one of the khaki-uniformed men. They led me down a dimly lit corridor that stretched like a tunnel to nowhere. We'd gone only a few yards when they stopped at the right side of the dark hall, in front of a great steel door.

The door slid to open: it was ajar now. Standing in the six-inch opening, peering out, was a large, full-bosomed woman who, when she saw us, moved to slide the door open and stood aside so we could pass through. In a blur I noticed a full-to-the-floor costume and black hair that was pulled tight back from an angry face. I heard the harsh spate of a Turkish exchange between her and the woman I'd followed, then a grating sound as the heavy door closed with a clang behind me.

I was inside the prison cell.

Withdrawn and exhausted from the many shocks of the last days, I seemed robbed of my usual acuity. Normally I would have quickly taken in the details of this new environment and sized up the implications for me. Instead, I received only a series of impressions: a large room and many women, dressed oddly, sitting on floor, on beds. Beds—endless beds, reaching to the ceiling. Iron posts, paint-flaked walls—and a din. Voices, so many voices, so many people. Black hair and olive faces—curious brown eyes, wide and staring—looking away.

I was wounded, more frightened than I'd ever been, vulnerable, yet passively accepting all the unknowns ahead. But in that brief, shaky moment when I glimpsed, for the first time, the place that was to be my home—my world—for who could say how long, another part of my head was making an acute observation.

Boy, it said, this is *really* different! Not too many people will ever have the chance to see the inside of a Turkish women's prison cell. You better take notes.

PART II

Throughout my stay in Buja, any ideas I formed about the prison, how it looked or what might have been its size and structure, were restricted by the boundaries of the cell I occupied, the corridors leading to the lawyers' visiting room, things I gleaned from the limited knowledge of three English-speaking prisoners, and my own imagination.

With my arrival, the population of the cell block, Yeni Bolum-ı, Kadinlar Koḡus (the mailing address, it meant New Building, Women's Cell #1) reached forty-four. Three and a half weeks later it had swelled to fifty, among whom were murderers, thieves, drug sellers and users, prostitutes and madams, women who sold children's bodies for the sexual pleasure of adults and some who sold children for other purposes, and old women whose offenses, in some cases, seemed to have been no more felonious than being too poor to maintain themselves. I never learned how "new" the prison was; it may have been erected within the previous ten years but you couldn't prove it by me. Given the quality of Turkish materials and construction and what appeared to be a characteristic inability to provide regular maintenance, the interior, at least, looked much older.

I have reason to believe our cell block was one of hundreds. Thus it follows that if each "dorm" could accommodate fifty prisoners, the total population of Buja might have been several thousand miserable souls not counting the solitaries locked away in tiny windowless cells deep in the subbasement. That such sinister caverns existed I have only on rumor, but Americans have solitary cells in their prisons, why not the Turks?

Of all the prisoners who agonized within those wet and cold cement walls a mere hundred were women. In addition to mine there was a second women's koḡus in another wing of the building, but there were no other Europeans or Americans in either of these units. Not so among the men.

Male *turists* fell afoul of Turkish law in sufficient numbers to warrant a cell block exclusively their own: Americans, Swedes, Germans, Italians, Egyptians, English, Syrians, Yugoslavs. With the exception of four or five Kurdish women in my cell, I was the single female alien, and while I could have communicated, albeit haltingly and ungrammatically, with Germans, French, or Spaniards, Kurdish and Turkish were the same to me—unmelodic and incomprehensible.

In this wholly alien environment, bewildered, numb, barely able to comprehend the fate that had befallen me, I was certainly unable to think beyond the moment to its greater implications. Like a reeling drunk overwhelmed with the need to stabilize my vertigo, I reached out for something solid, something recognizable, any familiar locus to which I could cling until the ground stopped moving beneath my feet. There was none.

Prisons are not nice places: not in the United States, not in Turkey. Nor, do I imagine, anywhere else in the world. They offer inferior accommodations, the cheapest available food, questionable companionship, the chronic, incipient danger of overly controlled rage, and a lack of constructive activity that leads to demoralizing boredom.

My previous knowledge of prison life was limited to a sixteen-month employment as a group supervisor in a California state-run school for wayward girls. For me, at twenty-two, it was a beginner's position that led to the Los Angeles County job in probation. That had been a long time ago, and at the time, I was one of the staff, a "guard" in charge of prisoners, not myself an inmate denied free will.

Then I was in my country, communicating in my language to prison authorities and prisoners alike. We interacted according to American customs and laws, all familiar and comfortable. Here, intensely feeling that much was expected of me, I didn't know what, in fact, was acceptable conduct on the streets, let alone in prison. Handicapped by a lack of social skills, I was terrified of making a serious social gaffe that would bring down the wrath of the guards and alienate the potential goodwill of my companions. Indeed, lacking language I neither knew what was expected nor could I follow the simpleist directions. How could I even select from among the prisoners those who might serve as good models of prison behavior?

What I *was* able to draw upon from that past early experience was a visceral familiarity with and a knowing expectation of the tensions that cook under the pressures of forced confinement, making me anxious in the extreme. This, together with the devastating humiliation of finding myself officially designated a criminal deserving of confinement with other criminals against the Turkish state, served to heighten that anxiety and deepen my depression. I felt in mortal peril: threatened physically and, worse, emotionally.

Against the wall, I didn't know how I could help myself except to learn of the skills I would need for survival. My ignorance was abysmal. My need, immediate. The task seemed overwhelming. Despair washed over me like molten lava, burning into my soul, threatening to drown me under its searing weight.

How we behave in the crises of our lives is not so much determined by cerebral decisions as it is by visceral reactions honed over a lifetime of trial and error, which is another way of saying each life is a unique learning experience. We develop our own style in part by imitation of significant role models and in part by the attitudes we hold about ourselves and toward life itself.

I belong to the Scarlett O'Hara school of survivors. What I cannot change I refuse to consider—at least until tomorrow, or when I see a chance or find a way to change it. This technique requires the submergence of feelings, a process I'd already begun on the dock in Izmir. That blossoming, hardening glass structure had been built to contain incapacitating fears, humiliation, terrors, and disbeliefs, the self-pity and pain for family, all of which was counterproductive to survival.

The structure, by its very nature, was fragile. Eager to think, I was unwilling to feel and made myself numb—numb and yielding. Adaptation was the key to survival, I believed. So repressing an assertiveness that has always been a significant part of my personality, I set myself the task of learning and adapting.

Lutfi, the woman who had rescued my belongings, thereby rescuing me, became a self-appointed alter ego. And because of her ability through language to forge a link between me and the Turks who peopled this new world, I handed her my will, relieved as a child who, lost in a shopping mall, suddenly rediscovers his mother. I was, for the moment, saved.

Lutfi gloried in her role of instructor and protector and, making herself very important, got me through the first days. In that moment our personalities fit like two parts of a jigsaw puzzle: it was a function of her deep-seated need to manipulate that made her such a good rescuer. But it was unnatural for me to be dependent, a condition I'd fought against all my life. Therefore, as time passed and I grew more confident, we had to clash. But in no way does that detract from the place of importance Lutfi will always have in my heart nor this acknowledgment of the debt I owe her.

So it was that on October 3, 1983, some time after eight in the evening, having passed into the confines that were to be my world for the foreseeable future, I followed this frenetic, confident woman into a dormatory room alive with women, color, and noise. Stacked wall-to-wall and floor-to-ceiling with triple-bunk beds, the room had a single bed made up with a pretty pink printed spread in a sheltered corner of the room. There she dumped the articles she carried and made me drop mine.

"My name Lutfi," she said. "You sit."

"My name is Gene," I answered, gratefully obeying.

"This bed belong lady in charge, Gin," she informed, saying my name as best she could. "She not here. Come tomorrow. Tonight you sleep her bed. She give bed tomorrow. She come eight in morning. No be afraid, she nice woman."

"Lutfi," I repeated.

"Lütfye, my name. Everyone call Lutfi. Is more easy."

She was a tornado in motion. Her long, curling hair stood out like an overgrown Afro, softening the angles of her long thin face. She found an empty locker and began folding the clothing on the bed where I sat dazed. Shuttling between the bed and the tall, narrow, steel locker, she stacked everything neatly inside, placed my two pairs of elegant summer sandals together on the bottom, and thoughtfully left me with the one nightgown and robe I'd remembered to pack as well as a pair of white, wood-soled clogs. Then, begging an unused padlock from one of the hovering women, she secured the cabinet door. Before giving it to me, she placed the key on a large safety pin that she insisted be attached to my clothing to be carried everywhere I went. I thanked her and promised to follow her directions.

Lutfi was protectress and manager. She thought to offer an apple, which I accepted, having eaten very little that long and arduous day. It was sweet, delicious, and made me realize I was ravenously thirsty. Childlike, I asked Lutfi for water, which she dispatched one of the other women to fetch. Urging me to undress (the other women were already in their night clothes), she insisted I "not be ashamed, we all women here." Showing me the toilet, she taught me its rules—"No put paper in hole. Paper make toilet not work." And when I saw there was no paper at all, she generously gave me tissues from her own meager supply.

At 9:30 she climbed into her own bed, the second level of a three-story bunk, where she lit a cigarette and picked up some unfinished knitting, leaving me in my bed, eyes closed against the overhead light, ears shut to the cacophony of noise in the room: women's voices talking, murmuring, laughing, crying; music and voices coming from a black and white television sitting atop a large white refrigerator in the corner of the room; water running somewhere in the background, splashing against cement; blankets scratching, slippers shuffling, papers turning, knitting needles clicking—all an undefined, blended amalgam of sounds in the background. Up to that moment I hadn't noticed the television or the refrigerator on which it stood, nor counted the beds or the women or really taken in the outlines of my prison surroundings.

Anxious thoughts and nightmarish images clouded my mind, rising from the dark corners where they'd been hiding. Wanting to shut them out, I tried to focus on the sounds in the room and for the first time heard men's voices. They were coming from the corner ahead of me and in front of the window, and as the music swelled, with a shock of recognition, I realized what I was hearing was the theme music of "Winds of War." But how could that be? It was impossible!

Energized by disbelief, I jumped from the bed and dashed to a position where I could see the set clearly. I had to verify what seemed impossible. And I did.

There was Robert Mitchum.

He was speaking Turkish!

The moving shadows on the screen, all familiar, all Americans, opened their mouths and, in voices I did not recognize, spoke to each other in Turkish.

Of course it was dubbed. How odd they sounded. But how wonderful to see their faces. Like stumbling upon friends in the loneliest place on earth.

"It's an American show," I said excitedly, as if Lutfi didn't know. "Winds of War."

"Yes," she said, unimpressed, "We have 'lot."

I stood fascinated, eyes on the screen, unwilling to have my countrymen out of my sight, although the familiar faces speaking unintelligible words in the voices of strangers, in the end, only added to my confusion. A cloud of unreality encircled me, and depressed, I returned to my corner bed.

I needed sleep. I was determined to try.

I have never been able to sleep unless it was dark and quiet. In part I blame my parents who, lacking foresight, conditioned me all wrong. The remaining reason was an early-formed assessment that the world is a dangerous place in which I must not, incautiously, let down my guard.

In these unusual circumstances, Valium over exhaustion, I was, not withstanding the above, sinking into sleep when I was startled by a female voice close to my ear offering a messianic message in very good English.

"Don't be frightened," it said. "I want to help you. And I can help you. Everything will be alright."

I wanted to see her, this angel of mercy, and, squinting, looked out from beneath the covers where I was shielding my eyes from the light, to see a small, brown face close to mine. I tried to thank her but she wouldn't allow me to talk. "Tomorrow," she promised, "I will talk to you tomorrow." And she was gone.

Someone else speaks English, I thought. And a better quality than Lutfi's.

The knowledge comforted me.

When I awakened, the room was quiet. Everyone was asleep. Although my watch said it was 2:30, the room was as bright as when I'd gone to sleep with my head beneath the sheet and blanket. It was the water I'd drunk before sleeping that awakened me. I had to go to the bathroom. Having in mind the crude toilets and the mysteries of their use to which Lutfi introduced me the night before, I placed a tissue in the pocket of my robe, and not wanting to disturb my sleeping roommates but unwilling to walk barefoot along the long stretch of damply cold cement, I slipped my feet into the clogs that thoughtlessly but, as it turned out, luckily, I'd taken from the ship. Carefully, almost stealthily, by stepping solidly and squarely, I made my silent way to what can loosely be called the lavatory area.

The toilets and washroom were in a small space that lay between the room with the beds and the steel door separating the dorm from the corridor through which I entered the night before. Could I have passed through this area just hours before? Tired beyond endurance, I'd not really seen it; certainly I'd failed to identify or commit to memory its true parameters on that first journey. Now, although tired still, I was sufficiently alert to perceive and retain the raw practicalities of this essential facility.

To the right, hanging waist high from the wall and thrusting aggressively into the room, was a large, gray, cement trough over which jutted, like gun-barrels thrust through a fence, two naked, unadorned, widely spaced pipe spigots serving as faucets. As I passed, seeing the water that gushed from one and dripped from the other, I was appalled. Sylvia had reported, as our bus approached the city on its way to rejoin the ship, the growing concern in Izmir, Turkey's third largest city and her home town, over a water supply that was already drastically inadequate to meet the requirements of Izmir's burgeoning population.

Anxious because my own hold on life was precarious, I moved to take responsibility to save this precious, life-sustaining fluid and tried to shut off the flow. But the handles turned too easily, the threads were stripped, and I only managed to diminish the flood. I moved on.

Against the same wall, but past the trough, were two shoulder-height partitions, one of which separated the wash place

from the toilets. The other divided the remaining area into two
cubicles, each being a toilet stall. Between the cubicles on the
right and a place for storage (including the can into which used
paper was thrown) to the left, a narrow aisle gave entry into the
toilet stalls through wooden doors that, hanging crookedly on
ancient hinges, swung inward.

I'd looked into both cubicles the night before with the caution of a novice forced to a choice without sufficient knowledge
to make a judgment. Having survived that initial experience I
met this second examination with increased confidence. The
first stall had a porcelain floor plate complete with footrests and
a three-inch-diameter waste hole. The floor plate of the second
stall was marble. In all other respects the two seemed identical
to each other and not dissimilar to the toilet facilities at the first
comfort stop of the overland trip except they were missing a
wooden overhead cistern and pull-chain for flushing.

Here I saw an exposed vertical pipe that carried water from
a spot two feet from the twelve-foot ceiling on the rear wall,
down through a flanged opening just above the floor. A crude
technique, it obviously served, minimally, as a flush. Protruding
out of the right partition, well forward of the "toilet" plate and
about eight inches above the floor, an exposed pipe poured a
steady stream of water into an already full shell of a forty-six-
ounce tomato can that, in turn, spilled a continuous cascade of
water across the gray-brown cement floor, a further waste of
water that only added to the chilling damp that permeated the
prison.

Choking down involuntary revulsion, I stepped into the
marble stall and waded through the water to squat over its
accommodation. Earlier, in the porcelain compartment, the
water had risen above the thin soles of my shoes. This time my
feet stayed dry, and I determined to wear only the wooden clogs
from now on. I could detect no differences in the two toilet stalls
but thought I managed the squatting with less stiffness and the
clothing with more skill. Practice does make perfect.

Back in bed, I buried my head under the covers and fell back
to sleep.

Startled by the slightest noise, I awakened twice before the
day officially began, the first time to see a short, round woman
in a "granny" nightgown and bare feet moving between the

window wall and the tiers of sleeping women, parting the undulating waters of their collective breaths, snores, sighs, and restless turnings as she floated toward the front of the dorm and the lavatories. Seeing my raised head, she smiled sweetly and put her finger to her lips, "Shhh." Beyond her, through those thrusting windows that ran the length of the room, it was still night.

The muezzin's call, faint, far away, and exotic, commanding the faithful to the first Muslim prayer of the day, awakened me again before 6:00. The 1955 visit to Istanbul had introduced me to the haunting sound of Islamic worship. I remembered well the Arabic music, lilting and at the same time mournful, and imagined the muezzin himself, robed, turbaned, arms outstretched, standing high above the street on his little balcony atop a graceful minaret. This coming back to consciousness to the melody of the muezzin's call brought a flood of remembered images—of mosques and minarets and flowing Arabic writing designs upon those temple walls, intricate patterns in colors of carnelian and lapis, of malachite, amethyst, and gold. I envisioned rays of late-afternoon sunlight, violating the mysterious, dark, cavernous interiors as they angled sharply through narrow, arched windows to catch centuries-old dust before falling upon a many-carpeted floor below. And I knew, without question or self-delusion—although the muezzin's song in modern Turkey was most likely a recorded message—I was alone and in a foreign land.

My roommates around me were still sleeping. Again, I slept too.

The next awakening, at 7:00, marked the start of my first full day in prison and initiated a routine that was to rule all the days to follow.

Shocked out of that last, early morning sleep by the sound of a harsh male voice scratching itself out of a low-fidelity loudspeaker mounted on the wall above my bed, I jerked awake. Squawking into the silence, this stream of unintelligible Turkish galvanized the room into frenzied activity. The other women were arising, hastily pulling on robes, taking up sweaters and shawls. Not knowing what to do, I searched for Lutfi and saw she was still abed, looking as drugged as I felt. Disentangling herself from a quilt that enveloped her like a cocoon, she jumped to the floor, pulling the quilt after her, and rewrapping herself like an Indian, she called me to follow. As I'd slept in my robe I was already dressed to join Lutfi and the rush of women crowding at the dormitory door.

"Where are we going?" I breathed, anxiously.

"Soldiers come," she replied, pushing against the crowd.

"Why are the soldiers coming?" The thought of soldiers with their cold, mocking eyes and rifles at the ready frightened me.

"You see," she answered. Then added, "Count prisoners. We go down. Come."

Immediately beyond the dormitory door, to the right of the narrow passageway leading to the wash basin, was a cement stairway I had overlooked. Carried along in the current of silent women, we descended it in a crescendo of galloping feet, to reach a lower floor the existence of which was unknown to me until this moment. At the bottom, the women, with me following, jumped over or sloshed through two water-soaked yards of cement before squeezing through an open door where, as the women fanned out, I saw we were standing in a large, outdoor, walled courtyard. Lutfi shoved me into her favorite spot in a forming line of women that began at the door and, following the contours of the prison walls, ultimately became a square.

"Not smoke. Not talk," Lutfi instructed, standing at my side. Yes, I nodded compliance. Next to her, silent and motionless in the dim morning light, there was opportunity to examine my surroundings as well as the women of cell block #1.

The yard, enclosed on three sides by the external walls of the prison building, was surprisingly clean. The light breeze stirred no discarded candy wrappers, nor did the thin sunlight catch the glint of any abandoned soda cans. The fourth enclosing wall, separating us from the outside, was of cinderblock. Ten feet tall, topped with another three feet of sharp-toothed wire, it may have tempted prisoners whose families lived beyond its barricade but discouraged all realistic thoughts of escape. No loose mortar, no crevice, no ledge of even the narrowest depth on which to get a toehold or handhold was in evidence, and one pipe only ran the full height of the barrier, a conduit about the size and gauge of a rainspout, pinioned to the wall's porous surface by three flimsy metal brackets. The penalty for failure was sufficiently harsh as to discourage the most desperate or foolhardy from attempting escape by this means. Who would want years, even months, added to the remainder of an unserved sentence? Hard time made harder by diminished privileges.

The women were a diverse group, representing every age, size, and female body type, yet homogeneous in racial traits: here were women with skin the color and clarity of English honey, with eyes that were luminous brown, black-lashed, almond-shaped, and glowing darkly under black, gull-winged brows, with hair so heavy and straight it seemed to frame each oval face in rich waves of soft, deep, dark brown. There were exceptions: time had streaked gray the heads of the older women; bleach and henna, employed to correct nature's oversight, showed dully and falsely on two only where, incarceration making regular ministrations impossible, dark roots were slowly taking over.

Lutfi's hair was fair, not quite blond, but her eyes were blue and her complexion light. These features looked genuine and they were, she confided some days later. "My family all have my color hair. We come from near the Russian border. Don't tell anyone." Russia is a dirty word in Turkey.

Some women seemed too young to be there at all, some too old. Invariably these shriveled, bent crones, unwilling to abandon the ways of their ancestors, wore scarves draped cunningly about their heads, necks, and foreheads in a simulation of veiling, outlawed by Atatürk. By holding an end of cloth under the nose, they hid as much of the face as possible from the eyes of the men who were expected.

There were other differences. I felt I could distinguish, even in nightclothes, the country women from those city bred by body language alone. The former were slow-moving and by their posture signaled deference, yielding, a wish to serve. The latter altogether seemed less withdrawn, more spontaneous and free, and of this group, there were seven standing together whose appearance and attitude set them apart from everyone else.

Youngish prisoners, they had the look of modern college students. Their hair was cut short, boyishly so, and they bunched together wearing blue jeans and sullen faces so that the bunching and the blue jeans and the sullen looks all proclaimed defiance and a tacit rebellion. In time I learned my perceptions were remarkably accurate. These girls, indeed, had a special camaraderie, having been imprisoned on account of antidemocratic and procommunist activities. Lutfi called them "the terrorist girls" and most of the other prisoners seemed to avoid unnecessary contact with them. Apart from everything else, their education isolated them from the other women, the majority of whom were illiterate. They were college educated and, for the most part, bilingual. French seemed to be their second language.

Shyly I examined these companions, searching their faces for one I thought I would remember as the woman who sought to give me comfort last night before I slept. I couldn't identify her but was shocked to discover several children in the yard, at least two of whom were nursing infants. I was moved to ask Lutfi for an explanation of why children were in prison, but I remembered her instruction for silence and held back until after the soldiers had come and gone.

At last they arrived. There were four, two wearing blue uniforms, two in khaki. Three were very young, one—I believed him to be in charge—was middle aged, and all strutted like important peacocks. There were no smiles although there was a greeting—all very serious—that I couldn't understand. And each carried a gun, a rifle, or a revolver. The grimness and the guns intimidated me, so except for some sidelong glances at Lutfi for directions on what to do, I stood stiffly silent looking at my feet in the white sandals with the thick wooden soles, ashamed and humiliated.

I watched a pair of blue-clad legs and a pair of khaki scissor across my horizon as the men walked the line counting women. Obeying an urge to scrutinize their faces at close advantage, I looked up and was surprised to see what was for me the only familiar male face in all of Buja: my soldier "friend" of the suitcase. His eye caught mine and his face eased into a slow, real smile, forcing me to struggle not to weep. In this alien place where men seemed indifferent to women except as objects, his sweetness moved me to tears.

At last the blue-uniformed head guard, who had been checking the reports against a roster, gave a nod of his head to indicate a satisfactory tally was made. Then, envoking a perfunctory,

"Allah go with you," he abruptly turned to lead the uniform parade back into the building as the women broke ranks. The "roust" was over. As Lutfi pulled me roughly into the throng of moving women and rushed me up the stairs, I wondered, What's next?

Back in the sleeping dorm Lutfi elbowed her way into a ragged line of women crowding close around a table, no more than a board with four legs painted the color of pea soup, near the front of the room. Seated before it was a caramel-colored woman. She was trying to keep order, trying to maintain her composure, and attacking a tiny paper with the stub of a pencil. Telling me she had to stand in this line, Lutfi introduced me to a young woman standing just beyond the melee and ordered me to go with her. Obedient in my confusion, I followed her to "my" bed.

"You okay?" she asked politely, a frown of tender concern pinching her forehead.

"I'm okay," I answered in some surprise. "You speak English." She was not the one at my bedside last night. Could there be *three* women with whom I'd be able to communicate? I wondered.

"Little. Not good." Her voice was a cool caress. "My husband American soldier," she explained. "I learn English from he. I Neshe (Neşe)"

"Neshe," I repeated. "My name is Gene."

"Gin," she said, "Lutfi tell me Gin."

"I'm glad you speak some English," I sighed.

"You be okay, Gin, we take care. You be eat with us, Lutfi and me, nodder girl. She not talk English but very nice."

"Thank you," I accepted. "What must I do."

"Nothing you do. I call when time. Boss lady come soon."

In the lapse of conversation I studied Neshe, deciding she was very pretty. Her heavy dark hair was pulled back and held at the nape of her neck with a blue ribbon, exposing a heart-shaped face and fine features. Her skin, smooth and unblemished, was the color of heavy cream that had been tipped with cocoa. But the arresting aspect of her sweet, composed face were large, expressive onyx eyes so openly given, so lacking in guile I felt as if I were peering into her soul.

"When will we have breakfast?" I asked, thinking about

thyroid and vitamins that I wished to take as soon as possible but preferred to swallow on a full stomach.

"We see soon," she answered, "Lutfi get number."

"A number?"

"Yes," she nodded earnestly, "number say when we can use fire to make toast. Women make every day list, say when get cook. If lucky we use fire number three, number four. Sometime we not lucky. Then eat maybe eleven, twelve morning."

"I see," I said, but I didn't. "The prison doesn't give the food? Doesn't cook the food?"

"Prison give food. Not good. Give bread, give olive, honey. Bread good, olive good. Sometime honey good, sometime no. Not cook food. Other food prison give not good. You got buy other food for not get sick. You got money?"

"I have some," I answered, remembering the lira Atilla had pressed into my hand in the taxi. "How much money do I need?"

"How much you got? I tell if enough."

"Seven thousand Turkish lira," I answered. It was worth about $28 American. "Is that enough?"

"Is plenty for now, Gin. When man come sell food, you want buy? Cost a hundred lira."

"One hundred?" I asked. "Is that all?" What kind of food could you get for forty cents that would be nourishing and edible? "Are you going to buy?"

"Not know. See. Sometime food good, with meat. Sometime no. If good, Lutfi, me buy. Give some Sara. Sara have no money. You want buy?"

"If you buy, I'll buy. Let me know. I'll give you the money. And Sara? Is she the other woman who eats with us?"

"Yes."

"I'll share with Sara, too," I declared, taking my cue from Neshe.

"It be good, Gin," she smiled.

"Good," I repeated, believing I'd successfully passed an important first test.

I was still bewildered by the method of obtaining food, by the "cooking fire," and the competition for a place in line to use it. Why didn't one person cook for the whole dorm? Why was there such a scarcity of "fires" that someone was always forced to delay breakfast until noon? What was a "fire" anyway? And where was the kitchen? I couldn't imagine. It would take more energy than I had at that moment to dig for answers. Though it was only 8:00, I was already exhausted. I'd just have to learn as life unfolded.

Lutfi returned at this moment, unhappiness written plainly on her tense face. We would be sixth in line to use the fire. Neshe said that meant it would be 10:30 or later before we would sit down to breakfast.

I didn't care. My mind had returned to the United States, to a life I believed was mine but to which I was prevented from returning. Torn by an ingrained and overdeveloped sense of responsibility, all I could think about was the overwhelming list of obligations, bills, appointments that would not be kept and what I must do about it all. If I couldn't meet my obligations, someone else must be advised of them and would have to take over for me. What a mess to dump on another person, I anguished, reexperiencing the seriousness of my situation and its repercussions.

Fury against the Turks rose in me for the first time. Did those coldhearted bastards think I had no life back home? Did they think it was okay to throw a person in jail eight thousand miles from home as if this act had no consequences? Did they think everything back home would take care of itself? How in the hell did they think I managed to pay for a cruise that brought me here to this blackhearted, backward country to spend thousands of dollars that benefited their pathetic economy and robbed me of freedom? Did they actually believe that money, in the United States, didn't have to be earned? That it appeared like magic in the pocket?

Resentment gave me energy.

"I need to write some letters," I announced, "and I have no paper, no envelopes."

"You need?" Lutfi responded, "I have. I give, you buy from canteen, give back."

"Yes," I agreed. "How do I buy paper and envelopes?"

"I show," Lutfi said, "Come today. We buy for cook, for wash clothes. You eat with me and Neshe and Sara, you give money to pay some."

"Yes, I want to pay my share."

"List come, I show. You need stamp and maybe other thing."

"Thank you, Lutfi. Thank you. If you could get me the paper now . . ." My need was urgent; I didn't want to wait.

"I get," she said. "You need something write?"

"Oh," I said, confused, trying to understand what she was asking. "You mean do I need a pen?"

"Pen, yes. You need?"

"A pen I have. Just paper and two envelopes, please."

"I get," she said, darting off toward her locker.

Neshe observed this exchange in silence before announcing her intention to wash and dress. Saying she'd see me later, she left.

I also thought it a good idea to wash and get out of my night clothes, although what I really felt like doing was returning to bed as I noted many other women had done. A near silence had fallen upon the room. Women were quietly padding to the washroom and back, some stood dressing at lockers, or sat on beds crocheting and knitting. The rest had metamorphosed into blanketed humps in their beds.

Anticipating visits from both Ludan and Atilla, I forced myself from the bed to the locker. Its key was pinned to the fabric of my robe, and disengaging it, I began an attack on the padlock catch, which was held together with what looked like twisted coat-hanger wire. Once open, I stared at the meager selection inside, deciding what to put on. Other problems plagued me that, at the time, seemed insurmountable.

I had no towel, no soap, and very likely a lot of other necessities about which I couldn't discipline my mind to think. Aboard ship, compacted into a space the size of a small closet, everything required for the comfort of passengers appeared like magic every day. It was clear the prison felt no obligation to provide what I, and everyone I'd ever known, considered the minimal staples of civilized existence. It was all too difficult, so much "asking" offended my image of myself as an independent person.

I stood there immobilized, wanting to give up.

With a clairvoyance and sensitivity I learned to count on, Neshe appeared from behind a bulwark of beds and lockers carrying a towel and small container of soap. "Gin," she said, "you keep towel 'till lawyah bring for you. Tell when you want soap. I give."

Wanting to hug her, choking back tears of helplessness and gratitude, I thanked her. "There are a lot of things I'm going to need," I remarked. "Can you help me make a list for my lawyer? She's supposed to visit today."

"Lutfi help make list," she answered. "I be togethah with you, if you want."

"I would like that," I said, thanking her again.

"Tesh (teş) a kur, we say, Gin. It mean 'thank you' in Turkish. You say, 'tesh a kur.' "

"Tesh a kur, Neshe. Very much."

"Chuock (čok) geuzel (güzel) . . . very much."

"Tesh a kur, chuock geuzel, Neshe."

At the trough, standing back from the rough edges of the crude basin to wash, I quickly discovered both faucets offered cold water only. Checking with Neshe, I was told "our side" of the building did without hot water in summer. This is already October, I reminded her. She assured me that at some undisclosed time before winter came, the "odder side" would be deprived as we became the beneficiaries of the prison's limited ration of heated water. How I would manage a bath and hairwashing, something to be faced very soon, seemed a question too fraught with disappointment to ask.

I was dressed and brushing my hair without benefit of mirror when Hikmet, the custodian, entered. I knew at once who she was.

She strode through the door, a stream of harsh words and an entourage of women trailing behind. Lutfi, alerted to her arrival by this strident proclamation, exploded onto the scene. Pushing the others aside, she let loose a torrent of rapid Turkish for which it wasn't necessary to know the language to comprehend that Lutfi had just usurped from the others the telling of the story of an American who had been delivered last night.

While Hikmet darted glances, which she made no effort to disguise, in my direction, I had my own chance to observe the lady who, reputed to be "nice," had the power to make my life easy or hard. And also to identify two women who stood by her side—one, elephantine among so many gazelles, the other, normally small, open-faced but guarded-eyed—as prisoner/lieutenants designate.

Hikmet was sturdy, as all prison guards ought to be. She had made her entrance into the room with some of the swash and stride that I remembered from newsreels of Mussolini, but she was definitely female. Small-boned, soft, deep-breasted, and round-hipped, her feet clad in slim two-inch navy pumps to match a patterned scarf at the neck, she just missed being stylish. Her face was pretty, though a bit sharp, and artfully and becomingly applied with makeup. Standing perhaps four inches over five feet without shoes (as she often did) I couldn't say what it was about her that I didn't like except, from the start, I thought she was a posturer. Maybe it was the deliberateness of her body movements or the way she composed her face to present to the world the person she wished to be and not the person she was. Very likely it was because as she listened, mostly to Lutfi who wouldn't let go, her features pursed in a look that said, "You have my complete attention," all the while her eyes darted about the room.

I intended to treat this lady with extreme caution.

Hikmet, a woman who, wanting to be modern and fashionable, hennaed her hair and wore it in a style derivative of that worn by American film stars of the 1960s, was in fact a female whose life had been deeply marked by the rigid traditions of premodern Turkey. Father's chattel, without choice of her own, she was given in marriage at the age of thirteen to a man of his choice. Now in her early thirties, looking young, well-groomed, and attractive, she was a mother and grandmother and the "arranged" marriage long ago disolved.

With less than a high school education she had managed to attain what to Turks was an enviable career in the prison system as a guard. It was understandable that without hope of further promotion, she protected her position, one offering no job security, jealously and, I thought, with some degree of fear. The hours required were unbelievably long—she was on duty twelve hours a day, six days a week and on call twenty-four hours *every* day of the week—and for a recompense that, by American standards, was dismally inadequate. For all this devotion she was paid the equivalent of $20 a week on which she was obligated to support herself and help her children. To supplement her income she took advantage of the opportunities her work afforded by "doing favors" for prisoners who had access to money.

That we shared a career experience was something she didn't know, something I would never tell her. What, in another time and place, might have brought us closer, was irrelevant here. Indeed, given Hikmet's fundamental insecurities—especially in dealing with people whose educational accomplishments exceeded hers—I believed the less she knew about me the better.

Having worked at her job in my youth, I'd formed opinions of the responsibilities that accompanied it as well as a standard of competent performance, so I confess, there were times I found myself judging her actions somewhat harshly and times I thought them reprehensible. To her credit she took her role seriously and was often kind. But the basic principles guiding her decisions were self-promotion and protection.

While I was sizing her up I saw she was taking my measure, and when she made no attempt to mask a calculating shrewdness that lit her piercing eyes, I knew that Hikmet was not as smart as she tried to appear. At least one of her shortcomings was a tendency to underestimate her "legal inferiors."

When Lutfi and the others had finally run out of words, preparatory to greeting me she fixed a smile on her face that flexed lips and cheeks but never reached the eyes. Only then did she address me.

"Gü nyden, Gin," she said in a voice calculated to to be cordial but, under the circumstances, seemed overly cheerful.

"She say 'good morning,' " Lutfi prompted, loving her role as interpreter. "You say, 'Gü nyden, Hikmet.' "

"Gü nyden, Hikmet," I repeated obediently and without difficulty, thinking how much more like good night it sounded than good morning.

"Chuock geuzel!" Hikmet squealed, smiling broadly, gesticulating congratulations and patronizing me with too much praise. It was easy to repeat the sounds that still hung in the air between us; the trick would be in remembering them the next time they were needed.

I knew, standing before her, a bewildered and exhausted middle-aged woman out of her element and frightened to be in this alien place, I presented no threat. This was not the moment for contests of who was smarter or who was in charge. Hikmet was in charge and I was smart enough to know it.

As one would behave toward a child, she tried to coax a smile from me. What had I to smile about? But she was persistent, and not wanting this challenge to be her first defeat, thereby incurring from the start her hostility, I did my best. Not a very successful smile, being designed only to give her confidence in my malleability, it seemed acceptable, for afterward she abruptly turned to other matters and let Lutfi take over.

I was assigned a bed, she said, pointing to a lower bunk in the center of the front row, where she and Neshe, sleeping one above the other on the adjacent tier against the wall, would be close by for translations. And, I observed privately, where Hikmet could keep an eye on me.

As soon as the decision was made, Neshe came forth with everything needed to make it up: sheets, pillow case, and a pillow. Already on the bed, covering the soiled ticking of a lumpy mattress, was a scratchy khaki blanket. One of the silent prison angels who always seemed to be at hand in these first days of my anguish contributed another.

Neshe made the bed. I was not allowed to help, and when she was finished, in the spirit of gift-giving rather than pride, she showed me it had been done the "way American like," something "I learn from my husband." I felt drawn to this elfin girl-woman who intuitively sensed that as much as I required practical aid, I also needed to build bridges between the life I was living and the life I'd lost. My bed would become an American shelter in this sea of Turkishness.

Sitting cross-legged atop the the bed, conscious of an unyielding hardness no adornment could disguise and the compacted cotton wadding that bunched beneath my thighs, stroking the inhospitable, coarse-fibered blanket under my hand, I felt centered and strengthened. I had a place I could call my own. In recognition, Lutfi brought the stationery—several sheets of eight and a half by eleven pulp-quality, blue-lined paper and two thin square envelopes. Giving thanks, I bent to write two of the most difficult letters of my life.

The first was to Jimmy. I was crying before I began.

In choosing to write first to Jim rather than either of my sisters or my brother, I acted instinctively. My older sister,

Robin, in Germany for the year with her husband, seemed too far from home, and though loving, we were not close. I felt very close to both Naomi, the youngest of the family, who lived in Los Angeles, and Gordon, our only brother, in Connecticut not far from my home. I knew them to be bright, devoted, and fully competent under fire but believed they would be so devastated upon hearing what happened to me, their ability to function objectively could be impaired. The idea of imprisonment raised specters of personal demons; *my* imprisonment would threaten their emotional equilibrium.

Despite our divorce, which had occured ten years before, Jim and I were also close. He was family and, like a blood-relative, he would be deeply roused and immediately mobilize to protect and rescue me. Unlike them, I knew he wouldn't panic.

Pen poised to start, knowing the contents of this letter would be shared by all, I wondered what I could tell these people who loved me? How did I explain a calamity I could hardly understand myself? In the main I wanted to reassure them, to say I was physically well, emotionally strong, and relatively safe, although I wasn't at all certain the last was true. My first words were an apology for being the agent of their anguish. Because of me their lives would be turned inside out, their feelings scraped raw. My innocence aside—I was the reason they would suffer so terribly. This knowledge was my deepest agony.

My imagination was ripe with visions of their disbelief at hearing the news from the cool, dispassionate voices of State Department professionals. As if I were there, I followed the frantic incessant telephoning from New York to Westchester, Los Angeles, Washington, D.C., to Turkey. I knew they would rally as that initial disbelief became horrified anguish, the anguish turning into bewilderment, frustration, and finally, fury. It was the anger that would propel them to mount a valiant effort to have me released, and admiring their resourcefulness, I prayed they would succeed. I, myself, felt helpless.

My contribution to a rescue would be twofold: to give them every fact of the circumstances of my conduct leading to the arrest, which no one but I possessed, and to do everything in my power to minimize the fears that imprisonment in Turkey can evoke. The film *Midnight Express*, based on the story of American Billy Hayes's incarceration in a Turkish prison, had done untold and unmerited damage to the reputation of the Turks as a civilized people and had horrified the sensibilities of everyone who had seen or heard of the movie. Dread that I was experiencing my own *Midnight Express*, I believed, would lie at the core of the panic my family was going to know. I had to convince them that Kadinlar Koḡus #1 was not like that.

I wrote Jim of the kindness of the Turkish women, said how much I liked and trusted Atilla Akat, and with reluctance prepared him for the possibility that I could be here for years. Because of this, I said, I'd be writing Paul, my lawyer, detailed instructions with respect to business matters. I closed by saying how much it helped me to know his loyalty, energy, and intelligence were working for me at home.

My protestations of the relative safety of Buja and the potential duration of my stay suggested a fear that I might not be believed: the first on account of understandable paranoia, the second out of a wish to reject the unthinkable. Over these things I had no control.

Before I could write Paul I was called to breakfast.

Neshe leading, we returned to the lower level to enter a large room directly below the dorm. It duplicated in size and structure the room above. Rectangular in shape with the same tall, wide windows overlooking the courtyard, it was at ground level and not nearly so crowded as the place where I slept.

Only along the interior wall and at the far end of the room were there beds, double- rather than triple-decked bunks, which left a spacious portion of the room free. Parallel to and below the windows, laid out nearly end to end, were three long tables with benches at either side. On the shorter of the two interior walls and to the left of the door through which we entered stood a bank of oversized metal lockers. Two-foot cubes, some of them with their doors standing ajar, they held the eating accouterments—plastic utensils, dishes, glasses, and other table paraphernalia—of the prisoners. They were also employed as larders for the storage of food belonging to "eating groups," being protected by padlock and key.

A place for four had been laid at the center table to which Neshe led me. Lutfi was already waiting, seated with her back to the window. Half the table had been set with a piece of brown and yellow oilcloth patterned in a geometric design and shaky white lines where regular folding had cracked the surface. The ragged and frayed edges told me it had been torn from a larger length. Plastic dishes, each of a different pattern and color, designated the four eating places. It may not have been the Wedgewood and embroidered linens I used to set a table when I entertained, but everything looked clean.

In the center of the cloth, served on smaller plastic plates, I saw the Greek-style olives and feta-type white cheese remembered from the bus trip. Beside them were a bowl of brown, viscous liquid I assumed was honey and a crock of dandelion-yellow butter. Several small, white plastic picnic utensils lay nearby, and at each place was a tiny, waist-pinched glass already filled with tea. Lutfi directed me to take the seat next to her. Neshe went to get Sara. I looked around.

A lot of women were in the room, perhaps fifteen or twenty, some of whom were eating at the two other tables alone or in small groups. Several were asleep with the bedclothes pulled over their eyes to obliterate the daylight and noise that filled the room, noise that differed from that heard on the floor above. Underneath was a blending of sound from the serving and eating of food, and of the cackling of women's voices; from the yard came the echo of feet on cement and of water sloshing against cloth and plastic. Rising above the hum came the piercing voices of small children and a baby's cry. Here, I realized, lived the mothers and children.

From my seat at the table, facing the beds on the opposite wall, I saw where bunks had been pushed together in pairs. Strung from the metal pipe rails on the upper beds, hanging down between the lower, I identified two "cradles" fashioned from small blankets and cloths. In one, a baby was sleeping. Withholding judgment, I observed and became acquainted with prison life. This was the way it was.*

Neshe returned with a small metal teapot and a young

---

*I later learned that children, five years of age and under, were allowed to live in prisons with their mothers. All of those in our cell block were still breast-feeding and had the benefit of the care and love of many women, while incarcerated.

woman carrying a plate heaped with thick slabs of buttered and "fried" toast that looked and smelled delicious. I guessed this was Sara. After she and Neshe sat down, Lutfi introduced us.

Sara seemed average in every way: nice-looking rather than pretty, neither tall nor short, hair that was frankly brown and straight, not lusciously chocolate or undulantly waving. Her sturdy body was round and well-developed but she could not be called overweight. Only her eyes were arresting: wide-set and black-lashed, they were two dark wells of hidden, pain-filled memory. Or so I imagined. Winging above them, black, thick, and gracefully arched, her brows framed a good-natured face.

Sara acknowledged my presence with a sweet, shy smile and some Turkish chattering that Lutfi translated as, "Sara say she glad meet you. Eat."

"Tesh a kur," I said to Sara, the only words I had.

"Chuock, chuock geuzel!" she squealed, giggling, and added something in Turkish that caused the others to laugh. I looked to Lutfi for translation.

"She say, except for you blond hair, you just like Turkish woman." I smiled at the thought. The smile made Sara happy.

The women were gracious; they served me first. I wasn't very hungry and helped myself only to the toast, which looked very good. Golden brown and crisp outside, it was moist and buttery soft inside. They watched me swallow a handful of vitamins, too polite to comment, and didn't press me to eat more than I chose, as if they understood it was too soon for a new prisoner to have regained an appetite. For me, watching the way they served themselves was a discovery of their individual personalities.

Lutfi ate carelessly, helping herself to whatever she wanted in full measure but without gluttony. Slender and reedy, she could eat well without adding weight because of her nervous energy and hyperactivity. Neshe took small portions and ate slowly with dainty reserve. Sara ate with the relish of a child, heaping honey on the bread and filling her mouth with large bites. When the three of us indicated we were finished, and only then, without self-consciousness she took for herself the last two pieces of toast and consumed them with pleasure.

Watching her during the meal, a woman who laughed easily and often, I couldn't imagine what offense this easygoing and ingenuous young woman could have committed. Wondering about the crimes of which other inmates stood accused or convicted was a general preoccupation but no one was so impolite as to ask.

While Sara continued eating, Lutfi, Neshe, and I smoked, drank tea, and talked. The conversation swung from English, excluding Sara, to Turkish, excluding me. Prodded by a sense of being too relaxed when there was much to be done, I reminded Lutfi of her promise to help me prepare several lists. She responded by tearing the wrapper from her pack of cigarettes —an unfiltered Turkish brand called "Samsun." Borrowing a pencil from a woman sitting at the next table, she was prepared to write. Together we produced three lists, all written on the back of cigarette wrappers, a supply of which Lutfi carried in her pocket and, I later learned, saved under the mattress of her bed. Paper of any kind was too scarce and too costly to be thrown away. I began to save mine for her, too.

Because foreign cigarettes were not allowed in Turkish prisons, Atilla had taken my English ones home with the bathing suit and blue dress we agreed would not be needed here. In turn, she had thoughtfully given me a supply of her brand to tide me over until I could buy my own. Now, I asked Lutfi to put first on the list four packs of Samsun. I preferred them to Atilla's filtered ones and it seemed only these two brands were available. Most women, though not all, smoked. And those who did, I observed, smoked heavily. I watched with horror as my own smoking increased, feeling powerless to do anything about it.

Lutfi made suggestions and recorded what I needed to buy: writing paper, envelopes, stamps, matches, toothpaste, facial-quality soap, and shampoo. After Sara volunteered to wash my clothes as she did for Lutfi and Neshe, I added laundry soap and bleach to the list. For this work the women gave her cigarettes and shared their purchased food. Instructed to do the same, I agreed but, privately, I decided to see that Sara got cash as well, because I believe in the right of people to make their own purchase decisions with money they've earned.

We added to my personal list items that were my contribution to the collective larder: a pound of butter, salad oil, canned tomato paste, which Neshe called catsup, and a chocolate spread no one had yet tasted but appealed to Sara and me, both lovers of chocolate. After some discussion I insisted that I share the cost of fresh tomatoes, salad greens, and onions, which completed the collective shopping items, glad these foods were available.

I wrote Atilla's list in English under the prompting of all three women. It included the following essentials: sheets, blankets, a pillow and cases, towels, wool socks, two pullover sweaters and a cardigan, plastic dishes, plastic flatware, and a plastic drinking glass. Plastic only was allowed in this prison, yet in spite of the rule, I saw more than one recycled jelly jar pressed into service for the women who couldn't afford a glass of any kind.

To the above I added two items I considered essential, toilet paper and a washcloth, and Lutfi begged for another. Coffee was barred by prison rule, but believing in the infinite power of America, she wanted "you lawyer buy Nescafé," so I added it to the bottom of the list.

Of the one thousand lira ($2) I turned over to Lutfi, nine hundred went for supplies, and the remainder, (fifty cents) was to pay for today's meat meal, which she and Neshe had approved.

When it was time to clear the table and wash dishes, the women, in deference to my preoccupied state, refused the help I offered, and I returned to the upper dorm with thoughts of the letter I would write to Paul.

Paul was more than a lawyer; he was a friend. I knew the enormity of the burden I was about to place on him, yet there was no one else to do it. Arlene, a good friend, was already taking care of the mail, turning over the motor of my car, watering plants. I knew she'd voluntarily continue those tiresome chores. But Arlene wasn't competent to make decisions required in my absence. Paul lived nearby, his office was in a neighboring town, he was an attorney. The confidence I had in him was rooted in the perception I had of his character and ability. He was hard-working, caring, extremely bright and thorough, but most of all he respected the priorities of his clients and saw his professional role as one of advising and implementing. When he took action he would try to do things the way I would have done them if I were able to manage my affairs myself.

With Arlene's help Paul could locate the things he'd need to take over: correspondence, paid bills, checkbooks. Unless I worked, the income from my investments wasn't enough to support the financial structure I was still building. Paul would have to sell some bonds—my security for retirement—to pay bills. I could conceive of a time, if I stayed here as long as Atilla said, we might decide to sell my car, my home, at the very least, to rent it. Even as I accepted these realities, they depressed me terribly. My God, I wondered, would it really come to that?

Realizing Paul needed specific information about my assets and debts as well as legal authority to act in my stead, I made a note to discuss the problem with Ludan: this and the urgent need to obtain more Synthroid.

Before leaving New York six weeks before, I'd made fifty aluminum-foil packets, each containing the daily dosage of vitamins and thyroid it was my habit and need to take. Now, looking up from the writing, I saw that Hikmet, who'd left the dorm soon after we met that morning, was back carrying the plastic bag in which I kept them and other useful medications. Waving the sack, she gestured me to see she was locking it all in a green wooden cabinet that hung on the wall over the head of her bed. I hoped, although there was no way I could ask, it would be available on demand.

It was another clear, dry Izmir day, and the sunlight flooding through the window warmed and brightened the room. I was addressing envelopes, relieved to be done with a difficult, emotionally draining responsibility, when Neshe stopped by to invite me for a walk in the yard.

"I must get my letters into the mail," I said. "They must get to America as quickly as possible."

"You send EXPRES. Three hundred fifty lira. I show you." Taking the envelopes, she looked them over. "No put prison address," she said, pointing to the open flap. "Need address of prison."

"What is the address?" I asked, ready to write.

"Lutfi tell," she said. "Not hurry, letter not go today."

"Mail doesn't go out every day?" I asked, chagrined to hear it. I *needed* these letters in the mail.

"Letter go three time week. Monday, Wednesday, Friday."

"And does it come every day?"

"Not come Saturday, Sunday," she said. But I couldn't expect mail so soon. It could be a week, even two, before I got letters from home.

"How long does it take for mail to reach the States?" I asked hoping, because of her husband, she'd know.

"Maybe week," she answered, "maybe more. But KONTROL read letter first."

"Do they read prisoners' letters before they mail them?" I asked, trying to remember what I'd written.

"Of course," she answered, but I could hear, "What do you think?" in her voice. "This why leave letter open. Not close."

"They have someone who reads English?"

"Sometime," was her enigmatic answer.

The threat was sufficient. I would be careful of what I wrote.

Having done all I could about home, I was motivated to go with Neshe. Exercise was beneficial. I would try to walk every day.

The yard, which I'd seen for the first time this morning (time was warped; morning seemed days ago, now), ran the length of the building wing: about forty-five feet. Its width was determined by the distance from the wall of our cell to that of the corridor leading to the visitors' cubicles in the main building, about twenty-five feet.*

It wasn't possible to get up a head of steam walking the perimeter of that courtyard. A number of things prevented it. First there was the unevenness of the cement underfoot, making it imperative to watch every step you took. Second were the prisoners: the older ones who, squatting alone, bent backs against the dormitory wall, attempted to ease the pain of arthritis in the warmth of an Aegean sun, and others who also walked or stood, squatted, and sat while engaging in congenial gossip.

---

*I didn't realize it at first, but our dorm didn't run the entire length of the wing. It stopped about fifteen feet from the end. When I discovered this discrepancy, I also became aware of two small windows three feet above ground level that were sealed with metal sheeting. One of the women, in answer to my questions, reported these were solitary rooms from which there was sometimes a banging on metal pipes and sometimes groaning sounds. Never did I personally hear any noises coming from an unknown source but, then, I lived one floor above and twenty-five feet away from that mysterious and dread-inspiring corner.

It was the third impediment to walking that truly slowed the pace: the clotheslines. Strung between the dorm and corridor walls, eight looping lines traversed the width of the yard from which, on every day I was in residence, hung five or six sheets, a like number of blankets, towels, trousers, shirts, dresses, blouses, sweaters, articles of various underclothing of all shapes and colors, and, of course, the diapers. A broken-field runner could not have managed a fast circling of what could not, in reality, be called an exercise yard.

Nevertheless, Neshe and I circled. Walking slowly in a clockwise direction, we nodded acknowledgment of friendly smiles, swung wide to avoid wet sheets, stumbled over cracked cement, and began to learn about each other. By asking questions I forced her to do most of the talking.

"You say your husband is American," I began. "Where does he come from?"

"South? I not sure. Carolina, maybe?"

"Have you met his family?"

"Not see family." She hesitated, momentarily uncomfortable. "Family be States. Yilmas be Turkey five year American soldier."

"Yilmas? That's your husband's name?"

"Yilmas," she repeated.

"Yilmas is not a very common name in America. I don't remember hearing it before."

"Husband 'come Muslim, take Turkish name, Yilmas Atagun."

"I see." It seemed a bizarre thing to do. Unless he was an American black. "What was Yilmas's name before? His American name?"

She thought before answering. "Not 'member," she said at last.

I was puzzled. Had he deserted her when she got into trouble? "Where is he now?" I asked.

Her eyes teared. "He be Buja, prison, like me."

Not wanting to probe I asked no more. But once having exposed her pain she wanted me to hear the whole story.

Yilmas (a.k.a. we shall never know), Neshe said, swearing me to secrecy, was not really her husband. Although they'd lived together for five years in an apartment in Izmir where Neshe enjoyed the relatively luxurious lifestyle of an American wife, they were unable to marry because Yilmas had a wife back home who would neither come to Turkey nor give him his freedom. Married a short six months before the air force sent him to Turkey, he had been trying to rid himself of this legal encumbrance for some time. The reason for her refusal to sever the marriage, Neshe explained, was grounded in Catholic dogma, and hearing this, I wondered what part this may have played in Yilmas's decision to become a Muslim.

The stalemate boiled to a crisis when the American wife showed up in Izmir and demanded her right to Neshe's apartment and its contents, including Yilmas. Adamant in his refusal to give her anything save a divorce, fueled by rage and immature judgment, Yilmas conceived a plan to break the deadlock and, at the same time, punish the woman standing in his way. He arranged first to plant hashish among her belongings and then to have the Turkish police discover it. For this he required Neshe's reluctant help.

"I tell him not good," she told me, "but he say he do. I not want help but he go 'way. Stay 'way three day an' I 'fraid not come back. I do what he want me do."

"What did he want you to do?" I was horrified.

"He say I call to police, say she have hash. I no want call. I be 'fraid. He say call from pay phone, they not know. I tell him it wrong, no want call. I cry, we fight. Three day, I ask not to do. But when I 'fraid he go 'way, I do what he ask. I call police."

"Then what happened?"

"Police believe wife she say it not be her 'hash.' We both arrested. Go to prison."

"Oh, Neshe, I'm so sorry."

"I sorry, too, but it be too late be sorry. We be prison now."

"Will you be here a long time?"

"Yilmas, he go out. American army help him. Soon he be go United States."

"You mean he'll be free?"

"Not 'xackly free, but he go States. Consulate make papers." She stopped walking and faced me, locking her eyes on mine. "You go home, too. Soon. American consulate take you out." Was this an accusation or a promise?

"I don't think so," I said. Had she some information I lacked?

"Yes, you see. You be free quick," she said, nodding. "You be American. Not stay prison long."

"I hope you're right," I said, full of doubt, not daring to count on easy solutions and writing off her conviction as more of the fantasy foreigners held about the miraculous power of the United States. When we resumed walking, I questioned her further. "What about you?" Will you be here long?"

"I be here five month. I not go home before two year more."

"Oh, Neshe. Just for helping Yilmas—something you didn't even want to do."

"It be true, Gin. But, I wrong. I afraid he go. Not come back. It be wrong."

"You still love him?" How could she? I was quick to make a judgment. A selfish idiot like that?

"Yes. Love Yilmas. Miss him. He write letter. I show letter. You read letter?"

"If you like."

We circled the yard for a last time, coming to a stop at the windows of the lower dorm. Tired, I suggested sitting awhile in the sun, and we dropped to one of the serviceable khaki blankets someone had left on the cement. Covertly I examined the other women in the yard and studied their clothing, which, in the main, was so devoid of the exotic it could have been purchased at any JC Penney's. Some women, however, irrespective of age, wore voluminous trousers in brightly colored prints, made of yards and yards of fabric that disguised the figure while allowing great freedom of movement. I'd never seen anything like them before.

"Are those pants or skirts?" I asked Neshe, nodding at the outfit nearest us.

"Pants," she answered. "I have. My mother make. She make for you. You want?"

"We'll see," I answered, unready for so drastic a sartorial change. "And those girls in jeans?" I asked, quickly shifting her focus to another question that intrigued me. "Who are those women?"

"Those be terrorist girls."

"What is a terrorist?"

"Girls have short hair, walk together, be together all time. They terrorist girls."

"Yes, I see them. But, what is a terrorist?" I tried again.

"Terrorist make problem for government. Not like government. Be all time against."

"Political activists?" I asked.

"Yes," she said, "what you say." But I didn't know if she understood what the words meant.

"Make plenty trouble for prison. Be terrorist men in prison, too. Lot terrorist men, girl prison. All time make problem."

"Where do they sleep?" I asked. "I haven't seen them upstairs."

"Be upstair when movie on TV. Was upstairs when you come last night. Tonight you see. Sleep downstair. I show when go inside."

The "terrorist girls" were out in force, walking the yard from dorm wall to prison wall. "I like you read Yilmas letter." Neshe returned to her central concern while my thoughts followed the masculine girls striding to a brisk cadence among flapping sheets and dangling trouser legs, five abreast, arms linked, like so many "butch" Rockettes. "You read?" she urged.

"Yes," I said.

Three yards from us Sara was squatting on her haunches, knees akimbo, alternately kneading and wringing clothes in hands reddened by bleach, and rhythmically rocking over a suds-filled, yellow plastic tub.

"I'll read the letters to you," I promised, and feeling her loneliness, asked, "Do you have family besides your mother?"

"Have family." Neshe answered, "Mother, father, sisters. Two sister marry American soldier, like me."

"Where do they live?"

"Live Izmir. I born Izmir."

"Do you get to see them?"

"Sunday, day for visit. Mother come. Father come. Sunday come soon be day for women visit. Mother come. . . ."

"Men and women don't visit on the same day?"

"Men, women not come same day. Father come one week. Mother come 'nodder week."

"The prison has a lot of rules," I said, despairing that I would ever learn them all.

"This be prison," she said solemnly. "Lot rule. You see. I show you."

The visiting schedule raised doubts that Atilla and Ludan would come today. This was Tuesday, not Sunday.

"My lawyer," I commented, wistfully, "and the man from the consulate, they said they would visit me today."

"Be cool," Neshe advised. "They come. You have visit from lawyah, from consulate when they want come. Not have come Sunday."

I believed her and was comforted. And I was increasingly sure, after "be cool," the "south," and Muslim conversion, that Yilmas was most likely black. The notion led me to consider how much more readily a black American might be accepted as an equal or better, given the desirability of U.S. citizenship, among Turks of olive complexion and fragile self-esteem, than they are at home.

With ample reservoirs of curiosity, I felt drained of energy. Aching joints signaled a demand for rest, and overall, just holding my body erect seemed hard labor. I suggested we go back so I could lie down.

It was cool inside the building. In silence we climbed the stairs and entered the dorm. At my bunk Neshe asked to bring her letters, but much as I wanted to grant so modest a request, with an apology I put her off and stretched full length on the hard bed.

Eyes closed, I could hardly imagine a time when I would feel comfortable here. Would I ever recover from this leaden weariness? It robbed me of strength and will. As exposure familiarized me with prison life, I felt increasingly dislocated and disbelieving, encased in a thick fog of unreality that made everything outside myself remote and far away.

What was I doing in this strange world? All that had happened since the dock was a dream, a nightmare I dared to think would vaporize when I awakened. Would I find myself home, on my own familiar bed with the cats purring at my side? Or was home the dream and this the reality?

Lying there, in the eye of the storm, I listened to the unique noises of the hive: the clang of metal against metal where, nearby, water was being boiled for tea; the brush of clogs against cement as women pursued their limited lives; water gushing from never-to-be-repaired faucets; and water cascading to the floor and sloshed about with a mop made of torn blankets, spreading the scourge of bone-chilling dampness.

From the squawk box on the wall came unexpected bursts of staccato Turkish rending the air with official announcements and competing with the hollow, rhythmic beating of palms against the bottom of an overturned plastic pail as women downstairs entertained themselves dancing.

Interlacing with these disparate sounds, like a thread pulling together the colorful patches of a quilt, were the voices of women: soft voices and loud, coarse or sweet, creating a hum punctuated by an occasional shout or a laugh. The murmuring chorus buzzed around me, delivering no message save that I was not alone. A noise conveying nothing, it served to weave the fabric of my surroundings into an exotic tapestry I'd not been educated to appreciate and to evoke images that separated me from my past and alienated me from my present.

This was not the world I knew. This was not my life. Where was I? Like an object without mind, will, or feelings, I'd been plucked from all that was familiar, all I believed in and relied on, from all I knew. Who was responsible? Fury, born of anguish, bewilderment, frustration, fear, horror, and helplessness, washed over me. It was the ship's fault—and the captain's. They had let me down. All of them. How could they have abandoned me? Abandoned me to a fate they could not begin to contemplate, a fate I did not deserve. It was the not the Turks' fault. They were running their country by their own rules as they had every right to do. The English, they were the cold, callous, uncaring culprits who let me go when they should have protected and defended me.

In that moment of passionate hatred, Lutfi chose to appear.

"Get up," she commanded in her abrupt way. "Soldier here. You get visitor."

Startled and dazed, I hastened to stand, feeling my heart quicken with nervous excitement at the thought of Ludan or Atilla being here. And I had so much to tell them.

"You take list?" Lutfi reminded, organizing me like a mother preparing her child for its first day at school.

"I have it," I said, fidgeting with my clothes and touching my hair.

"Be quick, Gin," she ordered. "No make soldier wait," and she rushed me from the dorm, past the stairwell, into a congregation of women blocking the steel door.

"Canteen here," she said explaining the crowd. "You 'list' come. I take. Look list, make sure all come. I pay, take money, give when you come from visitor. You go Euzgeul (Özgöl)," she directed, firmly thrusting me through the crowd and into the bosom of a tall woman with an angry face, the trustee, Euzgeul, whom I could now call by name.

Euzgeul, looking annoyed—a normal expression for her— grasped my arm and pushed me through the door while issuing an impatient order I couldn't understand. Afraid to move, I waited until Lutfi came forward and, shouting over Euzgeul's harsh voice, said I was to go with the soldier who stood waiting in the corridor. Trembling, from anticipation, fear, or merely weakness, I allowed the soldier to lead me down a wide corridor away from the cell block.

Upon reaching an intersection enclosed by bars and passing several soldiers and guards, I faintly recalled having taken this route last night, but when we turned left into the intersecting corridor and began walking past a series of cubicles that lined its right wall, I knew this was new territory and wondered if visiting took place here. An emaciated, unshaven man, seated opposite the stalls, was having his hair cut by a barber who apparently made house calls; no one was waiting for me; we passed without stopping.

Perhaps fifty feet down the hall from the intersection I began to see, dead ahead, we were approaching a soldier in a small guard station and noticed, to the right of it, a windowed room only slightly larger. Through the panes, now only ten feet away, I identified Atilla and Ludan standing together watching my approach, their faces etched with concern. Or so it seemed to me.

Relayed to the waiting soldier, I was escorted the last three feet to join my visitors, looking like relatives awaiting the surgeon's report of the outcome of a loved one's precarious operation. My heart turned over to see them so and it took a moment before I found my voice.

Atilla moved first, to embrace me, and Ludan held out his hand. Both wanted to know if I was alright. I said I was, that everyone had been very kind. We stood. It was an awkward moment.

The room was small but private. Except for the soldier who remained to supervise the visit, it contained nothing more than a picnic-sized table and two benches, and after we were seated —I on the prison side, they on the bench opposite me—I noticed, behind them, a walkway and door through which visitors entered without having to pass through the prison. It was a route barred to me, one more humiliating reminder of an unpleasant reality, but unwilling to spoil the pleasure of being with Atilla and Ludan, I made no comment.

On the scarred surface of the table was a metal ashtray caked brown with the oily sap of nicotine and gray with ashes. Bob Ludan, after helping himself to a cigarette and lighting one for me, began the interview by referring to notes on his ever-present yellow tablet.

"I've contacted the State Department in Washington to notify Jim LePere and Paul . . ." he stumbled over Paul's last name. "Yes, Attaguile," I supplied and, involuntarily, began to cry.

"You are alright?" Atilla asked, obviously concerned.

"I'm fine," I answered soberly, qualifying, "under the circumstances. I'm sorry to upset you. It's just . . . when I think of my family . . . how worried they'll be . . . I feel so bad. So bad."

"Yes," she said, handing me a tissue, "your family naturally will be worried." I wiped my eyes.

"Have you heard from them, Bob?" I asked, wanting yet dreading news.

"Not yet," he said.

I knew my family. They are among AT&T's best private accounts. "You will," I said. "You will hear from them."

Checking his notes, he looked up with reassuring candor. "I stopped in to see the director of the prison and left some reading material for you. It will help to pass the time." How clever he was, I thought. It hadn't even occurred to me I might read. "They'll be examined and then sent on to you."

"Thank you," I said. "It will be good to have something to read."

"Is there anything else I can bring?" he asked. Atilla drew on a cigarette and listened.

"I'm worried about my supply of thyroid," I said, checking my own notes. "I must have it every day or I'll turn into a basket case."

"Haven't they forwarded your medication?" Atilla inquired anxiously.

"It arrived this morning," I explained. "There's enough for a week. That's all. If I'm to be here longer I have to have more."

Asking for the exact name and dosage, Bob scribbled on the legal pad. This completed, Atilla took her turn.

"I have been to the court this morning," she reported, "and have filed a document requesting your bail. It would be better, I think, if you remain at a hotel instead of prison while awaiting your trials."

"Trials" was the word that caught my attention.

"How many trials will there be?"

"It can be many trials," she said without clarification. "That is why it is better if you are released on bail." She paused before going on. "I have not much hope they will grant the bail, but I try."

"Why not?" I asked, feeling in advance the insult of being considered a poor risk and more. Contemplating a lengthy stay for "many trials" lay at the heart of my worst fears.

"We shall see," she said, avoiding further discussion. "I shall return to the court tomorrow. For now we must wait."

"And if they don't grant bail?"

"I ask again," she said matter-of-factly and changed the subject. "You will require some articles of clothing for winter. I have seen you have brought with you nothing suitable for the cold weather that will soon be here."

"Yes," I nodded, handing her the Samsun wrapper. "There are a few women who speak English, thank God. With their help I have a list of the things I'll need. I'm most concerned about sheets, blankets, and towels. And I need toilet paper and . . ."

The soldier, so quiet until now I'd almost forgotten him, stepped forward demanding to see the paper I'd given Atilla. In a rapid torrent of fluent Turkish, holding up the list, she explained its contents. How stupid, I thought. What's the point of assigning a soldier to monitor our visit who doesn't understand or read English. Before going on I waited until the soldier, satisfied by her explanation, stepped back.

"I put sweaters and wool socks on the list, but as I don't need them yet and may be out before it gets cold, they can wait. I need dishes," I commented to Bob with a quizzical smile. "Can you imagine? Everyone has to provide their own dishes and silver." Not like America, our eyes signaled. "But, Atilla," I finished, "you'll see. Everything is on the list. Plastic only."

"I will get it," she said, reading. "I will have a chance for shopping Thursday. I will bring it to the prison on Friday. I will have news of the bail." She paused a long moment, worrying the lines of her face. "You must not count on the bail. I think it is not more than a 5 to 10 percent chance we shall have it."

"I don't want to stay here any longer than I have to," I said, quietly. "How can we speed things up?"

"It is too soon to speak of these things," she answered. "Wait. We shall keep trying the bail."

I tried to understand but lacked all concept of the shape of Turkey's legal system. All I knew was California juvenile court law. In Los Angeles where, as a probation officer, I had responsibility for seeing children's rights protected, no child could be held in custody longer than seventy-two hours—the clock started ticking from the moment of arrest—without coming before a judge who decided if further detention was necessary. Maybe Monday's trial was my detention hearing. And if the child remained in detention, he was guaranteed a speedy trial. One trial was all that was usually required. We never had "many trials."

"Yes, but the trials," I pressed. "Can't we get a fast court date?" Bob and Atilla exchanged looks. As if by mutual agreement, he answered.

"The legal process in Turkey can be quite slow, Gene, but there are a number of other options available that can be discussed in the event bail appears to be out of the question. Our main concern right now is that you are comfortable and have everything you need."

"Paper," I said, my mind easily redirected, "I need paper to write on." Bob wrote it down.

He asked how I was managing on food, which made me smile. In their audience, Turkish prison food became a funny topic on which I was the authority. Believing that neither Bob nor Atilla had access to previous intelligence on this esoteric subject, I reported everything I learned in less than twenty-four hours about the provision, purchase, and preparation of food, being careful to throw in the few Turkish words I'd memorized. "The *ekmek* is delicious when toasted with butter."

It was a joy to express myself in English words of more than one syllable.

"You see I'm learning," I concluded. "Luckily, I have a cast-iron stomach and food, believe me, is the least of my problems." I was worried about my financial affairs.

"About Paul," I changed the subject, looking to Bob, "I've been thinking a lot about things back home. I own property, there are mortgages, rents. Paul . . . can you tell Paul he'll have to sell some bonds? He has to know right away. I've written him a letter but he won't get it soon enough."

Ludan wrote as I detailed instructions for Paul. Conveying this information—knowing Bob's intelligence and reliability, trusting Paul to act conscientiously in my behalf—gave me a great sense of relief. Here was one concern, at least, I could let go of. There were so many others, few of which I could unload. In this grubby room, together with Bob and Atilla, I felt safe, not so dislocated. Acceptable, even satisfying outcomes seemed possible.

Soon after this the soldier indicated the visit had to end. With a sense of incompletion and dread, I accepted the inevitable return to the dorm, hoping those "otherworld" feelings could be held at bay for at least a little while.

To signal our compliance we stood, but in our reluctance to separate, we experienced another moment of awkwardness. From her open pack, Atilla offered a cigarette to the soldier and gave the rest to me. Bob shook my hand.

"I just want to tell you," he said in parting, "everyone at the consulate admires the way you're handling yourself in this difficult situation."

This unexpected praise broke through my fragile composure. Having experienced and, now expecting, the depersonalizing treatment directed to a perceived criminal, Bob's gift of respect went right to the core of my not-so-hardened heart. Shaken and crying, I left them as the soldier led me back the way I'd come. At the guard station, again I was transferred to another man who escorted me to the dorm. At the iron door Euzgeul, who even when she was smiling and clearly in good spirits had a shrill, harsh, piercing voice, let me in, still sounding impatient and angry. Euzgeul's worst fault, I learned, was a lack of warmth, not a hostile nature.

Inside, the hive was abuzz. My own world again retreated. There was no time to brood as Lutfi, just inside the door, told me in her excited way that lunch was ready. It was nearly three, and the women, having waited for me, were hungry. If she noticed I'd been crying she was too polite to mention it and we went downstairs.

The food purchased that morning turned out to be three portions of a Turkish-style moussaka that were served in the four-inch round, metal container in which they'd been heated. On the clean shabby cloth lay a golden, hard-crusted, foot-long loaf of bread from which Lutfi served torn chunks. The same bread from which our breakfast toast had been "cut." Provided by the prison at a rate of one loaf per prisoner per day, it was sufficient.

Neshe had prepared a salad of finely chopped greens and tomatoes and that, together with a warmed dish of prison beans doctored by Sara by adding onions and tomato paste, completed the main meal of the day. My appetite had not yet returned, but I tasted everything and found it good.

Bob's reading material arrived sometime after lunch. He must have scoured the consulate for anything that could be spared, for in addition to a paperback copy of John Fowles's novel, *Daniel Martin*, there were two three-week-old issues of the *Wall Street Journal*. Also delivered was a tiny packet fashioned of a folded scrap of notebook paper. Sent by the hospital for tonight's use, I was surprised to find it contained two yellow tablets I recognized as Valium, because I thought my supply was locked in the green cabinet with the rest of my medications. One 5 milligram Valium was quite sufficient to put me to sleep; I would save the second for another night. I felt gratitude and respect for the doctor's responsible decision to maintain control over the use of this potentially dangerous drug.

At 7:00 we were called for a second roust, a duplication of the first except that the women were dressed. Immediately afterward I was hurried upstairs by Lutfi and ordered to stand in the "medication" line, which already consisted of more than half the prisoners. I was amazed at the number of women who suffered from chronic conditions.

Hikmet was the medication dispenser. Upon noting my presence, she interrupted the routine to place my plastic bag in my hands, indicating through Lutfi I was to help myself. Wondering if this was a sign of special privilege or just a concession to the language barrier, I dug through the contents for the vitamins I would need in the morning and was startled to find my vial of Valium there. Now, instead of praising the doctor for his caution, I wondered at his carelessness. How many people should be trusted with so much temptation?

Planning ahead, I divided the vitamins so that, by reducing the daily intake, I could make them last twice as long. More than ever protective of my health, I left the Valium. I had no intention of leaving prison a drug-dependent vegetable.

This duty disposed of, Hikmet went home leaving Euzgeul, who immediately turned on the TV full blast, in charge. This was a signal for the women to change for the night and to find a well-located seat for the evening's entertainment. In a short time the room was crowded with women, as prisoners from below began collecting about the floor and on the beds at the front of the room. There was a noticeable avoidance of mine, a bed in an enviable spot for good viewing. I took it as a sign of respect for my rights, for which I was grateful. Undressing, myself, I stretched out, opened *Daniel Martin*, and began to read.

It was by agreement, having eaten lunch so late in the day, that Lutfi, Neshe, Sara, and I skipped dinner. Instead, Neshe reached under the lowest bed of her three-story tier to remove four apples from a great, round, red plastic tub, which she handed around to the four of us. Setting aside the book, I joined the group sitting together on the bunk next to mine munching the sweet, tree-ripened fruit. Looking around, I observed the scene: a replica of last night only I was no longer the audience. Having completed my first twenty-four hours in prison, I was now a member of the troupe.

The routine, the people, the food, the meager comforts, I

acknowledged privately, were not as bad as I'd expected. Nor as bad as they might have been. What was nearly intolerable, and unanticipated, was the dizzying sense of displacement that came and went and, when I allowed myself to think about it, the wrenching grief and anguish for what was lost and for my family, terrified and impotent, half a world away.

It was still early when, feeling drained from so tense a day, I took one of the Valium and picked up *Daniel Martin* again. On the TV Michael Douglas and Karl Malden were about ten minutes into a rerun of "Streets of San Francisco." Last night's disappointment had taught me watching TV only made me feel worse, but I couldn't help noticing how natural Karl Malden looked speaking Turkish. He had an angry, impatient face, one well suited to a language that sounded harsh to my ears.

I met the mysterious, English-speaking gnome before the evening was over and wondered if she only came out at night. I had just turned back to my book when she crept to the head of my bed. Holding a clipping torn from the morning newspaper in her hand, she confided it was about me. My head snapped around at the sound of her voice.

"About me?" I asked, astonished and anxious. Public exposure makes me uneasy, even in America. "What does it say?"

"It is only telling of your arrest. Would you like me to read it to you?"

"Please," I said, and she began translating.

" 'American woman, Gene LePere, has been sent to Buja prison last night after a hearing in the first court of Izmir. The American woman was attempting to smuggle several important antiquities from Turkey when she was arrested at the airport before she boarded her plane to the United States.' "

I was crying before she finished.

"It's not true," I protested. "They have it all wrong. I wasn't even at the airport . . . I wasn't trying to smuggle. . . ."

Her sad brown face leaned close and she patted my shoulder. "I am so sorry. I did not want to make you cry. It is not important. The newspapers always tell lies. Please try to forget about it," she soothed, and waited quietly while I composed myself.

"My name is Eminay (Emine)," she continued, smiling. "I have spoken to you last night. Do you remember?"

A tiny woman, with the saddest eyes I've ever seen, she

looked beaten, worn down, defeated, but her smile was sweet and sincere.

"Yes, I remember," I said. "You are very kind and I appreciate it. Tesh a kur."

"You are learning Turkish," she said, smiling her pleasure. "I will help you."

"Yes, I'm trying. I'd like to have your help." Her English was fluent and less accented than Atilla's. "Where did you learn to speak English so well?" I asked. "It is excellent."

"I have learned at the university," she explained. "Every Turkish university student must learn a foreign language. Also I continue to study. I have books I read every night. Sometimes I cannot find a proper translation in my dictionary. I will ask you. Will it be alright?"

"I don't mind at all. Please ask me. I hope I will be able to help you."

"I would also like to help you," she said. "Please come to me if you need anything at all."

"I will," I said. "Thank you very much, Eminay."

The Valium was taking effect. "You are tired," she observed. "We will talk again." And giving me another soft pat, she glided away. Pondering the infamy of Turkish newspapers and the wonder of English-studying gnomes, I watched her walk to the row of beds behind me, stop at the tier nearest the windows, and climb to the top bunk. Satisfied that I knew where to find her, I prepared to sleep.

At the head of the bed was a kind of pocket created by a blanket that was tucked under the mattress and looped to the rear of the pillow, over a string stretched between the side rails. Its function, I assumed, was a makeshift headboard, but I quickly found it useful, arduous as it was to open my locker, for hidden storage. Slipping the book into its recess, I slid deep into the covers, shifted and curled my body to make it conform to the lumps of the mattress, hugged the hard cotton pillow, willed the noise and shifting shadows to recede, and fell asleep.

The following days were much like the first. The nights as well. While the others sat watching TV, I slept. And during the night when they slept, I had the opportunity to enjoy a silence and privacy that evaporated with the intrusive announcement of the morning roust. In truth, my waking in the middle of the night was involuntary and cannot be ascribed to a need to be quietly alone. I woke once or twice every night because my sleep patterns had been disturbed, because I had a lot on my mind.

Regardless of whether or not I'd taken Valium—after the fifth night, I gave it up as an unnecessary indulgence—I awakened tense and anxious. It was handy to reach into the blanket pocket for a book and, in the dim light of the dorm, holding the book toward a bulb hanging behind my head, to push back unwanted, tormenting fears with *Daniel Martin*. When I finished *Daniel Martin* and no new book appeared, I read *Daniel Martin* again. Thank you, John Fowles.

During the day, even more than at night, reading became my great escape, and for this, novels were required. In them I could lose myself by participating vicariously in a life more like my own. Gripping literature was hard to come by, not because the consulate staff didn't try. This was Turkey, not the U.S. The *Wall Street Journal* hardly qualified as escape literature. It took a focused concentration my mind was too flyaway to manage, but the few copies I had came to serve an important function. Hung like curtains held between the mattress and supporting board of the bed above, they could be drawn together at night, shutting out the overhead light, and easily pushed apart at 3:00 A.M. when I wanted to read.

After I was given a writing pad, the possibilities for self-entertainment widened. Between writing letters or recording events and impressions, I could be found most of the time on my bed, reading or scribbling. It didn't take me long to understand that my bed, like that belonging to each prisoner, was now identifiably my "home," to be respected and protected from violation by the collective group. Beds, in their role as homes—a condition that might prevail for years—expressed the tastes and priorities of individual "owners." Decorated with pillows, quilts, photographs, and pictures torn from magazines, they were the place where prisoners entertained.

The second day of my residence, I received an invitation to visit a bed-home from a lumpish-looking young prisoner who approached my bed and addressed me by name.

"Gin," she said, "I like talk you. Come."

Believing there was yet another English-speaking prisoner

in Buja and determined to demonstrate my friendliness, I followed the short dumpy girl downstairs to her bed, a second-story bunk located in the center of the inner wall. Preceding me, she climbed to the upper level by placing one foot on a four-inch pipe protruding from one of the upright rails and hoisting herself aloft with a purchase on the horizontal one. Glad I was still agile and flattered to be perceived as equal to the task, I imitated her moves and followed her up.

Facing each other cross-legged on the narrow cot, I accepted a cigarette from the almost empty pack she held out and opened the conversation by asking, "Where did you learn English?"

In lieu of an answer, I received a grin and a light.

"Do you speak English?" I tried again, pronouncing the words slowly and distinctly while gazing intently at a face that reflected no understanding.

"English," she smiled, "English. Gin."

Hope died, to be replaced by mild panic as I pondered the length of a reasonable stay before making my escape.

I gave it something less than fifteen minutes during which time I labored to admire seven snapshots of her family variously identified as "sister," "mother," and other relatives, one of whom she demonstrated by closing her eyes and holding her breath, was deceased. In a lull of awkward silence and a voice remarkable for volume over quality, she broke into song, giving a repetitive rendition of the first line of "Yesterday," the only phrase she knew.

Meusheref (Müseref) was her name, Mishu for short. In the brief time we had together, I was transported from anxiety to pathos. Wistful and childlike, she was so eager to please and so anxious to be accepted as a friend, I could have wept. Before I left, she insisted I take one of her pitiably few decorations, the smallest and saddest of all red plastic roses on a crooked green stem, a gift I accepted with thanks and gratitude. A whimsical chance had brought us together, against all rational expectation; light years of education, culture, and experience separated us, yet human frailty had woven a bond sufficiently long and sturdy to bridge the span. Meusheref and I were peas alike in the same pod, and because she reached out to me, we established a communication.

I was born into financial comfort and reared by parents

blessed with social skills, skills we, their children, learned under their tutelage. Mingling with people of every station, we were apt to treat all with the same respect and dignity. As a consequence, I accept people at face value, freely crediting them with good character, fairness, and honesty until such time as their own behavior may cancel their credit. At home I enjoyed an unusually broad range of comfortable acquaintanceships drawn from all ages and strata of society. Within the circle of people I called *friends*, both men and women share common characteristics, all of which are significant to our friendships.

These people, from whom I draw strength and share pleasure, are above all energetic and alert; quick to humor and irony, dedicated workaholics, caring, kind, supportive, loyal, open, articulate, interested in the world, politics, and ideas, they are just quirky enough to be interesting. Intolerance makes them angry; beauty moves them with joy; some are rich and others live a precarious financial existence.

They read books, travel, go often to museums, believe in education and self-improvement, give their time to rational causes, and foster good government. They are professionals: doctors, lawyers, dentists, businessmen and women, teachers, musicians, dancers, actors, sculptors, painters, and administrators, who participate in life and take intelligent care of their minds and bodies. Among us language is cultivated as an art by which ideas can be precisely communicated. Challenged to find a single label by which they—we—might be characterized, I'd improvise the term, "hands-on intellectuals." Was it any wonder I felt myself lost and alone.

I never questioned how other prisoners might judge me for the use I made of my time though it was unusual to see them similarly occupied. So I was slow to grasp that, excepting Lutfi, and Eminay, who like me spent hours on her bed surrounded by books, pamphlets, and letters, no one else idled away the hours with reading or writing. Not even when Neshe, always accommodating, refused to write my list and the return address of the prison, did it occur to me it was a case of couldn't, not wouldn't. Eventually I understood that Neshe had never learned to read or write. Like most of the prisoners, she was illiterate. Only after I grasped this fact, I saw that Lutfi's rise to influence here was due only in part to her vitality and busybody personality.

A better explanation of her position as a minor power lay in acknowledging she possessed skills that were both scarce and crucial to the functioning of the community: an ability to read and write Turkish, to perform rapid and accurate calculations with numbers, and a useful sleight of hand with languages that dazzled Hikmet. Exactly where and how Lutfi picked up those smatterings of English, German, French, Italian, and Greek, I began to suspect was as a "party-girl." Her familiarity with English slang, and words like "pussy" and "fuck," tended to reinforce an impression that her former associates had not been precisely "top drawer." But I had no interest in verifying my guess; probing into lives and transgressions wasn't useful. This was a situation where less knowledge was preferable to more.

I thought Lutfi generous in sharing her gifts with those who lacked them, in part I estimated, because it gave her unusual access to gossip. There was nothing Lutfi loved better than being importantly "in-the-know."

Occupations helped make the time pass but few were available. Most women filled their days with washing, gossiping, laundering, mending, and other needlework. Card playing, chess, and other games were forbidden by the prison as dependent upon chance and therefore gambling. Anything that smacked of fortune-telling—the reading of tea leaves and other black arts—was prohibited. When Lutfi confided to me the supremacy of coffee grounds over tea leaves for their accuracy in revealing the future, I understood very well that, consistent with prison philosophy, coffee had to be barred.

Few of these pursuits attracted my attention; the women themselves, however, drew my interest. The notion that differences of history, geography, traditions, and language did not separate us from the common ground of being women and human beings made life livable. As nearly every prisoner had a knitting, crocheting, or sewing project in progress (using materials supplied by their families, donated by charity, or provided by the prison school—a revelation in itself!), I employed my own needlework knowledge as a way of connecting to them and discovered a variety of talent extant in the dorm.

One of the older women proudly unfolded, one by one, a

cache of embroidered linens she kept stashed under her ground-floor bunk. Impressive in quality and volume, it had been created under the aegis of prison teachers and accumulated over six years of imprisonment. There were goods enough there for three *generous* dowries!

Aysa, the smaller of the two prison trustees, was working a set of crocheted placemats and napkins for Hikmet, the matron. Using a fine-quality white cotton thread, she had worked a pattern of such delicate intricacy, I extravagantly admired the work and coveted the finished product. I also filed for future reference the idea that in the event I stayed, I could be taught to make a set for myself.

From the beginning Aysa took a detached but kindly interest in my welfare, sharing her supply of milk and cookies every morning so my first cigarette of the day wouldn't be smoked on an empty stomach, believing, she indicated, cigarettes to be less lethal when inhaled after food. She distained tobacco but not those who used it: defense of the nonsmokers' airspace had not yet reached Turkey. My interest in Aysa increased upon learning she and her husband had lived six years in Germany. In the most limited way, because *I* lacked the vocabulary, we were able to exchange a few words in German, which gave us a special relationship. But we never grew close. Aysa, only two months from release, was investing her emotions on dreams that beckoned beyond the prison walls.

On Wednesday, the second of my days in prison, we breakfasted early, Lutfi having elbowed her way to the head of the use-of-the-fire line. Afterward I saw to the mailing of my letters and fulfilled my promise to read aloud to Neshe one of Yilmas's.

As an amateur handwriting analyst, I thought the script suggestive of immaturity. Discovering the man through the text of his letter confirmed this hasty judgment as well as the earlier-formed belief he was most likely a black man raised in southern neglect. His language revealed a deficiency of education and ideas, but I couldn't fault his wild imagination. In it he alluded to an anticipated trip to Germany where he and his sergeant expected to consummate a "deal," the proceeds of which were to net him "three or four millions." Admitting to a lack of background references that might have put this forecast in a different light, I took it as the boastful bragging of an infantile mind. Only one category of transaction could, in one stroke, produce profits of such magnitude. It had to be illegal. And nothing I'd learned of Yilmas up to now gave me confidence he could conceive of or execute so sophisticated and risky a venture. The man was dangerously clumsy and impulsive. Consider the monumental failure of his last grandiose scheme, which landed Neshe and him in Buja, I told myself. The successful smuggling and sale of arms or drugs was beyond his talents. I condemned his judgment for being more than suspect; it was warped. This was not a man Neshe could rely on, and I wanted to tell her so. A friend protects a friend, and in good faith, I could not encourage her dependency on Yilmas.

Strongly as I felt, I was sensitive to Neshe's vulnerability and didn't have the heart to blurt out my indignation when Neshe, revealing her insecurities, solicited my opinion of her beloved. Instead, I cautioned her gently that making millions was unlikely to be as easy as Yilmas believed nor did it come without taking great risks and counseled, "Yilmas is heading for trouble and it might be better if you didn't count on him." She wanted desperately not to believe me.

The Yilmas discussions continued long after we left the letters and ventured into the yard for our walk. Neshe seemed to want to speak of nothing else.

"Yilmas be father of my little boy," she said. "He love Melek. Melek love Yilmas. Five year I live Yilmas. He be good to me. Have nice apartment, good life." Stooping, we ducked under a wet sheet. "I tell prison women Yilmas be true father to Melek, but I tell to you true. Yilmas not be father."

"Who is Melek's father?" I dared to ask since she was being so candid.

"Husband be father," she said, "same like father to older son. I be have two son. Big son be twelve year, live with husband family. Melek," her eyes softened with tenderness, "be five year. Soon have circumcise. Make big party." Her face clouded, "I not be home for party. Mother, father take care Melek, make party. It be happy time."

I was receiving information faster than I could process it, and my mind was alive with questions: about Neshe's husband and Muslim circumcision and why had they waited until Melek was five? But before I managed to ask, Meusheref with Lutfi hard behind ran into the yard grinning and calling, "Gin, Gin."

"Soldier come," Lutfi pronounced, catching Mishu open-mouthed. I hesitated, not expecting a visit today, but was commanded by Lutfi, "You go. Consulate wait."

Looking for Bob Ludan, I was startled to find two men dressed in civilian clothes waiting in the visitors' room. Strangers to me, I had no time to make assumptions as the bearded one held out his hand and, speaking English with a British accent, introduced himself as Father Geoffery Evans, Anglican priest, and the man with him as Father Eugene Nee, American Catholic priest. Why they were here I couldn't imagine and waited for an explanation. Instead of words, Father Nee stepped forward, reached out, and, pulling me toward him, squeezed me in a rough embrace. Startled by his abruptness, frightened, vulnerable, and totally confused, I began to sob, and Nee, looking for words to calm me, only added anger to my discomfort by proclaiming in a voice full of confidence and an accent straight from the Emerald Isle, "Ye'll be home in no time, Gene; all ye got to do is write yer congressman."

How dare this weirdo insult my intelligence by suggesting release is as easy as that!

As I struggled to escape his grasp—what right had he to hug me? I didn't even know the man!—I saw, over his shoulder, another horror taking place. Into that little room came trooping the saddest ragtag bunch of disreputable-looking men I'd ever seen anywhere except on New York's Bowery. I couldn't prevent myself from drawing back, aghast.

Poorly dressed in what were little more than ill-fitting rags that hung loose and wrinkled from emaciated bodies, unshaven and unwashed, eyes hollow with boredom and despair, they were identified as the English-speaking male tourists of Buja prison, here for their weekly visit with the local English-speaking priests. One of them, I knew, had to be Yilmas. I identified him, looking more aggressive than despairing, as the one whose skin was the color of Hershey's milk chocolate.

It took hours to overcome the shock of that encounter with Father Nee, and I agitated until Lutfi transmitted my demand to Hikmet I would never have to face the man again.

Sensing the Turks' disdain for Jews, I'd purposely avoided

discussions about religion, but in view of the vehement Turkish prejudice against Christian religions, my antagonism against the priests may have been perceived more favorably by prison authorities than was my intention.

When Ludan arrived with Makbule, whom I hadn't seen since the fateful day in court, I covered my bet by begging him to tell the director of the prison to excuse me from further participation in all "English-speaking tourist visits," though, calmer now, I realized the priests were undoubtedly well-meaning. It was the Catholic priest, I told him, who offended me by his roughness and unrealistic suggestions, not knowing that Bob, in the performance of his consulate duties, met weekly with Major Nee, American air force chaplain, to discuss the condition of American prisoners in Izmir.

Neither did I anticipate, not in the most soaring flight of my imagination, Eugene Nee, "The Knute Rockne of the Priesthood," would become a valued friend.

The reason for Bob's unplanned visit was that he had a paper for me to sign. Having to do with the Privacy Act, it was a State Department release by which I alone had the right of deciding to whom information about my case could be given. Naming Paul Attaguile and Jim LePere, I signed.

I wondered why Makbule had come (after all, she was only a secretary at the consulate) and tried to find a reason. It was true she carried and gave me a secretary's note pad, the fulfillment of my request for writing paper, but Bob could have handled that assignment without her. Perhaps male members of the consulate, like gynecologists, choose not to examine females except in the inhibiting presence of a member of the same sex? Or maybe in their infinite kindness and tact, she had been sent in case I wanted to discuss a matter too delicate for a man's ears? It was more likely, I concluded, her coming was a gesture of support for a woman alone in a degrading situation.

I liked Makbule. She typified, in a way Atilla did not, the Turkish woman of fantasy: diminutive, sweet-faced, soft-spoken, yielding. Without being insipid, Makbule was kind, concerned, and competent in a way utterly unlike any American woman I knew. I could feel her pulling for me, wishing things to go well. I was glad to see her for any reason.

Seeking news of the bail request, I was told no report had

yet come to the consulate. Still, needing to hear something concrete and hopeful, something that promised a realistic strategy, I seized this chance when Atilla was not present to question Bob about the likelihood of circumventing a three and a half year prison term. His reply was not an answer. "Are you being treated well?" he asked.

Each time I exposed my aching need to be free, Bob's knee-jerk response was to ask about the treatment I was receiving. Each time he asked, I answered the same: "I am being treated very well." Although I appreciated his concerned protection, I couldn't seem to get through to him that physical conditions, minimal standard though they might be, were something I could handle. It was the isolation because of language, the sense of cultural dislocation, the boredom and rot of the mind that threatened me, not the food. I had a terrible, gnawing perception that the life I was living in Buja was not mine. "I'm not sure," I said squarely, holding his eyes, "I can live this way for three and a half years."

It was true. In the first hours and days of incarceration when I considered the options available—those pitifully few of which I was aware—suicide as an alternative to long-term imprisonment was not overlooked.

I have long believed suicide to be a viable option. Not to be elected carelessly, being so irreversible an act resulting in a condition so permanent, it is, nevertheless, the ultimate decision that restores control to an individual who feels robbed of personal choice in everything else. The method for my ultimate "escape" was worked out when I saw how easy it was to obtain Valium. I thought it too soon to start stockpiling as I hadn't exhausted either curiosity or hope. Just knowing the option was on the shelf, available and waiting, brought relief.

Bob kept hidden his reaction to my admission but exposed one of the alternative possibilities heretofore unrevealed. There was something called "prisoner exhange," a foreshortened version of which he supplied.

A treaty had been signed between Turkey and the United States agreeing to the exchange of nationals imprisoned as foreigners in the two countries. Upon return to the country of origin, each prisoner was theoretically supposed to serve out the remainder of his sentence. But in practice, Bob explained, if, as

in my case, the United States had no criminal statute compara-
ble to that under which the prisoner had been tried in the
foreign country, upon transfer home prisoners were quickly
released. As forty-five days would elapse from submission of
request to transfer, I asked Bob Ludan to start the process immediately. He said he was already looking into it.

Ludan was the very correct foreign professional, limiting his
interactions to the search for and transmission of information
between me and my family, keeping the State Department informed as my case progressed, and, above all, making sure my
human and legal rights were never in jeopardy. On a more
personal level I found him very kind, and his continuing frequent inquiries into my health and other needs struck me as
sincere and caring. Given the enormity of my isolation, I may
have invested his visits with more personal feeling than was the
case, but each time I saw him his presence warmed me, and
increasingly, I came to admire his intelligence, to count on his
integrity, and to lean on his judgment. Young as he was, Bob
Ludan was a person who inspired confidence.

And so was Atilla. Their visits were the highlights that
marked the slow-passing days.

After two days at Buja and a series of confrontations with
the limitations of its resources, I was better able to identify the
things I could buy on my own and those for which I would be
forced to rely on outside sources. During the same period the
agitation of the past five days settled down to a livable level of
anxiety bringing with it increased clarity of mind, and I began
recalling issues, previously overlooked, that had to be addressed.

In anticipation of another visit the following day, I began a
new list for Atilla and Bob. It began with provisions that included facial quality soap (the canteen had sent laundry soap
instead), fresh fruit (I wasn't yet aware the prison provided it),
more books (how many times could I read *Daniel Martin*?), an
English-Turkish dictionary, 5,000 Turkish lira every week (an
amount Neshe calculated was necessary), and stamps of a de-
nomination larger than 15 Turkish lira.* I added a note to find

---

*A 15 Turkish lira stamp mailed a letter anywhere in Turkey, but my mail
to the United States—sent the fastest way, EXPRES, required a minimum of
350 or more, depending upon weight. Two extra sheets of paper could add

out if Bob could get me more Valium in the unlikely event I used all I had or might get from the clinic. And, out of an anxiety I couldn't control, I noted another reminder for Bob about the Synthroid. The remainder of the list, two items, concerned responsibilities to others.

As my six-week cruise vacation was to have placed me in New York on October 8, I had made an appointment with a New York client for October 17. It was clearly a date I wasn't going to keep, and I wanted Bob to ask Paul to call and make my excuses. Paul, I trusted, would give whatever explanation he deemed necessary and appropriate.

The next item, saved for last, caused me the most consternation, and I had put it off as long as my conscience would allow. No longer could I delay revealing to Ludan a complicating matter concerning my family.

All of my life I'd avoided trading on the family name and connections. No one here or on the ship knew my father was Joe Hirshhorn, a self-made maverick millionaire, collector of modern art who, before his death in 1981, had donated some eight thousand pieces of art to the nation. On the Mall in Washington is a museum bearing his name—The Joseph H. Hirshhorn Museum and Sculpture Garden, one of the jewels in the crown of the Smithsonian Institution. With a brother and sister named Hirshhorn, I saw no way to avoid the involvement of people, including some in high government positions, in Washington, and thought Bob had a right to be forewarned. I told him the next day.

It was one of the hardest things I had to do, blowing my cover, and I waited until everything else had been discussed.

Makbule was present but not Atilla, who sent word that the court had turned down the request for bail. Despite having been warned in advance of the probability of this outcome, I took the news with keen disappointment and foolishly gave into a resurgence of hope when Bob reiterated Atilla's intention to submit

---

as much as 40 Turkish lira to the cost, but stamps of denominations larger than 15 Turkish lira were not available from the canteen. The faces of the envelopes of the first letters mailed to my family, except for a small area reserved for name and address, were entirely covered with 15 Turkish lira stamps bearing the blue and white face of Atatürk.

a second request on Monday. With Bob taking notes, I ran down the items on my list and turned over the key to my *Sea Princess* stateroom, carried off in blithe ignorance when I debarked Friday last.

Finally there was nothing more I could find to delay, what was for me, a terrible confession. I told him about my father and suggested the repercussions that might echo from this indisputable fact of my life.

Although unfamiliar with the world of art, where the name Hirshhorn is readily recognized, Ludan was swift to react with concern that a "connection" to a museum could have a seriously detrimental effect on my case.

"Neither my father's private collection nor that of the museum contains works of art that predate the nineteenth century," I protested. "The thrust of his collecting was in American paintings and the majority of those are by artists of the twentieth century. Among the sculpture there are earlier works, but not "ancient" by any stretch of the imagination. The museum is known as a *modern* art museum."

But as I labored to convince him, watching his face, I saw he was not. Worried about the court's perception of motive when the daughter of a museum founder was charged with smuggling works of art, he felt it was imperative that this fact be quietly kept from Turkish notice. As it was something I would not have willingly advertised in any case, the decision was fine with me, and I assumed Bob would counsel the others in New York and Washington.

I was gratified by the absence of any other reaction to the revelation that I was the daughter of Mr. Hirshhorn. In the United States this admission brought a predictable response, a heightened interest that became a burden. There was no reason Turks would have known of my father, either as an avid collector of art or money. As for Bob, I found it refreshingly obvious he had never heard of Joe either, when he asked for and carefully wrote down the spelling of our family name.

And when Ludan unexpectedly arrived to see me the fourth day in a row (a record for consulate visits, I'm sure), it was clear my exposure of the Hirshhorn connection had come not a moment too soon. The impact of family—insistent and forceful as their personalities—was being felt in Izmir.

After inquiring and receiving assurance about my health, in his understated way, and with a wry smile, he said, "I've had quite a few phone calls from the States. It seems there are a lot of people concerned about you."

"My family?"

"Yes, and others." I waited for explicit news. "I've read a biography of your father," he interjected. "He was certainly a very . . . colorful man."

I didn't want to talk about my father. I wanted to know how the living were bearing up.

"Who of my family has called?"

"Your sister Naomi called from California; Jim LePere . . ." he was tracing the list of his notes on the faithful yellow pad, ". . . I've talked to Paul, Jim's brother, Richard, and Robin in Germany. And the consulate has received a long telegram from your brother, Gordon."

"Are they alright?"

"They are . . ." he paused, choosing his words carefully, ". . . naturally, very worried."

"Oh my God, naturally." I swept my hand across tears that had begun to flow. "Did you tell them I was alright? Did you tell them it's not like *Midnight Express?* Did you . . . ."

"I did my best," he said. "I let them know you are physically and emotionally well. . . ."

"It's worse for them than it is for me," I interrupted, "don't you see? I'm here. I *know* what's going on. They're so far away . . . they don't know. They're imagining the worst. The absolute worst." To this there was no response.

"Your family has hired another lawyer."

"Another lawyer?" I was alarmed. As much in the dark about their activities as they were about mine, I also imagined the worst. "What about Paul?"

"This lawyer has been hired by your family in addition to Paul. They've asked me to have you add his name to the release so he has access to information about your case." At my hesitation, he added, "It's entirely up to you. I brought the document for your signature, but it's your decision."

My family has hired a lawyer to help me, I reasoned, denying a seed of anxiety deep within my subconscious. The least I can do is to allow him whatever information he needs.

At my nod, Bob pushed the papers and a pen across the table. I signed and, in doing so, recalled something I'd thought through the night before.

"Paul needs a power of attorney," I said. "I've asked him to pay bills and liquidate some bonds and haven't given him the legal power to act in my behalf."

"I can write something up right now," Bob said, readying the famous legal tablet. As an afterthought, he went to his brief-case and, removing a sheet of paper, held it out to me. "I happen to have a copy of the telegram your brother sent. Perhaps you'd like to read it while I'm working on the power of attorney."

I took it and began to read.

We are a verbal family, high on words and stringing them together, but Gordon carries this pleasure to excess. I have sometimes thought him to be in love with the sound of his own voice, infatuated with the thoughts he imposes. In an earlier time he might have been a successful purveyor of snake oil.

His telegram was articulate and insistent. It was also long, repetitive, and filled with more than a little "blowing into the wind." Addressed to: The Honorable George Schultz, Secretary of State, and Members of the State Department in Washington and Turkey, it began, "Dear Sirs,"

I address you in behalf of my sister, Gene Hirshhorn LePere, the daughter of Joseph H. Hirshhorn now deceased, who is being held without legitimate cause in the prison called Buca in Izmir, Turkey. My sister, Mrs. LePere, is incapable of having perpetrated the crime of which she is accused, to wit: the smuggling of antiquities from Turkey where she is now forcefully prevented from returning to her home and a family deeply anxious of her safety.

The importance of our father's contribution to the United States is well-documented. Numerous friends of the Hirshhorn family, distinguished colleagues, and government officials join me in seeking the fastest possible means of freeing my sister. As her brother, only living male relative and head of the Hirshhorn family, in their name and hers I strongly urge you to take the necessary steps to secure Mrs. LePere's

release whilst she is yet in sound condition and to
protest the unconscionable actions of the Turks in
this deplorable matter.

As the diplomatic representatives of the United
States, the responsibility to protect the life and liberty
of my sister is incumbent upon you. I charge you to
undertake this mission soonest with every
consideration for her safe and speedy return.

It went on for another three paragraphs filled with more of
the same.

When I finished reading, I lay the sheet of paper on the table,
feeling vaguely uncomfortable. Two feelings assailed me simul-
taneously: gratitude for my brother's unquestioning loyalty,
and embarrassment at his blatant bravado. Bob, across from me,
was still writing; about half the page was filled with his even
penmanship. While I waited for him to finish, I wondered what
he thought of Gordon's wire. What impression would a stranger
form of this man after reading it? As for myself, I felt used.
Instantaneously filled with guilt, I resorted to a private and
bitter humor. I can say one thing for Gordon anyway, I thought,
he has no aversion to using the family name as a club.

"He can be a little pompous at times," I said aloud when
Bob, finished, looked up.

"It's impressive," he commented with the barest trace of a
smile, and handed me the completed statement to read and sign.

Back in the dorm I had a lot to think about.

I should have been relieved to learn the family had taken
action. But there was anxiety, too. Who was in command of
their decisions? Were they working in concert under the
rational guidance of Paul and Jimmy? Or was everyone acting
independently? Would they let their anguish propel them to flail
about in every direction? Who hired the new lawyer? And who
was paying for him? Gordon didn't have any money. He was
heavily in debt. What would I have done in their place? There
were no maps to follow in this uncharted territory, and the
explorers were crazy with worry. I would be, too, if I were in
their place.

I thought about Naomi, imagining her in the kitchen of her
lovely home in the Hollywood hills, spending her waking hours
weeping into a telephone variously connected to Jimmy, to Gor-

don, to Paul on the East Coast, to Bob Ludan or Atilla Akat in Turkey. Naomi was inordinately sensitive and her feelings lay close to the surface. Once an inveterate hand wringer, she had outgrown such overt expressions of weakness and learned to have confidence in the real strength of her character. She, I thought, would be able to exercise the influence of her good judgment upon Gordon's forceful, and sometimes impulsive, ideas.

I was the older sister but it was Naomi to whom I, who kept up a front for most people, was able to reveal myself in weaker moments. Her tender and nonjudgmental identification with the sensitivities I preferred to hide made it possible for me to let down my guard with her. Although I had already written a number of letters home, because Naomi represented a place where weakness was acceptable, I had yet to write one to her. Needing all my strength to push down feelings, I was afraid that any contact with her would put me in touch with my pain, that given permission, I might begin to feel sorry for myself and in so doing, I might break down. That was something my pride wouldn't allow. Not looking at my pain and not feeling sorry for myself was all that prevented the hardened glass backbone, that was keeping me upright through this terrible ordeal, from cracking.

For Gordon to try to "rescue" me was fitting. In his lifetime, only three years fewer than mine, I had "rescued" him—or tried to—more times than either of us remembered. Bonded as "middle" children in a family of four and by the gift of similar talents and interests, we'd spent a lot of time together as we grew up. As children we also shared a rebellion against the constraints of a middle-class, upwardly mobile family as well as the consequences of revolt, being on the receiving end of a fair amount of parental disapproval. I viewed Gordon as brilliant and persistently aggressive, a combination that could be effective in setting me free if, and this was the core of my anxiety, he could set aside his own self-interests and concentrate on mine.

Richard LePere's involvement in the family's efforts to obtain my release was interesting news. The LePeres were a caring family of energetic strategists. Although no longer a legal member of their large clan, it was a sign of their generosity and loving spirit that I remained in their eyes, and mine, an in-law of good standing. Indeed, shortly before I left on my cruise in August, we'd spent a delightful weekend in Washington, D.C., at Richard's home, celebrating his and Mom LePere's birthdays in what had become an annual family event. The LePeres were great and Richard was one of my favorites.

A self-employed magazine consultant and the youngest of eight children (Jim was fourth from oldest), Richard was, like the other LePeres, a self-made success. When we first met he was a gangly, smart-mouthed seventeen-year-old. Now only thirty-eight, his "smart mouth," supported by a remarkable intelligence and a Herculean work schedule, had made him one of the best paid and most highly respected men in his profession. I suspected it was because Richard lived in Washington that Jim had sought his help.

Richard was a formidable addition to the rescue team, and realizing how many good, smart, competent people were working to free me both in Turkey and in the United States, I was more accepting of the small part I was forced to play in shaping the final outcome. It was my responsibility to "be cool" while I was waiting.

I began keeping a journal on Saturday, October 6, at the suggestion of a well-behaved rabbi whom Ludan brought to the prison. During the brief visit this calm man accepted in good grace my refusal of his offer of a copy of the Old Testament. I welcomed, in addition to the idea of keeping a record, two little, yellow, soft plastic ear plugs for times when the din of the dorm seemed intolerable.

Having no experience in journal writing, I used it to record everything I found interesting, including the new Turkish words I'd been learning.

October 6. Biliorum, which means "I know" has little use for me since there is little I do know, but I like the way the word rolls off the tongue and try to use it when I can. A second expression, "au tur," I have frequent need to use as women are always coming to my bed and I can invite them to "sit down" in their own language. During these visits we order "chai," tea.

Chai was an important feature of prison life. Indeed, with only three "fires" available in the cell block, paid for by periodic collections from the inmates and bought outside the prison by Hikmet, its significance was obvious by the fact that two were reserved for the production of tea from eight in the morning until eight at night, while only one was spared for meal preparation.

Prepared in the Turkish manner,* the tea was very good. As tea was the only hot beverage available in prison I, who disdain tea to the extent that even in Chinese restaurants I never indulge, drank it frequently and learned to enjoy it. Served in characteristic Turkish beverage glasses (the same as those used for coffee) from a round metal tray, each glass cost 7 Turkish lira, less than 2 cents, which included the unlimited use of sugar to which one helped oneself from a bowl with the tiniest spoon I'd ever seen.

The women who had the job of "tea ladies" made some small profit from their twelve-hour work days. Thus, it was a job for two women for which there was considerable competition among those without funds and with the most minimal skills in arithmetic. A record was kept of every glass ordered by every prisoner throughout the day. Each evening after the kettles were put away for the night, the "tea ladies," carrying their record book, made a circuit of both dorms to collect the monies owed. It amazed me to discover, as I paid my nightly bill, I was consuming tea at the rate of seven to ten glasses daily. The rites of tea drinking also gave me an insight into something far more important, how much the absence of common language distorts our perception of people.

When the women came for my money they invariably looked to Lutfi for translation of the sum due, despite the fact that Turks use Arabic numerals just as we do. By taking their record book, miming my wish to know which was my account,

---

*To prepare the tea, two large kettles are used. The first, filled with water, is placed directly over the fire to boil without a lid while the second, containing a suitable amount of tea leaves, is set atop the first. As the water below comes to a boil, the tea leaves are steamed open. When the water in the lower kettle is boiling, it is poured into the upper kettle and the tea is allowed to steep before serving.

reading the amount they had totaled, and handing them the exact sum in lira, I gave evidence of an ability they'd overlooked and eliminated the need for translators. I saw by their faces it was a revelation. It was a revelation for me, too.

How often, I realized, now that it had happened to me, we arrogantly assume someone who doesn't speak our language is stupid or ignorant. As an American, where every day I encountered new immigrants, I cautioned myself to be more careful not to make that mistake again. Recalling my grandmother, who arrived in New York at thirteen years of age and alone, and my father, who came when he was seven, both without a word of English to help them adapt to a new culture, I felt a profound sense of unity with them and drew strength from the knowledge we shared a common experience.

The tea ladies also provided hot water for bathing, at least, if Neshe was to be believed, during the times when none other was available. For the princely sum of 50 Turkish lira (20 cents), beyond the purse of many, you could buy a kettleful of boiling water. Of course, hot anything depended on having fuel.

October 7. In the four days I've been here we've already been without fuel for a twenty-four hour period during which there was neither tea nor warmed food. But today Hikmet bought new "fires" and I took my first bath in one of the toilets (the one with the marble inset). The boiling water was given to me in a metal drum about 18 inches in diameter and depth. You need a second plastic pail in which to mix the boiling water with cold, creating a substantial amount of the right temperature.

Neshe and Lutfi together provided the equipment for the bath including soap, towels, plastic pails, and scoops. The toilet stall being tiny, no more than five feet square, with Lutfi's participation, the door perforce stood ajar and I stood naked on the cement floor amid buckets and pails feeling very exposed as the other women milled about taking care of their own needs.

It is a known phenomenon that under crowded conditions cultural courtesies will develop to provide a semblance of privacy. Japan, a small, overpopulated country full of ancient wisdoms, provides an example in which downcast eyes and deafened ears are the reasonable substitute for "space." I thought this same phenomenon was also present in the women's dorm at Buja.

In Turkey, bathing is not a daily ritual to be undertaken in the privacy of one's own tub as it is in the United States. Rather, in Turkey, it is an infrequent excursion to a public bathhouse and the occasion can take on aspects of a communal sport. In Buja, the bath, I saw, was a social activity in which many women might participate but, exposed as I was, the experience didn't seem to violate my sense of personal modesty.

After my body was clean, Lutfi, having wisely saved some hot water, attacked my hair at the wash trough. I can't remember ever feeling so refreshed. It was wonderful!

Sitting before the one mirror in the room, with curlers and clips borrowed from Eminay, Lutfi set my hair and loaned me a scarf, which I tied around my head, allowing it to dry overnight while I slept.

> October 9. Sunday is visiting day. Yesterday a lot of people bathed and washed hair. Today, Sunday, everyone is on edge. You can feel the tension in the air; women worrying if someone will come to visit. There have been a lot of sharp voices and a lot of crying. Euzgeul has been shouting like an angry condor in a harangue that goes on for twenty minutes.
>
> At my insistence Lutfi explains the problem. An old woman wishes to avoid her turn at housekeeping. For two years this woman has side-stepped the mopping; some pitying woman has always taken her place. But though the argument continues through the day and into Monday, this poor, enfeebled, sick old woman finally loses. She is forced to take her turn.

The dorm was kept surprisingly clean, being swept and wet-mopped every morning and evening, by the inmates. This, in part, explained the perpetual dampness of cement floors and the reason why two inches of water stood in a low spot at the foot of the stairs, from the top of which a bucket of water was spilled before the stairs were mopped. Whatever remained at the bottom afterward, typically, was ignored.

There were other routines around which trouble brewed like maggots in garbage. Toast making was notable among them. After the fighting for a place in the cooking list, new arguments broke out every day in the "kitchen" because some group was too slow using the single "fire." One day, when I'd been there less than a week, Hikmet, in a petulant snit, decided there would be no hot breakfasts at all. This dictum lasted two days before she relented. Her reason for reversal was because she "didn't want Gene to have a bad impression of Turkish jails to take back to America."

I understood very well that I was a unique presence in the dorm, being both a curiosity and, through no fault of my own, a kind of "celebrity." Almost everything about me was different: my appearance, language, orientation, customs, posessions, and the imagined influence of my citizenship in the glamorous country from which I'd traveled to their humbler shores. I had the impression that, in addition to their innate kindness, my tender-hearted Turkish cellmates believed I should not have to experience the indignities they willingly suffered as their natural lot. A good example was my eating group's continuing unwillingness to allow me to help prepare, cook, and serve food or to clean up after meals. Another example was the offer I had from one of the women to give up her "good" mattress for my "bad" one.

Even Hikmet wanted to make special allowances for me. When she understood I took pills every morning, thyroid and vitamins, not wanting me to swallow them on an empty stomach, she invited me to share her breakfasts (the first prepared regardless of the list) and to eat at her table. To all generous offers of special privilege I gave thanks and a firm refusal. Special treatment was counterproductive to acceptance. I needed the goodwill of my fellow prisoners.

But I accepted my value as a pleasant diversion. The women took a definite interest in my clothes, especially my night-clothes, a slinky, revealing, white nylon gown and green (not silk) Chinese robe. I got many approving comments on the coat-of-many-colors dress that I wore once a week when my usual uniform (navy slacks, white, sleeveless tennis top, and white cotton jacket) was in the wash. They examined my lipstick and lip brush, a jar of blue cream eye shadow, and the Avon moisturizer I applied morning and night.

The odd Mishu, patronized by the other women, approached me as I was brushing my teeth, wanting to know—by sign language and grunts—what the green fluoride rinse was and could she try some. Within three days of my arrival, Lutfi had appropriated my travel mirror, which magnified the smallest pore into a crater. She enjoyed it so much I let her keep it until I was released.

There is no doubt that the most magnificent trick I had up my sleeve, one that gathered a large crowd the first time I performed it, was the removal, cleaning, storing, and replacement of my extended-wear contact lenses. It took a full-time guard, usually Neshe, to watch over the bottles and case while I went into the next room to wash my hands on Sunday nights, when I removed them, and Monday mornings, when I put them back in.

Turkish women with access to department stores and television found nothing unusual in my clothing nor I in theirs. The modernists (about half the women) looked quite smart when they dressed up. But the outfits worn by the peasant and older women were a considerable curiosity to me.

Each day they donned a shalvar (şalvar), the trousers I'd first noticed in the yard. Flowing nearly to the floor, usually made of a brightly printed cotton, it looked like a skirt but was, actually, a ballooning pair of trousers with a wide crotch that fell around midcalf. Held at the waist with elastic, it afforded an inordinate amount of comfort and great freedom of movement. On the upper half of the body was worn a pullover sweater or blouse over which they often added a crocheted or knitted vest. I was seriously considering Neshe's offer to have her mother make a shalvar for me.

One might assume Turkish underclothes were similar to ours, but I never got to see any. In a room where thirty-five women dressed and undressed, by some sleight of hand they managed to disrobe invisibly. I was not so adept, it would appear. Lutfi confided to me that my habit of removing my underpants from beneath my nightgown before retiring had drawn unfavorable comment from one gossipy old crone.

I worked hard to minimize the differences between us, building bridges with the Turkish women over common experience and feelings: grief, fear, anger, and our womanhood from which sprang a love of children and the ease with which we cried over our many losses. Most of all we shared a bitter impotence for the lack of control over our lives. My hopes for the future were in the hands of my family and the lawyers. Time dragged between visits from Ludan and Atilla, on whom I was dependent for everything.

My court date had been set for October 27, Ludan told me at a visit on Monday, October 11. I was excited now that there was a specific target date. In a frenzy of hope and prayer, not wanting to fool myself but at the same time fantasizing, I imagined that somehow, against all odds, I'd win the day and be cleared to go home.

Now Bob presented me with a new problem.

"Your family wants to send someone to see you."

"Why?" I asked.

"I've repeatedly assured them you are physically and emotionally well, under the circumstances," he answered, "but they want to have a representative verify your condition."

"I see," I said, understanding their need because I understood them.

My family's indigation over my situation echoed my own. It was intolerable that I should be incarcerated in a Turkish prison, presumed guilty until I could prove my own innocence. As Americans, nothing in our individual or collective lives had prepared us for this situation. And being about eight thousand miles removed from the scene of action enflamed their sense of impotence and fed every irrational fear for my safety. They just wanted to see for themselves that everything that could be done was being done. We are alike, really. Always needing to be in control.

"Who do they want to send?"

"I have told them it is up to you."

I knew immediately who *couldn't* come.

"Not Gordon or Naomi," I said, "they're too emotional. I can't handle their fears and anxieties; I have all I can do to manage my own." Jim? "Not Jimmy, either. He has a very short fuse. He'd be arrested for punching someone out fifteen minutes after he arrived in Turkey."

I tried to imagine one of them here in the visitor's room, greeting me, sitting across the table. . . .

"Richard LePere or Paul Attaguile," I said, firmly, "No one else."

"Richard or Paul," Bob repeated, and waited while I thought some more.

"Richard," I said, finally. Richard would be best. He was street smart, laid back—and I could count on him to hide his feelings from me.

It was decided.

Atilla confirmed the court date later that day. When I said how hard it was to wait more than two weeks, she told me, "Gene, you are lucky to have your court so soon. They are putting other cases in December. It is perhaps because of the consulate it is heard so quickly." I was lucky, I realized, and happy, at last, there was something *I* could do: plan my defense.

I insisted Atilla call Charnaud and the examining custom inspector as witnesses in my behalf. *They* knew I wasn't attempting to hide anything. She agreed. Making notes, she treated me like a partner as we discussed strategies and persuasive arguments.

But without allowing me to lose heart, she did not encourage any real hope that the coming hearing would be the last.

Before leaving, Atilla reported that she and Makbule had completed the shopping. Everything I needed would reach me today, except the Nescafé, which had been disallowed by the prison authorities. I hugged her and asked her to thank Makbule before returning to the dorm.

I lived in two worlds. In one, in the visitors' room, I experienced brief moments of being a familiar self, a competent, active participant in directing my life. In the other I returned to my role as displaced person, incompetent and passive in the acceptance of the Turkish world that I inhabited. Shuttling between them, I experienced in full how much my present existence was divided.

October 12. Today I have received my first mail. A letter from Yilmas. I wrote him last week at Neshe's insistence because she said he was experienced in everything I needed to know about getting home.

In an erratic hand and impossible spelling, Yilmas

offered discouragement, disenchantment, and one line
of comedy. The letter began, "Dear Sister, Welcome
to another planet—Turkey. . . ."

The women were disappointed about the Nescafé
but, luckily, I remembered I had the powdered coffee
packets from the ship. There were eight. We used
four today at lunch . . . with cold water. It still tasted
good. I have given the remaining four to Lutfi to keep
for the group's use another time.

The things Atilla bought arrived yesterday. I was
so happy and excited to have my own stuff. It made
me feel more at home. The sheets are so pretty and
the blankets of soft, warm wool. When my bed was
remade, I bought tea for the whole dorm. It was a
celebration. The party cost 500 Turkish lira, about
$2.00. A cheap price to pay for a bit of happiness.

The pain of women filled the dorm. It was bred of many
things: of the petty competition and unexpected kindness, of a
despair that drove some prisoners to vent their frustrations
upon their most defenseless sisters, the women without money,
influence, or power. They were the ones who suffered most:
having to eat the meager prison food without benefit of cooking
because they didn't have the twelve lira to pay for "fire"; to wash
their bodies, their clothes, and their dishes without soap; to sleep
without sheets, covered only by one scratchy, hard prison blanket. These women, treated almost as if they were nonpersons,
often retained a dignity that was astonishing and helped themselves by working for those who could pay.

The dorm was the world in miniature and had its share of
personal drama about which I had Lutfi to thank for learning.

One of the inmates was an old, very old, pathetic woman
jailed because "she sell hash." Her time had been served but she
couldn't go home. She still owed the prison a fine of 70,000
Turkish lira, about $280. It might as well have been a million.
She had once been considered rich, the owner of a home and
business. But while she was in prison, her alcoholic son sold her
house and posessions, and because her daughter's husband
didn't like her, he refused to pay the fine for her release. Women
from both cell blocks had already collected 30,000 Turkish lira

and later would raise the balance among themselves to set her free. I gladly made a contribution to the fund.

Four middle-aged women and a new-born baby entered prison soon after I did. Lutfi, who had a subscription to one of the daily papers that reported their lurid story in three columns of detail, told me why. They, and four more women, assigned to the other dorm, were arrested for their participation in a baby-selling racket. Operating a delivery clinic for indigent and ignorant women (one of the arrested women was allegedly a doctor), they told the mother her child was born dead. Then they sold it. The baby who came in with them wasn't theirs. It had been rescued in the arrest.

I recoiled to think what had become of the children already sold, for these women hadn't concerned themselves as to the use to which the babies might be put. Few buyers were simply childless couples, and most infants had been sold into sexual and other kinds of slavery.

I used to watch one mother and child check out of prison every morning at seven after the roust and check back in twelve hours later. She appeared to be on some kind of "work program," spending only nights in the prison. Her bag of baby clothing and supplies, even the baby's diaper, were prodded and poked by Euzgeul twice a day looking for illegal contraband.

It was the stories of the women I knew best that most interested me. Because I found her so good-natured and easygoing, Sara's was probably the most surprising.

She was serving a twenty-year sentence for the murder of her husband, whom, Neshe and Lutfi both reported, she had loved very much. Six years had already been served in a small jail near her native village where the killing took place, but she had been transferred to Buja for medical attention. What her ailment was I never found out.

I couldn't guess what possible reason, barring an accident, Sara would have for killing a man she loved, but Lutfi, in her slang English, made the circumstances clear.

In Turkey, she explained, especially in the country towns, traditions prevail unchanged even today. There, as Sylvia let us discover, men continued to idle while women worked in the fields and at home. Enjoying his male-granted right to play, Sara's husband had learned from other women techniques of love-making more sophisticated than those to which Sara was accustomed, techniques she found repugnant and believed immoral.

Sara was unwilling when he asked her to submit to anal intercourse; a heated argument ensued. When she was adamant in her refusal, he used a large knife to force her submission. After the act was over and he lay sleeping, Sara, outraged and physically hurt, asked herself why, if he loved her, had he caused her so much pain and humiliation. In her anguish, seeing the knife on the pillow, she took it and stabbed him repeatedly, crying out, "You hurt me. Now see how it feels."

Lutfi said that after the anger passed, Sara, unaware her husband was dead, kept trying to rouse him. Unable, she had been grieving ever since.

This story was related as we sat drinking tea after the noon meal. Sara watched my face as Lutfi told her story. Aware of what I heard, her large, brown eyes were sad and knowing. From time to time, she participated by filling in a detail or confirming what had been told, which Lutfi then translated for me. At the end I felt as sad as she looked. With good behavior, Sara could expect release in five years, but her future sounded bleak to me. Her only child was being cared for by her in-laws, who were unlikely to accept her back into their lives.

Lutfi's story I had to piece together for myself. The bit she told me was no more than the tip of the iceberg.

She said she'd been arrested in 1980 for smoking one marijuana cigarette, that she'd been put in a hospital from which she'd escaped. For three years she had managed to avoid the law, during which time she had hardly ever used marijuana "because my husband, he no like I smoke." She was rearrested and her original sentence lengthened from three to five years because "I escape from hospital. That why."

Lutfi's husband wasn't really her husband. The fact that they weren't actually married led to an incident that revealed a defect in what I had previously thought was only an animated, perhaps high-strung, personality.

On the second Sunday after I'd arrived, Lutfi was called out with other women from our dorm, and although prisoners' vis-

its with their families were restricted to no more than ten minutes,* she returned unexpectedly soon to the accompaniment of
a great pounding on the steel door and many loud, attention-
getting wails.

Swooning in the arms of several attendant inmates, she was
half carried to the lowest bunk of her tier, where she writhed,
half-fainting, and generally wept and wailed while women scur-
ried to wet clothes with which they mopped her face and
worked to calm her.

My bed, where I'd been writing, was adjacent to the one
where Lutfi was half-reclining, so I had a clear view of what
happened. Neshe came to assist, leaning over the prone girl who
whispered something to her. I saw Neshe nod, then climb to
Lutfi's bed where she dug under the pillow and came up with
a small plastic bag. It was full of blue and white capsules. There
must have been twenty of them.

Neshe extracted two, climbed down, left the room, and returned in a half-minute with a cup of water that she gave to Lutfi
with the capsules. In a smooth gulp they were gone, and in a few
minutes Lutfi had grown calmer. As with everything, I had to
wait for a translator to learn the reason for Lutfi's outburst.
Neshe told me.

In a visit from her brother, Lutfi learned that her "husband"
had been arrested and was currently imprisoned (in Buja). Legally barred from visiting Lutfi because they were not married,
he'd tried to circumvent the rules by presenting her brother's
identification at the gate. He was caught.

From this incident I began my education on Lutfi's drug
usage and dependency and was also sharply reminded of the
rigidity of the Turkish mentality.

Visiting rules were narrow and restrictive, unwilling, it
seemed, to take into account human needs and feelings. Worse,
incarceration for so harmless and forgivable a "crime" smacked

---

*Prisoners' Sunday visits, restricted to members of their families, were
conducted at the individual booths that lined the hall to the room where I
had mine, under the supervision of soldiers. This larger room, where the
length of visits was more generous, even an hour, was primarily for the
use of attorneys and their prisoner clients.

156

of overkill. I never learned how long a sentence the Turks deemed fitting for this minor infraction of rules.

> October 13. My court date is two weeks from today.
> Why do I have such dire thoughts about its outcome?
> . . . Mrs. Akat has repetitioned the court for my
> release on bail and hopes to hear today. Arrangements
> to pay the bail have been made by Jimmy in New
> York but I don't expect it. Why I cannot say except
> there is a dark, masculine, punitive, judgmental issue
> here having to do with women and foreigners and
> prerogatives of insecure countries. I do not expect
> release on bail. I do not expect acquittal in two
> weeks. I cannot convert my sentence to a fine, so I
> expect three to six months of continued confinement
> and then a prisoner exchange to the U.S. The whole
> thing is a disaster. How easily it could have been
> averted. So easily. I try not to dwell on changing the
> past. It is not possible.
> The American Consulate came again today. They
> had the vice consul* with them, Bob Ludan and
> Makbule. They couldn't be nicer. I will add a
> 'smuggling' specialist to the attorney list to work with
> Mrs. Akat.
> I grieve over Naomi, Gordon, Jimmy and the
> others. I must try to write Naomi now. I fear the
> trial and that they will convict me . . . . Then the
> prisoner exchange, two, three, four months. I know
> the Consulate will expedite . . . .

The reports I received through Atilla and Ludan were beginning to depress me as every meeting made it increasingly clear there was no easy way out. Whatever fantasies I'd been harboring that somehow my family would work a miracle were slowly dispelled because I saw how little of substance was being done. The "smuggling specialist" seemed an act of desperation in the hope of finding any kind of leverage by which to pry me loose. So far the only specific actions the family had taken was to hire an American lawyer and to suggest the hiring of another Turkish one. Did they know something I didn't? Did they know

---

*Beauveau Nalle.

everything I did? What good was all of this accomplishing except to spend my money? Or were they planning to pay for it? The vice consul didn't have answers to my questions any more than Bob did.

Unlike Ludan, who had completed only one year of a two-year assignment in Turkey, Beau Nalle was an older man who had taught for years at the American University in Istanbul, Atilla's alma mater. In foreign service, he'd been stationed in Turkey some years more. Less formal than I expected a man of his rank to be, he expressed concern over my health and offered to lend books from his personal library for me to read. When I explained that the prison routinely tore the covers from all hard-bound books, he backed off gracefully.

In front of him, at my urging, Bob gave a full explanation of "Prisoner Exchange," which, in ignorance up to then, I had held as my ultimate hope should all else fail. The conditions were time-eroding. For starters, keeping in mind the tortuously turtle-slow Turkish trial system, forty-five days must lapse between a finding of guilt and the submission of an application to begin the process, which, if then expedited, would take another six to eight weeks. This news so depressed me, I considered entering a plea of guilty if it would speed things up. Now that the novelty had worn off, I wasn't just restless to go home, I was terrified of having to stay in so stultifying a place.

> October 14. The food is boring—day in and day out
> the same thing. Soups made with vegetables cooked to
> death, potatoes, starches, starches, starches. Beans of
> 30 different kinds; macaroni, rice, lentils, barley. And
> bread. We purchase "borek," a triangular, flaky
> pastry, and the hot food which is most often stuffed
> peppers with rice and no meat. Sara adds onions and
> tomato which is tasty but it all becomes boring.
>   There is a lot of nervous knuckle-cracking by all
> the women.

The cracking of knuckles was so widespread I wondered if it were a national habit. While I try to avoid making generalizations, it was impossible not to try to understand the meaning and cause for some of the things I observed. For example, Turkish women have the most extraordinary eyes. It is a trait too universal to be accidental.

I was struck by them time and time again. Set wide apart, they are dark, mysterious, clear, and luminous, delicately outlined with curling black lashes and crowned by brows that arched above them like black gull wings.

Remembering the traditions from which these women had only recently* been liberated, I ventured the guess that these eyes must be the result of a process of natural selection, taking place under conditions that prevailed for centuries. I knew that women here had been swathed in yards of veiling that left nothing uncovered but the eyes. By what other physical characteristic could the choice of a suitable bride, the mother of one's future children, be made? Those ladies who looked out into the world with the most seductive, compelling, lustrous, beguiling eyes were least likely to remain old maids. Case closed.

The soldiers and guards, television, and the memory of the traditional dancers in Pamukkale† gave me the data for a second hypothesis by which to explain the observable gracelessness of Turkish men that was singularly different from the smooth, seductive body movements of the women.

Where grace and seductive movement had always been cultivated in the Turkish ideal of woman, I realized it was only in this century that Turkish men had begun to move away from the military man as the masculine ideal, fostering a stiff, precise, and awkwardly regimented bearing. Now, for the first time, the Turkish male has new role models acquired from other cultures, especially through the varied entertainment media, that are showing him new, graceful ways to use his body. I think the Turkish male is still very awkward because he hasn't had time to adapt fully.

Speculation about the last example was most intriguing, but being especially ignorant when it comes to languages, I mention it with all humility. My conclusion is so tentative I must offer it more as a layman's question than as a hypothesis.

I was much struck by the fact that the Turkish words for yes

---

*1924.
†This town's name has two apparently legitimate pronounciations: Sylvia said Pa mu ká lay and Bob Ludan called it Pa mú ka lay. I say it Sylvia's way.

and no—*evet* and *hyer*—are both two-syllable words, and I found it near to impossible to speak either of them with a modicum of finality. My familiarity with foreign languages is decidedly limited, but in all the Romance languages, and in German and Dutch, and in Russian the word for "yes" and the word for "no" have but a single syllable, just as they have in English.

It is infinitely easier to spit out a one-syllable word in anger or confirmation. No! Yes! But I have yet to hear the Turkish "no" pronounced in a way that is a convincing closeout or a Turkish "yes" that bites the air. My question: can people who say *evet* when they mean yes and *hyer* when they mean no be believed? As a people, does their language express a clear and firmly fixed position? Or should one understand that a "yes" may mean a "no," and a "no" a "yes"? Is this the reason why there is often a subtext to Turkish dicta?

I have no answers. Only questions.

From my bed where I spent most of the hours of the day, I could see a calendar hanging on the wall over Hikmet's bed. A Turkish calendar, it took a few days to get used to seeing Saturday and Sunday dates in two columns together at the right side of the matrix. I glanced at it often, as if frequent checking would make the days pass more quickly.

Sunday, October 16, was a date I willed myself to obliterate. For me it would not exist. October 16 was my fifty-seventh birthday, and I could not see the humor in knowing it would be spent in a Turkish prison.

Apparently I succeeded for, though my journal entry for that date was lengthy, there is no indication I'd given birthdays a thought. Repression takes considerable energy.

October 16. I was tired this morning, and for the first time since I arrived, I went back to bed after the 7:15 roust. I slept about forty minutes and dressed for breakfast after which I had a good brisk walk by myself. Lutfi's manipulations and intrigues threaten to cause Neshe problems so we have agreed to spend less time together. . . . Jealousies are ridiculous here but L is a consummate manipulator. She rushes for center stage no matter the play or drama and injects herself totally into the role of Star. I, the American, belong

to her, although she speaks only fair English and
understands far less of what I try to convey than
Neshe. Be that as it may, survival requires games and
I will attend to L as much as seems casually proper
and necesary. N is likely to be here longer than I and
needs an atmosphere of acceptance which L seems
able to rob anyone of.

My initial dependency on Lutfi diminished as most aspects
of prison life became routine. Thus I was better able to stand
back and see her as she really was: a nervous, hyperactive, drug-
dependent narcissist complete with all the concomitant self-
serving, manipulative, and attention-drawing behavior. She was
always onstage and often working behind someone's back to
elevate herself by diminishing others.

I had often wondered why Eminay had approached me
like a frightened bird on two occasions but always seemed too
busy to develop a more open friendship. I had learned she
was college educated like the "terrorists" downstairs and a
practicing pharmacist. She could be found on her bed studying her books and writing long letters to a sister every spare
minute of the day. Her family, obviously one of culture and
refinement (Eminay played the viola and longed for classical
music), except for the sister, was either dead or had disowned
her.

Although she professed, and demonstrated, goodwill toward
everyone, she kept very much to herself. The reasons for her
imprisonment are, even now, unknown to me, but what I could
see—what anyone with eyes and feelings could see—was the
depth of her pain. She was as sensitive as an exposed nerve,
vibrating with suppressed feeling. I suspected it was the incarceration itself, a humiliation she couldn't shrug off, that had
wounded her so terribly.

I saw in her myself a few months hence: a fish gasping on
a dry dock, surrounded by humans who could survive breathing
the unnourishing atmosphere of this bleak prison.

Eminay would have felt more fulfilled had she been able to
use her knowledge and skills for the betterment of the other
women, if she had been given even the smallest bits of responsibility. I learned it was Lutfi who, by a dogged campaign of jealous and false undermining, was preventing Em-

inay from enjoying more respect and meaningful occupation.

The woman had withdrawn and was paralyzed by fear. A fear I began to understand, not from the head as an intellectual concept, but in the belly where it took hold and began to grow inside me after Neshe and I adapted our preferred behavior on account of the incipient danger of Lutfi's influence with Hikmet.

Of course, in the final analysis, it was Hikmet who was to blame. Her relationships with the women were safely superficial; she relied on Lutfi and fat, boisterous, gossipy old Nuran —alleged to be an in-law—for her perceptions of conditions in the dorm and what to do about them. It was the perks of her position that Hikmet enjoyed; she was ill-suited to the responsibilities that accompanied them and unbecomingly familiar with the women she was paid to oversee.

> . . . Friday HKMT had her legs waxed. In front of
> everyone she pulled off her pantyhose while one of
> the country women worked over a wax that was made
> of sugar, lemon and water, pulling at it, like taffy,
> until it was the right consistency and applied it in
> strips along the front of HKMT's calf. Then she pulled
> it up, bit by bit, systematically removing the hair.
> Both legs were done in about a half hour.

The depilatation didn't end with the legs. Hikmet removed her sweater and had her armpits stripped, pretending it didn't hurt although afterwards both axillae were greatly enflamed. Getting dressed again, she left the dorm only to return soon after when, in sign language bordering on the lewd, she let me know that by the same process her pubic hair had been removed. She was now as clean as a little girl.

This practice, which I was later told by a doctor is not confined to women, probably has some sexual implications that a sociologist specializing in Turkish customs might illuminate.* However, there were some things I prefered to be kept in the dark about: the condition of Hikmet's armpits and groin were definitely two of them.

---

*I have since learned that hairlessness, in the Muslim religion, is believed to improve one's chances of getting into heaven.

October 17. Late Saturday, after most people were in
bed and watching shitty TV, there was a militant
rhythmic shouting in the lower dorm. All the 'chiefs'
got up: Euzgeul, Ayse and Nuran (the gossipy old fart
related to Hikmet). I got up, too, out of a sense of
self-preservation and nothing else. L, of course, got up
to be center stage. Euzgeul went to the door and set
up a terrible pounding. All very ominous. But
nothing happened. The chanting stopped and
everyone went back to bed. The contained anger and
frustration is pent up and one day will explode like a
volcano. The fucking TV blasted until midnight last
night. I can't stand it.

I felt I had attained a kind of tranquility and acceptance, but
as the structure that supported it was eroded, I grew less com-
placent and more tense. First Neshe and I found it necessary to
pull back from each other. I had learned to look over my shoulder and, all too often when I did, found Lutfi watching me. Now
the security of mealtime was threatened when Sara announced
her intention of pulling out of the group. She said she'd be
happier eating alone, but Neshe later told me the real reason.
Lutfi had gotten off some nasty cracks aimed at Sara's Achilles'
heel: her healthy appetite unsupported by funds to pay for food.

Unwilling to put pressure on her—although her desertion
made me uneasy—I said, through Neshe, only how much I liked
her and how sorry I would be if she left. In tears, Sara stuck to
her decision, and I knew it was because she was too proud to
give Lutfi the chance for another cobra strike.

Without Sara, whom I instinctively sensed had been the
balance wheel giving our group stability, I wondered who
would be the buffer for Lutfi's sudden flashes of anger.

October 18. I spent an hour with Bob Ludan and
Makbule and was told about Richard LePere, the
trial, attorneys, etc. Doubt things will be settled at
the first trial. Trying for bail again. Bob thinks my
priority should be getting out of prison on bail. I may
not have to remain in Turkey for the balance of the
trials. That's a new notion to me but it seems it can
sometimes be done. Bob will be in Europe for three
weeks starting October 22nd. I will miss him terribly.

He's been wonderful to me. He says Richard's in
Ankara now! Will be in Izmir Wednesday (tomorrow)
and here Thursday. He's supposed to have a couple of
lawyers with him.

   Makbule will translate at the trial. I've asked her to
make sure she translates every word I say. She's asked
for a statement of the events to study before the trial.
I am preparing it between now and Thursday.

Looking forward to Richard's visit, writing the text of my
story for Makbule's use, and preparing for the coming trial
preoccupied my waking hours and interfered with sleep at
night.

   My appearance worried me: it was important that Richard
be able to report, honestly, to the folks at home that that I looked
well. I planned for another bath and hair-grooming session.

   The anxieties that oppressed me clouded my judgment. The
newest argument I'd dreamed up and planned to discuss with
Richard and Atilla Thursday was intended to persuade the
court I should be released by what amounted to blackmail
through economic manipulation. The argument was laughable
and counterproductive:

   . . . think about the dollars American tourists *would*
   and could bring in if they weren't too afraid of the
   police state because of the way they have treated a
   57-year-old respectable lady who'd already spent $2,000
   here but who would make sure the Turkish tourist
   industry would *never* see popularity with either
   Americans or British.

The judges, had Atilla allowed me to say those things in court,
would have locked me away forever or ordered me to a psychiatric ward. The journal entry shows a deterioration in ideation
and self-expression. There was a desperation about the energy
I focused on the coming trial, a desperation growing out of all
I knew, felt, and believed about a future life for myself here,
especially as the realities of prison life grew increasingly clear.

   October 19. Suddenly a flurry of activity and Turkish
   instruction. Police women are here to search our
   quarters. . . . The locker must be left open, I am told.
   Just take your money. I follow instructions and the

crowd downstairs into the yard and pass the pretty young soldier women in their smart khaki uniforms, nicely coiffed and made up. They are bunched together waiting for us to clear out so they can do their job.

Ten minutes or more Neshe and I paced the yard and when we saw the prisoners reentering the building, we followed them. At the door the women soldiers were lined up, single-file, all the way up the stairs. They "frisked" each prisoner as she entered but I was asked, "American?" and they moved to let me pass when I answered, "Yes, American." But I raised my arms for a "frisk" because I wanted to hate them for all the women, including myself.

One of the soldier women ran her hands softly over my breasts and waist and let me go. I went up the stairs, passing a woman soldier on each step, feeling angry, humiliated. And, when I entered the dorm I could see my bed had been pulled apart; my books and papers strewn about, the bedclothes pulled out at top and bottom. I channeled my anger into re-ordering my bed. My locker had been searched but not really disturbed.

The cell-block searches were conducted about every two weeks and exemplified, for me, not only the indignities attendant on imprisonment but also my changing status. I had always sensed the innocent ignorance of my foreignness would give me protection from the many threats and humiliations of prison life. I also understood it would be temporary, that, in time, being less a novelty, I would blend into the general scene and lose the advantage I'd once had. When the soldier women had searched the dorm last, neither my bed nor my locker had been touched. In two weeks my status had slipped. I could *not* stay here long and be safe. Underscoring my fears, that day the smouldering tensions erupted in violence as the "terrorists" opened a protest and Hikmet's "wardens" tried to subdue them.

It was a fight card with two main events. The initial outbreak occurred that afternoon when the militant women marched up the stairs to the upper dorm. As soon as I heard the angry voices, the trampling feet, heard the screams and saw the shoving crowds, I scrambled off my floor-level bed to find safety on higher ground—Lutfi's bunk. The fight rolled into the dorm, a mob scene with all the attendant noises and action.

Then, somehow, the "loyalists" managed to push and shove the "revolutionaries" back down the stairs and I could hear the battle continue to the sounds of screams and slaps and heavy furniture being bruted about downstairs.

> By this time many of the mothers had escaped to the upstairs with their babies. The din was frightening. I took one baby into my sanctuary before the mother left to return to the fight below. The hate, terror, fury, rage that was unleashed around this place was very frightening. You could sense it, heavy, in the air. The turmoil continued with outbreaks that rocked the floor below for over an hour.

Sitting together on my bed, Lutfi, who'd fought among the loyalists, and Neshe, who had stood on the fringes of the battle, got into a hair-pulling, face-slapping contest and had to be forcibly pulled apart. Even quiet, shy, soft-spoken Sara had been stirred by the unleashed violence. She ran through the dorm raging and storming her indignation about something I couldn't understand. I watched her climb to her third-story bed directly behind mine, fling outraged accusations at Hikmet, who sternly talked back, then, primatelike, swing to the floor to rush about, weeping and raging some more.

Safe on my perch, I did not know I was frightened nor had I any awareness of the effect so much uncontained emotion had had on me. But when the tension finally eased and the rooms grew quieter, my composure broke and I silently began to cry.

I remember hearing ignorant laymen, especially when I was young, talk about people's nerves being "on edge" or saying so-and-so's "nerves are weak." Too much stress, fear, panic, and depression, I guessed, could make a person hypersensitive or overreactive to stimuli. My traumatic experiences in Turkey had resulted in my "nerves being weak."

The afternoon didn't pass without Lutfi reaching under her pillow for the cache of pills and popping two for *her* nerves, yet when I was ready to do my hair, she washed and set it, tying it up in her headscarf again.

We had three "counts" that day and no dinner: everyone was

emotionally drained. Eminay, weeping pitiously, told me Hikmet blamed her for the problems with the "revolutionary" women, issuing warnings and threats of making her life more miserable than it already was.

It was after eight when Hikmet went home, and as the movie began—it was *Citizen Kane!*—a protesting chant began again downstairs. Instantly Euzgeul, Nuran, and all the major brutes took off for downstairs. This time they went prepared. Ayse and Euzgeul removed, from under Hikmet's bed, two large wood boards to use as clubs. I was shocked to have Lutfi tear her scarf from my head and wrap it around her own before she followed them. Neshe, who stayed out of it this time, posited Lutfi's need for the scarf as a prevention against having her hair pulled as it had been in the earlier battle.

This skirmish ended abruptly when blood was drawn: a revolutionary "girl" and Lutfi were wounded and taken to the doctor for stiches. All fighters, and even some passive partisans, were placed "on report," reducing morale to a new low. The penalty was "no visits for one month." I was angry with Hikmet, critical, based on my "professional" experience, of her inaction. The episode had been mishandled from the beginning and could have been prevented.

There is always a moment while the storm is gathering, when a calm, firm intervention will deflate swollen emotions the same way an angry boil can be drained before it bursts and spreads its contents over healthy flesh. I had watched and waited for Hikmet to face the lower dorm agitators, to acknowledge their pain, and, by the balm of her strength, to contain their behavior. Instead, frightened and ineffectual, she sent her "gunsels" to subdue them—as she always did—thereby trying to put out a fire with gasoline.

For a community of prisoners full of repressed rage to exist under such weak leadership is to invite disaster. Everyone feels unsafe. There is no one who will protect them from their bottled-up emotions.

More than ever I wanted out. More than ever I was invested in the outcome of the trial, in possible bail, and in knowing the plans my family had developed to get me home. I could hardly wait to meet with Richard, Ludan, Atilla, and any other lawyers who had joined the rescue team.

October 20. I have dressed carefully and applied my
makeup and am waiting to be called to the visitors
room. I don't know what time that might be but I am
ready.

I think about how the police women search this
place for weapons—guns, knives, scissors—none of
which are permitted. The women make knives from
torn pieces of the sides of tomato cans with which
they cut bread and slice onions and other food. To
cut wool and thread they either bite it or burn it with
the lighted end of a cigarette. These are weapons, too.
But the Turks have blind spots and do not realize it.
And what about the sharp-pointed, 12-to-15 inch
aluminum knitting needles? How ridiculous!

It is now just about 11:00 AM and the loudspeaker
has begun to blast Turkish music, reminding me that
for the past 2 days we have had unrelieved Turkish
music playing at ear-splitting decibels. It played all
through the melee yesterday. It contributes to the
tension here and could easily have abetted the riot. It
gets my nerves very up-tight. The only place to avoid
it is in the yard.

I wish my visitors would come. I need to get away
from the throbbing, vibrating music.

At 1:30, wearing a white, nubby cotton, knitted skirt, and a
charcoal gray, long-sleeved, pullover sweater Atilla bought, I
walked to the visitors' room. After nearly three weeks in prison,
the guard trailed instead of leading me. Richard LePere was
there, standing alone, looking out the door, waiting. As he em-
braced me and I cried on his chest, I remembered how uncomfortable the LePeres are with emotional demonstrations of any
kind. Richard had been selected to visit precisely because this
was true.

"I must say, Gene," he said, pulling away and forcing a
smile, "you certainly do find the most unusual places to take a
vacation."

We both laughed, which helped to ease the unreality of
meeting in such a bizarre environment.

The guarding soldier watched as I sat down on my usual
bench and Richard took a seat beside me, seeming to be fascinated by Richard, handsome and relaxed in his expensively

cut gray suit and with the suede Hartmann briefcase that lay
open-lidded on the scarred table.

"Bob Ludan is waiting with some Turkish woman from his
office," Richard explained. "I asked him to give us some time
alone."

"Makbule," I said. "That's good. "Is Atilla coming?"

"No. She and Jim Schroeder are together. He had hoped to
meet you but we're leaving tomorrow and he wanted to go over
your case with Mrs. Akat.

"Who's Jim Schroeder?"

"A lawyer from this firm in Washington your brother
hired." There was another awkward pause as Richard weighed
his words and, I thought, how much to tell me. "Your brother,
Gordon," he went on, emphasizing the name with what I read
as sarcasm or controlled impatience, "has gotten ahold of a couple of hotshot lawyers who are trying to run the show. This guy
Schroeder is okay. We flew out together." He paused meaning-
fully before continuing. "There's another one . . . from New
York, coming in time for the trial."

There was so much I wanted to know and so much Richard
wanted to tell, my questions stumbled over his answers. I asked
about the family and learned how each was handling the crisis.
It was the preoccupation of their lives from California to Germany via New York and Washington. My brother had alienated
Paul, who refused to deal with him. Richard had taken over as
moderator. Jimmy was taking care of my real estate investment
together with his own. Although they had tried to contain the
spreading of alarm throughout a large network of family and
personal friends, there were a great many calls. It was Jimmy
who, staying at his phone day and night, fielded them, calls from
people who had learned of my predicament and wanted to offer
their contacts and efforts to the fight for my safe return.

The soldier's presence was a constant reminder of the restrictions of time. It wasn't long before my interest returned to
more practical concerns.

"Why so many lawyers?" I asked Richard, "I've been told
you want to hire another lawyer from Istanbul. I have confidence in Atilla. I don't think I need another Turkish lawyer."

Richard waited, then answered. "Look, Gene, we've been
doing the best . . . It's hard to know the right thing to do.

". . . I may have made a mistake. . . ." He shifted on the bench. "I hired another lawyer in Washington . . . agreed to pay him ten thousand, blind . . . who knows? We're shooting in the dark. This other one, Gant, from New York, is another of your brother, Gordon's, brilliant ideas."

"You don't like him," I said. It wasn't a question. Richard and I understood each other.

"Not really. But I only met him once. We had a big powwow in Washington. Paul came down. There's a terrific guy. Your brother, *Gordon*, was there."

Richard knew my brother's name; he knew *I* knew his name; both of us knew I had only one brother. Yet every time he spoke his name he said it the same way, "your brother, Gordon." I got the message. Richard was disgusted or angry. Something about Gordon had turned him off. The word pompous came to mind.

"And Jimmy?" I asked. "Was Jimmy there?"

"No. He said he didn't need to be there. Didn't want to be in the same room with Gordon."

"I see," I said, unwilling to waste time on things I couldn't do anything about. "What else?"

"Well, Paul's concerned . . . he's worried about your money . . . how much all this is going to cost. Gordon's lawyers . . . Your brother's been a busy little bee. He's got some other tricks up his sleeve . . . cloak and dagger stuff. . . . Anyway, I need to know how much you think all this is worth to you?"

In one stroke Richard confirmed my dark suspicion: my family was spending my money. This is not a thing we Hirshhorns feel even the slightest bit comfortable about. Maybe no one does. But what choice did I have?

"My God, Richard, how can I put a price on my freedom?"

"Yeah," he nodded, "but how much? Give me a number."

I felt trapped.

"Well," I said, making a tentative stab at it, "I figured about thirty thousand. . . ."

"How does ninety strike you?"

"Ninety? My God! Why so much?" He was talking about wiping out my future security.

"It may not be," he backed off. "I just want to get an upper limit."

"Well, of course, how can I say I won't spend whatever is

necessary to get me home. But ninety thousand? You're talking about a fortune."

"Let's not get hung up on that," he said amiably, and turned to glance at the soldier behind his back.

"Doesn't understand a word we say," I injected in a matter-of-fact voice.

"Okay," he said, "what about a motorboat? Can you operate one?"

"A motorboat?" I was bewildered, still thinking about the money, "I suppose so . . . if I had to."

"Can you read a compass?"

"No. What's this all about?"

"Now, wait a minute. It's easy," he said, making a circle with his hand. "There's three hundred and sixty degrees. We give you the heading . . . you set it. Just like that, you're on a Greek island only twenty-five kilometers from the coast of Turkey."

"By myself?" I was shocked. "You expect me—alone, on the open sea, in a motor boat—to take myself out of here? You must be crazy!"

"We're talking extreme measures," he said, trying to calm me. "This is only if everything else fails. Listen," he continued, leaning closer, "if you get bail next week and they return your passport . . . that's it. Sayonara, Charlie!"

This was not what I'd expected to hear: that with all the efforts of so many clever, energetic people and an obscene outpouring of funds, in the end it was I who would be expected to run every risk, brave every threat to get myself home—and in such a dangerous, foolhardy way. Where did I get the boat? How did I pay for it? What had happened to negotiated strategies, legal loopholes, appeals to the reason of rational Turks? Richard's visit so far had been a litany of utterly depressing bad news.

"It doesn't sound to me as if you have much hope," I said, quietly.

"That's not true, Gene," he tried to assure me. "This is the final backup plan." Turning, he reached into his briefcase to extract an envelope, "Here you are," he said, handing it to me, "some pictures of your favorite nephew."

The soldier, alert to the possibility of an illegal exchange, leaned over the table. Satisfied when he saw the photographs, his eyes fell on a miniature tape recorder in the briefcase. In an attitude of curiosity rather than threat, he tapped Richard on the shoulder and indicated his desire to know what it was. Richard, by pantomime and demonstration, explained while I sorted through pictures of Richard and Carol's little boy, Alex, as well as photos taken when we'd all been together in Washington at the birthday party in August.

There were other photos: Gordon's wife, Helen, and their three girls. Looking at these tangible connections to home, gave me a sudden and heartbreaking realization, of how starkly alone I really was.

Ludan and Makbule entered the room at that moment. After the greetings, I got right to the point.

"I want to know if there is a real strategy for my release. This thing can't just continue to drift. The court hearing is a week from today, and I want to know if it's possible I can be found innocent at that time."

"That's doubtful," Bob answered. "Typically there are a series of hearings that can take months to conclude before any finding is made."

"I want to expedite matters . . . by entering a plea of guilty if that's the only way."

"That's a possibility," Bob said, "but I'm not sure how much it would help."

"It would make it possible to start the prisoner exchange sooner. We'd have the guilty verdict we need."

"I don't think it works that way in the Turkish legal system. You'll have to consult Mrs. Akat about it."

"Their legal system seems ass-backward to me," Richard injected. "Don't you think so, Bob?"

By now, even *I* knew better than that.

"Richard," I explained, "it's not that their system is wrong, it's just different from ours and we don't know how it works or how to manipulate it effectively. Our legal system is based on English law. There is a presumption of innocence that favors the accused and a body of common law by which our laywers can develop legal arguments and cite precedent to sway the judges. In Turkey it's very different.

"Yes," Bob took up the explanation, "Turkish law is founded

on Napoleonic law in which everything is based on statutes. Legal arguments are limited to the revelation of pertinent facts and special pleadings." He smiled. "I'm not sure why cases seem to take so long or why there are so many trials. The Turks just seem to be slower. For one thing, their constitution doesn't ensure a "speedy trial" as ours does. On the other hand, our legal system has been known to grind out justice slowly, too."

I wanted to tell Bob about the riot—the reason I felt getting out of prison was so urgent a matter—but I didn't want to alarm Richard. Weighing the choice, I decided it was more important to lay all the cards on the table. I would have to trust Richard's discretion as to how much to repeat to the family. Interrupting the discussion of strategy, I related the full story, ending with my fears.

"I can't stay here much longer, Bob. It is growing increasingly dangerous. There are so many intrigues. . . ."

"I've told you, Gene," Bob interrupted, swiftly concerned, "I can make arrangements for you to be moved into the hospital."

"I've resisted transferring because it would isolate me more. I feel so isolated now, even in the dorm where I have the companionship of women, three of whom speak some degree of English." I'd given this some thought. "Let's see what happens at the trial. If I'm going to be here a long time, I'll move to the hospital."

"So we're back to the trial," Richard said.

"Yes," I said, feeling defeated.

"Gene," Bob said, "I wouldn't look too far ahead. I think you should concentrate on getting out on bail. That's the most important thing."

"But what are the chances of bail being granted? Twice already Atilla's requested bail and twice the petition's been shot down."

"Things are looking more favorable for bail," Bob said. "I think there's a good chance."

"What's different now?" I asked, not believing him.

"Listen," Richard said emphatically, "a lot of big guns have been brutalized in D.C. over this mess. Think of it like this, we've shot an arrow into the air, we don't know yet where it's going to land."

"I suppose," I said, wearily. "What else?"

"About Mr. Yilset," Bob said, and seeing the question on my face, "the Turkish attorney your family wants to take over the case. . . ."

"Take over the case?" Whose idea was that?

"It is understood that if Mr. Yilset represents you, he'll be in charge and do the talking at the trial," Richard explained.

"I don't like that at all," I said, annoyed. "I know Atilla and I trust her. Who's this Mr. Yilset, anyway?"

Richard answered. "He's supposed to be an expert in smuggling cases and very well connected. In other words, he's got friends and influence."

"I assume he'll come to the prison to meet me before the trial."

"I presume," Richard agreed.

"In any case," Bob continued, "in the event he is to represent you, you'll have to sign another notarized power of attorney for him."

I nodded. I wasn't comfortable about these developments. "I'm not so sure about this Yilset," I said again. "and I'm not sure why Mr. Gant is coming either. It seems to me he won't be able to contribute to the trial. He's not licensed to practice law in Turkey, is he?"

"I'm sure he's not," Richard said, "but he's supposed to have a lot of friends here, people he can lean on to clear this up and get you home ASAP."

"Let's hope so," I said. "Oh, God, how I hope so."

The visit was winding down. What else could be said?

Makbule had been silent during all the discussions. We had spoken frankly, as if she couldn't understand or wasn't there. Silence was so characteristic of Makbule, I wondered if Richard, who was usually a tactful person, may not have forgotten she was a Turk.

I handed her my carefully written defense. Of the people here in this room, all of whom who gave me comfort and support, only she would be with me a week from now. I hoped she wasn't offended by anything that had been said.

I looked at the two men sadly. Richard's visit I accepted as a gift of his precious time; I'd expected him to fly in and rush back. But it was hard to accept Bob's desertion. He had stood at my side through this whole terrible ordeal. He had become, in my mind, a lifeline of security against lurking, as yet unknown, threats.

Then I remembered something that Neshe had told me.

"Bob," I said, "I understand they handcuff prisoners and take them to court in a big van with a lot of soldiers." The thought of it made my stomach clench into a hard fist.

"I don't know," he said.

"It sounds pretty awful to me. Do you think . . . might they be willing . . . after all, I'm not your dangerous criminal type, to leave off the handcuffs?"

"I have no idea, Gene," Bob replied sympathetically, "Let me see what I can find out."

It was time to part.

"Tell them I'm okay, Richard. You can see that I'm okay."

"I'll tell them," he said, embracing me. "Take care of yourself, Gene, and listen, I know you don't like the idea, but don't be surprised if Yilset shows up at the trial."

I wept saying good-bye to Bob and tried to be a good sport. "Have fun wherever you're going," I told him.

"This has been planned a long time," he apologized, "I've put it off too long already."

Makbule assured me she would study the pages I'd given her and asked if I needed anything for the trial.

"A pair of pantyhose," I replied. "It's gotten too cold to go barelegged."

This time I waited until they were gone, waving as I watched them walk down the hall. Then I was escorted, dejected, back to the dorm.

October 21. I feel very let down. Very discouraged.

If I once felt safe here—safer than I did on the ship —that condition has changed. It was only an invalid's respite, a moment of recovery from the terror of the days since the Friday return to the ship to the Monday night's sentence to prison.

At this moment I feel dreadfully unsafe. The feeling certainly may have begun with the "riot" but seemed to crystallize with Richard's visit. Perhaps I expected some magic of American persuasion—clout cum money—would open doors. Even Bob Ludan's leaving adds to the despair.

I sense some change in HKMT toward me, possibly because I witnessed the riot. Neshe's woes with L and with HKMT are also discouraging. Neshe is strong—and impotent; potentially a victim, as we all are.

. . . I did not sleep well at all last night. Perhaps I should have taken a Valium, but one almost needs to feel numb or safe to take one and give way to undefended sleep in the midst of so much threat. Thank God for the books Atilla and Bob have brought. They provide better escape from reality than sleep or drugs.

Richard's notions of a good way for me to get home were at the root of my despondency. If the family's options had been reduced to such preposterous, *desperate* plans, the future loomed very bleak, indeed. I had prayed for a break on the 27th: everyone washing his hands of a very hot potato. Somehow I'd held on to what I now saw was a fantasy. The meeting with Richard and Ludan had opened my eyes at last. Nothing was going to be so simple; the legal process would drag on and on; it could take six months; it could take two years. I asked myself if I had the courage and the strength to manage and answered myself. I didn't.

Atilla paid a visit that Friday morning providing a safe receptacle for my grief and a sensible resource for answers to my questions. From her I could always count on compassion modulated with direct, refreshing, no-nonsense information.

"Dear, Gene, you must understand there is only the smallest chance for acquittal at the twenty-seventh, but I have been talking with a great many people and I believe it is 85 percent chance for the bail."

"Richard was talking about me getting a boat and taking it to a Greek island. . . ."

"This talk is foolish! Why does he speak of such things? Now I tell you, and I am usually right, I am sure it is is 85 percent you will have the bail. You understand, you will not go free from the court. You must return to the prison—but only for a short time.

The bail will be paid and I will bring the papers for your release. Then you will go out."

"And if there is no bail?"

"There is something else I believe can help you. We will have elections in November, only a few days after your trial. It is usual for an amnesty after such elections and you will go free. I believe there will be an amnesty."

I had heard talk of amnesty in the cell block, dismissing it as wishful thinking.

"You think there will be?"

"I believe so. The candidates have said so."

"And it will include me?"

"It includes even those who are imprisoned but not yet found guilty. That is you. It will not be so soon. Perhaps in May it will come." She waited as I mulled that over.

"Now," she continued, "since I believe you shall have bail, I would like that you stay at my home for your first night out of prison . . . that is, if you will like to come to me."

"Oh, yes, Atilla, how kind you are," I said, weeping again.

She smiled. "I am glad you will like it. I have hoped," she said. "Now, we will speak about the trial."

She told me what the courtroom looked like, where she would be seated, about the judges and the prosecutor and where Makbule and I would stand. I told her about the handcuffs and she nodded. "Yes," she confirmed, "this is so. There is nothing that can be done. I am sorry."

Choking down the humiliation invoked by painful images of the preparation and trip to court, I chastised myself for anticipating future agony. Take each thing as it comes, I told myself. Everyone must do it and if they can stand it, I can, too.

"I shall buy a dress for you to wear at the trial," she said.

"No," I said, "I'll wear the same dress I wore at the last one."

"You will need a coat. It is cold."

"No. I have a sweater. I'll wear my own sweater."

"You will be cold."

"No. I come from a colder climate than this. It is not cold to me."

"You will need shoes."

"No. I will wear the same shoes as before. Stockings are

what I need; I have none here. Makbule has promised to buy them."

"I will make sure that she does."

Atilla liked Schroeder very much, saying, "He is a very nice gentleman and smart." Of Richard she went farther, calling him "a remarkable fellow, so young to have made such accomplishments." Promising to come again before the trial, she left me in a much better mood, praying for acquittal or bail.

Atilla is so caring, I was sorry to refuse her offer to buy clothes but she cannot know how important it is to me to wear my own things for the trial. Everything here is alien: the people, the food, the culture, the legal process. I cannot feel alienated from myself, too. I must wear my own U.S. clothes. It will help me restore a sense of myself.

. . . Lutfi has knitted me a pair of Turkish booties using the left-over wool from her "husband's" sweater she finished last week. They are green and white, very pretty, and warm. I thanked her sincerely. It was supposed to be a surprise but Sara gave it away. But, this kind act doesn't really help. Neshe dropped out of the eating group today.

She says she needs to be alone, to eat alone. But since I'd just written a letter for her to Yilmas asking for 10,000 Turkish lira, I wondered if she was short of funds and offered to lend her some. It isn't money. It's Lutfi.

Lutfi's self-preoccupation was fascinating in a kind of horrible way. She never passed a mirror without checking her appearance, and often, when the rhythmic sounds of Turkish music filled the dorm, she took a scarf, wrapped it around her hips, and danced seductively before any small crowd she could find.

She was a sensuous-looking woman. Slim, she had full, heavy breasts that were rarely confined in a brassiere. She affected loose-fitting, v-necked sweaters and silken shirts that she left open to reveal her stunning cleavage. More than once I saw her delight the other women with a trick I'd never seen before. Gripping her right breast with two hands, she aimed it around the room and with appropriate accompanying sounds of "ack, ack, ack, ack . . ." machine-gunned down some imaginary foe. It was a surefire laugh.

Neshe confided to me, in a whispered hiss, how much she'd come to hate Lutfi. I didn't hate her but I hated the trouble she was causing for so many women and I especially hated seeing my friends Neshe, Sara, and Eminay, whom I'd grown to love, being hurt. Lutfi was destructive and the thought of leaving her on the 27th gave me relief.

> October 22. Bob Ludan is on his way to Europe, I've had a new visitor, and Lutfi's turned the dorm inside out after swallowing a handful of her blue and white capsules.

The Anglican priest, Geoffery Evans, brought a British woman to visit. It was brave of her to come. Her name was Nancy Rust and she told me she represented a Catholic women's church group in Izmir, who would be happy to provide whatever I'd like to have while in prison.

I was moved by the concern of strangers, the support of women who had never met me. Nancy said the entire community of British and American women had been frightened by what had happened to me. It left them feeling terribly vulnerable.

"We are all saying prayers for you, day and night," she said.

"I'm sure it will help," I responded. "Thank all the women for me, please."

To her offers of books, yarn, knitting needles, embroidery, or any other kind of handiwork materials, I begged the question.

"If you'll add to your prayers the wish that I'll be released on bail at my hearing on the 27th, I may not need them. If I'm still here after that, I will take you up on your kind offer."

She hugged me before she left, brushing tears from her cheek onto mine.

Ten times a day now I was beginning a sentence with, "If I am still here after my court hearing . . ."

For the better part of the day Lutfi was ill. Pale and pasty-faced, she said she had a headache at breakfast and ate nothing. She sat with us, smoking and drinking tea. Within the hour back in the dorm, her voice had grown weak and her speech so

slurred it was incomprehensible. If possible, her color had worsened.

She lay on Nuran's bed in pajamas, covered by one of my
blankets, attended by Neshe (loyal in spite of her "hate") and a
flock of other worried women who bathed her face with wet
cloths. It was to Eminay, the enemy who'd suffered most at her
hands, that Lutfi confided her illness had been caused by an
overdose of the pills "I take for nerves." Once it was known
what was wrong, under Eminay's supervision, countermeasures
were taken.

A basin was brought and soapy water. With Neshe holding
Lutfi's clammy forehead, vomiting was induced. Then, taking
turns, two at a time the women walked her around the dorm.
By dint of this dramatic stroke, Lutfi managed to involve the
entire upper dorm in her "Camille" act until late afternoon. Her
old eating group rallied in relief at her recovery, and Lutfi was
well enough to have dinner with us that night. I was furious
with her.

I was equally furious with the prison authorities, Hikmet in
particular, who carelessly provided dangerous drugs for the
Lutfis of this world. A known drug user with a history of attempted suicide, my narcissistic friend had two red, ropy scars,
one on the inside of each wrist.

> Little by little it has gotten so that N is afraid to walk
> or talk with me. I am afraid to spend time with her
> for fear she will suffer and the same with E. I grow
> more fearful every day and I do not like it.
> . . . I am afraid about my writing: that I will be
> caught—or not allowed to take them out of prison. I
> find more ways to cover up the names and to scribble
> so no one can read my writing. I hope I can read it
> myself. I will reverse the letters in abbreviations and
> use pig-latin for special situations.
> . . . the trial looms ahead. Thursday, next
> Thursday. Court will be at 10:30 and I will be taken
> out about 8. . . . I will make up my face and comb my
> hair and try to look brave. I am scared to death.

I was only just beginning to understand what I came, in
time, to call the "Turkish disease"—fear. It is not paranoia,
which is being afraid without reason. The Turkish disease is a

reasoned fear, based on the knowledge that the individual is
always subservient to the State, is powerless against the State,
and that the State is jealous of its prerogatives.

This condition of generalized anxiety paralyzed Turks of
every class and category. It was not restricted to the lower levels
of the pecking order but infected everyone all the way to the top.
Living in an atmosphere where the air one breathes is con-
taminated with fear, one becomes infected with the illness.
There is no immunity from the disease in Turkey.

> . . . . ME [my new code for Eminay] is a wreck this
> AM. She reported a vivid dream she had last night in
> which she and I were climbing a mountain that was
> steep and very dangerous. "You helped me so much,"
> she said. I had carried her knapsack and, although I
> left her at one point promising to return, she doubted
> I would come back "because it was dangerous there."
> I did come back and helped her again.
>   She cried as she told me the dream and said she'd
> also cried in her sleep and was crying when she
> awakened. She doesn't know, she says, why she cries
> so much and I said, "because your heart is breaking."
> The symbolism of Eminay's dream is so obvious. The
> plight of these people, the intelligensia, is *frightful.*
>   . . . I can't stand all the shifting sand under my
> feet . . . . I've been told KH [my new code name for
> Hikmet] suspects me because "I don't want to talk to
> her any more."

In a decision that was typical of the Gene I used to be before
Turkey, I approached Eminay to act as translator for me. I was
tired of living under the threat of retribution—my own and two
of the other women who spoke English. I was going to have a
confrontation with Hikmet.

I come from a family that likes to confront. Though it has
been much abused, confrontation is neither a nasty word nor
does it necessarily imply anger. From the confrontation I sought
with Hikmet, I hoped for clarification. I had rehearsed my part.

Confiding in Eminay, I previewed, for her reaction, what I
intended to say: that I was isolated here, separated from my own
people and language; that without the women who spoke English I had no companionship at all; that it was essential to have

all three women available, not just Lutfi. Lutfi's English was proving to be untrustworthy.*

I planned a comparative assessment of the English-speaking talents of the other two women: Neshe didn't express herself well but understood everything; my having chosen Eminay for this delicate "confidence" was proof in itself of her demonstrable skills at understanding and communicating in my native tongue.

The confrontation, once we'd overcome Hikmet's reluctance, was successful beyond our hopes, bringing to light more than I'd bargained for. Hikmet revealed that the day after my arrival, Lutfi had reported my desire to donate to Hikmet one of three pairs of summer sandals in my suitcase. There were other revelations. Hikmet was obviously frightened of Lutfi and afraid for her job. Her insistence that we whisper, and her frequent checks to see if Lutfi was watching as we huddled in conference on one of the beds in the upper dorm, spoke volumes about the woman's insecurities. My God, I thought, everyone is afraid here. Even the guards.

In the end it was decided Eminay would be the sole interpreter approved for exchanges between Hikmet and me. And, "if I was still here after my court hearing," I would no longer eat with Lutfi, becoming a part of Eminay's eating group instead. In an unexpected bonus resulting from the encounter, Eminay was restored to a position of acceptance, being given several responsible jobs to perform including the dispensing of evening medications.

The intention to wait for the outcome of the hearing became moot when Hikmet witnessed an angry argument between Lutfi and me over the four remaining packets of powdered coffee.

October 24. . . . L announced two weeks ago she had given one packet to ME because ME said she longed for

---

*The TV had broadcast the story of the attempt of armed men to gain entry to a country club where Ronald Reagan was playing golf. Lutfi, reporting the story to me, said Reagan had been shot playing golf and was dead. Seeing my hysterical reaction, Eminay obtained the facts for me. This was my first clear proof that Lutfi was an utterly unreliable source of information.

coffee. I said fine. Today I asked her for the three
remaining packets which I wanted to give to ME. She
said okay but could she keep one for herself. I said
sure.

Later she returned the roll of TP I'd given her to
share among herself, s and N, to whom she'd never
given any. When I asked why she was returning it,
she said because I'd done a bad thing taking the coffee
back. I explained the TP had been a gift, the coffee she
was to have kept for the group. Since we hadn't used
it and she'd seen fit to give one away, I wanted ME to
have the others.

It soon became clear Lutfi's English wasn't up to understanding the difference between "give" and "keep for," and in
the course of the angry exchange I realized there were other
voids in her understanding. When, furious with her, I asked if
she thought I'd been "ungenerous" with the group, she said I
had. But, when I reworded the question, asking had I been
"good" to the women, she quickly said "yes."

It was Hikmet who put an end to the exchange. In a burst
of staccato Turkish she declared there were too many translation problems. From then on I ate with Eminay and the two
Kurdish women who were her friends. Neshe agreed to join us
in a day or two. I thought I would be happier, then—"if I was
still here after the court."

Within myself I felt demeaned by becoming a party to such
trivial and petty concerns. But in prison, life is very circum-
scribed and inmates lack opportunity to invest fervor in more
earthshaking issues.

Makule came last night with a notary. Richard—or
the family—did hire another attorney from Istanbul.
He will be in court Thursday and couldn't represent
me without this power of attorney.

After dark the evening of October 24, I was called into the
dimly lit hallway to sign the document that would permit Avi
Husamettin Yilset to be recognized as my attorney. Makbule
acted as interpreter. There was something about his name and
his arrogant demands to replace Atilla that made me reluctant
to have him on the case. It was very hard to know the right thing

to do. On the one side was my confidence in Atilla and a recent incident in which one of the prisoners, falsely accused and confined for four years, was released because of the competence and determination of her sole attorney—a woman.

In favor of Yilset was Eminay's advice that the more lawyers you had the better your chances, and my personal reluctance to move against Richard's decision.

Hesitating, I signed, but my anxiety forced me to tell Makbule before she walked away, "I did it, but I'm not happy about it."

October 25. This morning Atilla Akat came. I discussed with her the things which trouble me: that besides Gant, another attorney was coming from the States; that my family hired this attorney who speaks no English and whom I have not met.

It wasn't that I minded having Yilset's expertise available; I didn't want him to manage the case. If he were willing to subserve to Atilla, I'd have felt comfortable. His fees were an added cost that I would have been willing to incur under those circumstances. Maybe when I met the man I would feel better about him.

As for two lawyers from home, I thought one, Gant, quite enough. I wanted to put my foot down at the idea of two but without more information as to the reasons for his coming, I was torn by doubts.

When Atilla told me she had talked by phone with Yilset, whose plans failed to include a meeting with me—he was flying from Istanbul the morning of the 27th, just in time to appear at court and not a moment sooner—my mind snapped to an immediate and enraged decision. He's not coming. He doesn't have the courtesy and respect to meet me? I don't want him. And that goes for Washington, too!

In a highly agitated state, I instructed Atilla to go right to the consulate. "Tell them they have to stop both lawyers from coming."

Wisely, she suggested I express myself in writing, since the consulate might hesitate to act on her word alone. The resulting statement, written with her help, contained more than one sentence that was a jumble of her speech patterns and mine. Besides stating these men were not to attend the hearing, it gave the reasons for my request: Mr. Yilset was unacceptable because we'd never met, and that the other attorney, given he neither spoke nor understood Turkish and had no legitimate standing in a Turkish court, was an unnecessary expense. He would be relegated to a rear seat in the courtroom with the other spectators.

In an emotional frenzy I'd added a sentence deploring my family's willingness to spend my money for things that would be of no help except to assuage their own anxieties.

Not at all certain dismissing them was the correct strategy, at some intuitive level I felt great relief for having done so. The result of the consulate's action in my behalf (I later learned they had sent a telegram to the States containing, word-for-word, the statement as I'd scribbled it in the visitor's room) had repercussions that brought Beau Nalle and Edwin Gant, who had arrived in Izmir the morning of October 26, to the prison that day.

I was surprised to see them. Nalle introduced Gant before getting down to the real reason for the visit.

Gant looked sloppy in his wrinkled suit, which I noted and forgave since he'd just stepped off a plane after a long overnight trip that included three changes of aircraft. I thought him to be no more than thirty-five, although being overweight and soft made him look older. He had a paunch that hung, like a balcony, over a black leather belt that circled his hips rather than his waist. He greeted me in a manner I found too effusive and, therefore, insincere.

"Gene," he said, taking liberties as he took my hand, "glad to meet you, at last. I've heard a great deal about you from your brother, who asked me to send his love."

"Thank you," I said, instantly escaping into a formality reserved for people I don't trust.

"Your brother thinks the world of you," he went on. "He couldn't say enough about how smart you are and how resourceful."

"If I am so smart and resourceful," I replied curtly, "what am I doing in a Turkish prison?" and turned quickly to Nalle.

"Were you able to reach Yilset and the other man?" I asked, alert to the possibility of having been thwarted.

"We had no difficulty stopping Mr. Yilset from coming, but

I don't know if the telegram was received in Washington in time to catch Mr. Lasky from flying out. We won't know until tomorrow about that.

"Actually," he went on, "the reason I'm here is because your family was very troubled by your message. They think you've given up and . . ." He hesitated, looking for the best way to phrase what he wanted to say. ". . . they are concerned about your . . . mental health."

"They think I'm crazy?"

Beau smiled. "Something like that," he said.

"And you've reassured them I'm in my right mind," I said with an answering smile, "or have you come here to make sure I didn't 'flip out' sometime yesterday?"

"I can see you're okay," Nalle answered, "and I told them that already. I am sure you based your decision on sound reasoning."

Gant interrupted. "It may not have been the best course of action, you realize. This is a tricky situation."

"Have you met Mrs. Akat, my attorney?" I asked Gant.

"Not yet, although I've heard splendid things about her," he said, throwing off a faint aroma of the patronizing male.

"*I* know her, Mr. Gant, and I have the utmost confidence in Mrs. Akat. She knows me, she believes in my innocence. She's a fighter. I am satisfied I have the best legal help Turkey can provide."

"Yes," he frowned, "but Mr. Yilset is extremely well connected, if you get my drift."

"I understand you perfectly," I said. "What you may have failed to discover is that Mrs. Akat is also 'well connected.' " I shrugged, annoyed and upset to discover my decision treated without respect. "In any case," I concluded, "I have made this decision. It is mine to make. It's my neck and if I've made a mistake I'm the one who has to live with it."

From Beau I sensed no criticism. As had been my experience with Ludan, he accepted my decisions and respected my right to make them.

"I told your family I'd get back to them on this. They seem terribly concerned." I turned to Beau, crying now from the complex emotions that wracked me.

"You have to understand my family," I said. "They are so

frightened at the thought of prison, especially under these circumstances, their fears sometimes outweigh their judgment. If
any of them were in my shoes, they *would* have gone crazy or
would have killed themselves before now.

"It's easy for them to spend my money carelessly. It's mine.
And somehow they've confused the expenditure of funds with
getting me home. The more you spend the more insurance
against losing.

"I'm not made of money. My father may have been rich but
none of us has inherited a penny. The estate has yet to be settled.
What money I have I've worked hard for and conserved through
denying myself a lot of indulgences. While I wouldn't hesitate
to spend whatever's necessary, I'm not willing to throw money
away.

"I don't know that my decision was right. I have plenty of
doubts. But it seemed to me the ratio of lawyers," I glanced at
Gant who was taking it all in, "to client had grown excessively
high, particularly since I couldn't justify the need for more. I
saw no reason to give Mr. Lasky a free trip to Turkey at my
expense. Mr. Gant, I understand, has a specific assignment to
assist me if I am lucky enough to get bail tomorrow."

"You bet," Gant said. "I've got a lot of contacts here. I'll be
getting in touch with the minute you're out."

I didn't like Gant but I needed him. I was sure Paul wouldn't
have approved his coming if there wasn't a good reason for it.

"I believe we've covered everything except . . ." He reached
into his pocket and handed me a small, soft plastic envelope.
"Makbule asked me to give you this. She said it was something
you wanted."

Opening it I saw it was the pantyhose. Thoughtful, reliable
Makbule.

"Please thank her for me. I needed it for tomorrow."

"Speaking of tomorrow," Beau said, standing to go, "I'm
happy to tell you the director of the prison has made arrangements for you to be taken from prison without handcuffs."

At this news I began to cry, relief and gratitude washing
over me. Tension building over the last week and culminating
with yesterday's crisis had aroused in me a profusion of conflict-
ing emotions that shattered my control, robbing me of a determined serenity. How kind everyone was, how thoughtful. Even

the prison director. So much was riding on the outcome of the trial. Torn, I couldn't contain my impatience for tomorrow—and I wished it would never come. If bail wasn't forthcoming, would my family, in their despair, rail against me? Would I regret my decision of yesterday? My God, had I done the right thing?

But I had learned not to look farther than today, and the knowledge I wouldn't be manacled, my hands locked together, was a balm that soothed the turmoil in my brain and calmed the beat of my heart.

I asked Mr. Nalle if he'd be in court in the morning. Gant I assumed would attend. They were both coming, Nalle said, and asked for the last time if there was anything else I needed. When the two men said good-bye, Beau injected a note of uncertainty. He said, "We're not sure we'll have sufficient money for bail and, if not, your release may be delayed a day or so." What that implied, I didn't know.

The trial was all I could think about and getting ready for it was all that concerned me.

I had my fortune told today by a gnarled peasant
woman. She did it with a bunch of beans, a few
Turkish coins, two buttons and a cheap metal ring.
She said I would be released from jail at the trial and
two days later I would leave Turkey. How I pray she
is right.
Took a bath this afternoon and had an unbelievable
audience.

Three and a half weeks had passed since I'd entered prison a strange American lost and afraid of the unknown. Proof that I now belonged to this company of women was the attention I received on the occasion of my bath in preparation for the court hearing.

Where once they had given me a wide berth, recognizing and respecting I needed time to adjust, they accepted me now as just one of the crowd. Inside the toilet stall with the paraphernalia for washing, clothing slung carelessly over the shoulder-high partition, my privacy was casually violated by the women waiting in line to use the other toilet. Their language was Turkish and none of my translators was in sight, so I had no way of discouraging two of the women who reached over the stall door trying to wrest the washcloth from my hand so they could scrub my back and wash my hair.

Gesturing in every way I could think of to discourage them, their wishes overrode mine as they strained to do a service that is common in a Turkish bath. Stark naked, I wanted no part of it, but the stall wasn't big enough for me to elude them. Three days before, the door to the stall I was using had fallen from its hinges. Now, merely propped against the opening, the inevitable occurred. With two women pressing against it, the door gave way, and as it fell in on me, I gave a shriek of surprised embarrassment that brought women running from the dorm. Unhurt, the ridiculousness of the situation struck full force and I began to laugh. The two women giggled and the laughter spread until all of us were rocking with it.

I remember the laughter now with great tenderness and feelings of camaraderie for my "friends," the valiant, patient, resourceful, loving women of cell block #1, Buja Prison. Having cried together, having experienced so achingly each other's pain, it is good to remember the one time that, together, we shared the pleasure of laughter.

> . . . the old lady's fine money was collected in full
> today and she will go free tomorrow. I hugged her
> when I heard. All the women are very happy for her.
>   I must be ready to leave at 8 AM tomorrow. I will
> set out my things. I am anxious and will take half a
> Valium in the AM.

They didn't come for me until 8:30 the morning of the 27th. I'd been up since 6:00 and by 7:00 was satisfied with my carefully constructed appearance. Having been advised that prisoners wait all day at the court building without food, I fortified myself with a piece of pound cake, a tangerine, and two sesame seed cookies—food that was in my locker. After the roust I dosed myself with what amounted to two and a half milligrams of Valium and sat quietly on the bed to wait. My friends, on adjacent beds, kept me company, repeating good wishes and their belief I would be out of prison before the evening roust.

Hikmet arrived at eight. Dressed smartly in a navy uniform, she looked very pretty with a light-blue scarf tied at the neck of her tailored white blouse complementing the warm tones of her skin. Seeing her so attractively turned out I guessed it was she who would accompany me to court.

The waiting seemed interminable, as if the whole dorm were holding its breath. Neshe brought forth a woman who was willing to let me to wear two of her rings to court. Explaining that the rings had once belonged to a person now dead and that such rings bring luck, Neshe wanted me to wear them. Gratefully I accepted the woman's offer, placing her rings on the finger where, before entering prison, I'd worn my own. Then, taking the stranger's hands in mine, I let the pressure of my fingers and my smile speak my hopeful thanks.

When the call came at last, Hikmet led me through a throng of women waiting to touch, to hug, to kiss me, smiling and nodding their optimism and prayers. Beyond the steel door, side by side, we walked the one familiar corridor, passed through the barred intersection, and quickly, it seemed to me, entered a wide hall that led to what I thought could only have been the front door. Where were we going?

Outside, on a graveled drive, stood a large van where, instead of having to enter the rear, Hikmet gestured me into the very wide front seat and climbed in after me. At once we were joined by two men. One, in a business suit, got in through the left-hand door, sliding over the seat to my side; the other, also not in uniform but more casually dressed, after shutting the right-hand door, climbed into the driver's seat and started the engine.

Where were the other prisoners? Where were the armed soldiers? This privacy was a privilege I hadn't dreamed of.

On the drive into downtown Izmir, which took about twenty minutes, I sat between my keepers as quiet and unmoving as someone in the grip of paralysis. Staring ahead through the broad windshield—dazed by the sensation of being free—I saw along the route the people of Izmir negotiating their ways to work. At many stops stood long lines of people waiting for a bus. But I noted that this major thoroughfare, even at rush hour, was not clogged by commuter vehicles.

In the Konak the van came to a halt and I recognized where we were. It was the same building of the notary and the first court hearing. The driver remained with the car as Hikmet and the other man, flanking me, led us into the building. Because the courtroom was on the fifth floor, we stood before the only elevator, pushing buttons. But after a long wait, when it didn't come, Hikmet shrugged and led me to the stair. During the long climb there was no conversation, no talking. Hikmet simply took me by the arm and pulled me, like a child, wherever she wanted me to go.

On the fifth floor we entered a small and very bare room in which Nalle, Atilla, Makbule, and Gant were already present, standing instead of sitting since there was only one chair.

With translation now available, I learned that the man who had come with us from the prison was the director, himself. This private place, like the van, had been provided by him as a courtesy. "It is a very big concession," Atilla hissed discreetly, causing me to wonder who, in Washington, had so much clout. No one in my family, I was sure.

Here in this room protocol was tricky. Everything had been done because of me but, as I was the accused criminal, the Turks couldn't openly acknowledge it. They handled it by pretending I wasn't there and by making much over Nalle, whose legitimacy as a celebrity was indisputable.

Nervous, anxious, holding myself together, I took the unused chair, becoming a quiet observer. Because the room was small it seemed crowded, and the scene reminded me of nothing as much as a cocktail party. Nalle and Atilla reminisced about the American University, searching their memories for names the other would remember. Gant and the director stood together, trying but unable to converse. Makbule and Hikmet, standing apart, were the wallflowers: Makbule, due to her natural reticence and Hikmet, because English was the language in this room and because here, her authority was unimportant.

After twenty minutes a clerk opened the door to the hall to say the case would now be heard.

Atilla had described the courtroom well. It was approximately thirty by forty feet in size, and we entered through a door that opened from the corridor into the center of the room. Facing me, on the wall opposite the door, was a row of four windows overlooking Izmir. Spectator seating was to my right, separated from the stage on which the drama would take place by a low wooden barrier. The judges' bench, at the opposite end of the room to my left, faced it. Atilla, dressed in her black robe with red satin lapels, took a seat facing the room at a table near the dais, the windows at her back.

Makbule led me to the prisoner's bench facing the judges in what seemed to be the very center of the room. We stood and would continue to stand unless and until the chief judge invited us to sit. Hands clasped before me, I looked at the three men who would decide my fate. They, too, wore black robes with red satin that flashed, in that setting, like cardinals in a nest of crows.

The judge to my left was a small, old, round-faced owl. To my right sat a second whose angry, grim face frightened me. By his full head of black hair, I judged him to be considerably younger than his colleague. It was the chief judge, between them, who gave me the most heart. A gray-haired man with a kind face and intelligent eyes, he looked at me with what I thought was compassion.

To the right of the judges, to my left as I faced them, on a platform that raised him above Atilla but prevented him from rising above the justices, was the black-robed prosecutor. His face was too closed to read his character.

On stage, having assessed what I believed to be the full cast of characters, I still had no understanding of what purpose this hearing would serve for the Turkish State. I knew only what I hoped it would do for me.

As usual the proceedings began with an identification of the accused, forcing me to reply to questions I had answered before: my name, the names of my parents, the date of my birth, the address of my residence. Everything had to be spelled. Makbule translated. The typist, seated in front of the dais three yards from me, hunt-and-pecked the legal record. Now that the moment was here, I was calm. I had learned patience in Turkey.

The proceedings were slow, everything being said twice: in Turkish and English, in English and Turkish.

The meat of the affair began with the reading of the indictment after which Makbule was given time to explain what it said. After this the chief judge read "my" statement as interpreted by the judge who had sent me to prison October 3. As Makbule made the translation I was astonished to hear the story had been recorded more completely than I believed possible and was correct in most detail.

Eminently fair, the chief judge then gave me the chance to correct the record as it stood. Through Makbule I reminded the court it was *I* who had volunteered at the dock that the head was marble, not onyx, bringing about the inspection.

On this point I had hoped Charnaud would attend as my witness but Atilla, who had spoken with him as I'd requested, reported he claimed not to remember. I was bewildered and made angry by what I believed was a memory loss, on Charnaud's part, of the variety claimed by Bob Haldeman during the Watergate hearings.

Next came an opportunity for the judges to ask me questions. Old Roundface, demonstrating no curiosity, passed. But when it was Grimface's turn, he made up for it. Asking three questions, which brought out material I thought needed to be aired, he learned over the rostrum.

"Have you been educated or trained as an archeologist or geologist or do you read many books on the subject of antiques and archeology?" he challenged me accusingly.

"I have not been trained or educated either as an archeologist, geologist, or antiquarian," I answered, "nor have I read often or extensively on these subjects."

"Why have you bought these antiquities?" he asked angrily.

"I bought them because I thought they were souvenirs, not antiquities. I did not seek out the man who sold them to me. I had thought to buy some needlework and when I stopped to look at it, the man approached me. How could I have thought they were antiques when I paid twenty dollars for the three? I didn't have the training to know *one* was ancient."

And if I had known and the price was still ten dollars, I would have bought it anyway since I hadn't been told the removal of even one antiquity—openly displayed—was against the law and considered smuggling. But this I didn't say.

Grimface had one more question. "Is it allowed," he asked harshly, "to export archeological antiquities from the United States?"

The question was revealing. Didn't he know the United States has no reservoir of ancient Greco-Roman ruins to dig out of the earth and preserve as Turkey did.

"In the United States," I answered, "antiquities are not

lying about everywhere. The only places such things can be found are in museums, in the shops of dealers, and in the hands of collectors. Therefore, transactions with respect to them is considered legitimate business. Naturally it is legal to buy, to sell, or to export antiques."

I could not tell if my responses had swayed Judge Grimface to look more favorably on me, or what impression they had made on the others, but as no further questions were forthcoming, Atilla stood to interject a point for the defense.

"I am a well-known attorney," she said, "and I have taken this woman's case because I know she is innocent of this charge. As a Turk who loves her country, I should like to see the tourists come, but I feel guilty because we Turks cannot control our own people from selling antiquities. By this inability, we are entrapping the tourists.

"It is up to us, Turks, to stop the sale of such things rather than to arrest innocent tourists who may, unwittingly, have bought them."

I liked what she had said but couldn't gauge the reaction of the court.

Then, to my surprise, three witnesses were brought in: the two archeologists who had been at the dock and my blond antagonist from the Izmir Museum. Both women looked as I'd remembered them: one, willowy and smartly attired, the other, falsely blond and dumpy, wearing the same ill-fitting cotton suit and hostile expression.

The chief judge conducted the inquiry. In a patient, well-modulated voice he questioned the dock archeologists first, and although I couldn't understand what was being said, the exchange seemed to go smoothly. In the interim between their dismissal and the calling of the museum witness, while Makbule whispered that they had spoken in my favor, I looked around at the spectators behind me.

Beau Nalle was seated in the very last row separated by one from Gant. Between the two men whom I recognized was another I did not. A tall, slender, distinguished-looking man wearing a suit of West Point blue, he had the face of a Jewish Gary Cooper framed by soft, steel-gray hair. I judged him, in one swift glance, to be American, wondering if the telegram had been too late to reach lawyer Lasky before he'd left the United States. If it were Lasky, I thought he might prove to be more likable than Gant.

Now the blond beast took the stand, answering questions with impatience and arrogance. Without knowing what was said, I could tell she was arguing with the chief justice who, unruffled, continued a patient probing.

Her interrogation lasted rather a long time, and when she left the stand, Makbule said she had spoken against me and that the judge was trying to make her soften her position.

At stake, I later learned, was not the issue of the head's antiquity—there was full agreement on this point—it was rather its importance, rarity, and value, a fine point impacting seriously on the severity of the crime of which I stood accused. To the end, Blondie took an adamant position, claiming that "all antiquities are rare in that they cannot be manufactured now. . . . People have stolen too much from us. They must be made to stop."

There was more palaver, none of which was translated; then I was given the chance to speak in my own defense. Caught unprepared, believing the story, as it was already exposed, to be complete, not knowing what I could add that might be found compelling, I was still unwilling to let the opportunity pass unexploited.

"How can the court think," I pleaded, "that I would spoil six weeks of a once-in-a-lifetime vacation by taking such a chance if I'd had any inkling I was committing an illegal act in buying these heads? Since I had no knowledge about antiquities, I relied on the price as assurance I was buying only souvenirs."

Next came Atilla's turn to make her official plea for the defense. Standing, she addressed the judges in a forceful voice.

"My client is innocent," she said, "as I have already told the court. I believe this and it should be obvious that she has not known the good from the bad since she has bought two false heads as well as the real one.

"I believe the evidence shows this woman should be exonerated now. But if this cannot be done, because of her nationality and customs, because of her age and many health prob-

lems,* it is not good that she should remain in prison. I ask that
she be released on bail and remain in a hotel."

The prosecutor's statement, I thought, would be the most
telling. When he rose and began to speak, I strained to read, by
his manner or from Atilla's face, what his official posture would
be. But I had to wait for Makbule's translation to learn what he
had said.

He was not wholly against me. He told the judges he believed I had no intention to smuggle and concurred in Atilla's
request that I should be allowed to leave prison on bail.

Then the judges cleared the courtroom and retired to delib-
erate.

In the corridor, among the smoking, teeming hordes of troubled Turks awaiting their respective fates, I leaned against the
wall, trembling from the strain of what had passed and the
anxiety of waiting for the judges' decision.

Atilla was exultant. "The head judge is on your side," she
crowed. "He was acting as your lawyer, arguing with that
woman. There is something wrong with her. I believe some
unhappiness or disappointment in her personal life."

"You should be found innocent," Makbule declared, breaking her usual silence.

"At least," down-to-earth Atilla said, "you shall have bail. I
am sure."

Too anxious to speak, I said nothing. Hikmet squeezed my
hand and smiled broadly.

"The one judge," Atilla frowned, "he is against you. It is
possible he can be anti-American. We have such people here."

"I think you should be found innocent," Makbule repeated,
without her usual reserve.

Reaching into my purse where I had tucked away the remaining half of that morning's Valium, I popped it, unobserved,

---

*My "health problems" were one of Atilla's favorite special pleadings. The
hypothyroidism was controllable by medication—assuming I could obtain
a sufficient supply—and what other difficulties there were can be ascribed
to the slow process of aging. Teeth break down unless cared for; arthritic
deterioration is hastened by a cold, damp environment and a lack of
exercise. I was disinclined to ask her to forgo the health issues. Anything
she thought would help was okay with me.

into my mouth, swallowing it without water. The air, dense with smoke, was choking, and I felt ill from stress and anticipation and the noise of a hundred chattering Turks. Many lawyers stopped to compliment Atilla on her fine defense. Unused to so many people, I felt assaulted.

Why hadn't we returned to the room to wait? My knees felt soft, flabby, too weak to hold me erect. I wished I could sit down. Closed in by the bodies of my supporters, I shifted in an effort to find more strength from the wall.

"You have made a wonderful answer to this difficult judge's question, saying these objects are kept where they cannot be sold." Atilla returned to the trial.

"That was not what I was trying to say," I told her, protesting a compliment I didn't deserve. "It is only that we don't have ancient Roman and Greek cities in the United States."

"I have understood it differently," she interrupted, "and so will the judges. It was very good, your statement. I have used it in making my argument."

At this juncture my point was immaterial. Leave it. Who cares, it's done. Will they let me go? My heart leapt at the thought Makbule could be right. Oh God, if only I am found innocent today and this whole nightmare will be over.

The clerk appeared. Quickly we filed back into the courtroom, resuming our former positions.

As the chief judge began to read from a paper in his hand, involuntarily I took a deep breath, holding it until he was finished. Makbule translated.

"You are allowed to leave the prison. A bail of one thousand and five hundred American dollars has been set. The next trial will be on November 29, and if you don't appear for that hearing, you must realize this bail money will be forfeit. The court has demanded your birth certificate and your police record from the United States. They will contact Interpol to obtain them. That is all. Do you understand?"

"I understand," I said, weeping with relief and more. How could they think I might have a police record? The suggestion was humiliating.

I later learned the verdict had not been unanimous. Judge Grimface dissented. Of course.

The chief justice, having been assured by Makbule I understood the terms of the order, concluded the proceedings with a few words. Now, as if a cage of wild animals had been opened, the room was flooded with reporters; the flashbulbs of their cameras set the room afire with blinding lights.

Quickly Hikmet came forward and, taking my arm, pulled me from the spot where I still stood, too frightened and alarmed to move. Like a pair of broken-field runners we wove through the throng, out of the courtroom, and into the corridor. Rushing me to the stairs and seeing my fatigue, Hikmet helped me run five flights and out into the street. We had eluded the cameras but, as I learned the next day, not before some shots were taken.

Before I got in the waiting van, I noticed the man who had been sitting between Nalle and Gant, as he strode gracefully from the building. On his way to the street he passed within feet of me, and catching my eye, he lifted his right hand in a snappy thumbs up salute and smiled.

On the ride back to prison, reliving every moment of the morning, savoring the joy of victory, I wondered about the stranger who obviously wished me well. Not only had he left the courthouse without Gant and Nalle, but he had also made no attempt to introduce himself. This could not be Lasky, I decided. So who was he?

All the way back to the prison, Hikmet kept patting my hand and smiling. Her pleasure at my release was generous and made me forget, for a moment, her indifference to the people she thought her inferiors. Sleepy and yawning when we reached Buja, I was unable to alight without help from the van. Hikmet, seeing me falter, came to my aid and held my arm during, what seemed to me, the long walk to the cell block. It was only noon when we returned.

The women were waiting as the steel door slid back, and Hikmet, in a triumphant voice, wasted no time in broadcasting the good news. Then the women crowded around me, crying happy tears, wanting to know every detail.

I had seen this before—the generosity of these women. Condemned though they were to serving such long terms of incarceration as three, seven, eleven, and more years, powerless and without funds with which to appeal for release or even to improve the conditions under which they lived, they expressed a wholehearted outpouring of joy upon hearing of a comrade's victory against the system. It was a humbling thing to experience.

But I hadn't the strength to accept their hugs and excused myself to "lie down for just a few minutes."

Neshe came to sit on the bed beside me, her eyes full of the conflict she was struggling to bear—happy I was going and distraught at the loss. Her feelings mirrored mine.

If I could have changed that day's outcome, it would have been only to see the court declare me innocent and send me home with its blessings. I wanted nothing more at that moment than to return to the world from which I'd been barred, to the family who loved and needed me, to the friends and the work I felt so desperately deprived of. But a part of me also felt pain and guilt at leaving behind the women who had cared for and comforted me here. Of them all I had the tenderest love for Neshe—brave, sweet, loyal, compassionate, reasonable, sorely wounded Neshe who bore her disappointments with so much dignity. I was proud to call her my friend. And, of all the friends I'd leave in Buja, Neshe was the one I'd miss most.

It was Eminay who cried openly. Her dream, the meaning of which she was unaware, had come true. I was leaving her on the steep, dangerous mountain, and I feared, as she had, I wouldn't be returning to help her.

"I am crying with happiness because you will go home," she said. "For you to go home is better even than my going home."

I hugged her. There was nothing to be said.

The woman of the rings came, proud to have played a part in my release. Wearily I took them from my finger and, placing them in her hand, thanked her.

"Chuock, chuock tesh a kur. Tell her," I asked Nese, "it meant a lot to me to have them. I'm sure they helped me get the bail."

Soon Eminay called me to lunch. She and the other two women had risen early this morning to eat breakfast with me before I went to court. Because I had not anticipated their thoughtfulness and felt sorry to have disappointed them, I ignored my exhaustion and followed her, for what was to be the last time, to the lower dorm.

Even the revolutionaries, whom I'd been told were Communists, enemies of my country, came to the table to share my happiness and say good-bye.

I returned to find my suitcase on my bed. My "friend," the soldier who knew how to smile, had truly protected it for me. I emptied the locker into it while Lutfi, Neshe, and others assisted the packing by pulling the bedding from the "bad" mattress. Bringing strong cord, they bound the sheets, blankets, and pillows in a heavy bundle I was to carry out of prison.

It had occurred to me I might need these things, myself, should I be found guilty and returned to serve my sentence. But I preferred to leave all of Atilla's purchases for the use of indigent women. Eminay advised against it.

"Hikmet will take them home," she said, "It has happened before. The poor women who need them will not get to use them."

Sara, her eyes red from crying, joined us as we sat on the bed, now covered with only a prison blanket.

"Gin," she said, "I love you very much," and threw her arms about me, lovingly.

"I teach her to say this," Lutfi said, moving forward from behind the others.

"You did it well," I answered her, "Now, you must take care of yourself and not take so many pills again. If you do I shall hear about it and be very angry."

"I take care," she said. "I glad you get bail. You go home, soon, I think."

"I hope so."

Before I left I gave Eminay 250 Turkish lira, asking that she buy a jar of the chocolate spread for Sara, who liked to put it on the bread at breakfast.

"Don't say anything to her now," I asked. "Let it be a surprise after I am gone."

It was about four when Hikmet came to get me. The bail had been paid; Atilla, who was waiting in the director's office with Gant, had brought the court order for my release.

The moment was at hand; I was really leaving. Lutfi and

Eminay and Sara stepped forward to say good-bye. Smiling in spite of tears, we hugged fiercely and let go. I went to Neshe, who hung back, watching, her eyes wide and intense with feeling, but dry. Embracing her with all the warmth I felt, I kissed her cheek and patted her hair, promising I would get words to her through the American brother-in-law whose address I had in my purse on a torn scrap of paper.

Hikmet carried the suitcase into the wash area, while I, struggling with the heavy bedclothes, followed behind. Along our route, between the dorm and the steel door, many women from both dorms lined the way, touching and reaching to kiss me as I passed. Even Euzgeul, seven inches taller than I and unable to show tender emotion easily, bent to kiss me.

When the steel door slid back and I stepped to follow Hikmet to the other side, in a spontaneous burst of triumph, the women began to clap. Overcome by emotions I could not express, weeping openly, I turned toward them one last time before turning my back on the place that had been my home and the women who, by their loving protection, had been both friends and family for three and a half interminable weeks of my life.

PART III

When I left Buja Prison, I took with me not only clothes and bedding; I carried the infection I'd caught in Turkey. Imprisonment had changed me. Release was not what I expected.

For me, living in a foreign land and being unable to speak the language had not seemed threatening. At every port where the *Sea Princess* had put in, I'd roamed the unknown streets on foot, an explorer, discovering the land and its people. I had believed that by the simple act of leaving prison, free to move about within the country, I would quickly recover the strong personality I formerly had.

I soon realized this belief was falsely taken.

The trauma of events beginning on the dock had damaged some essential aspect of my ego. I was not the same. In part, debilitation was responsible. Continuous stress had emptied my reservoirs of energy and courage.

Being brave was a role I'd adopted before I was seven, wanting to carve for myself a unique position in a family where all the natural avenues to status were usurped by my two sisters, as oldest and youngest, and my brother, as only son. Lifelong practice at acting brave had given me a kind of real courage, I suppose. Long ago I'd learned the thing you fear is rarely as bad, in fact, as it was to anticipate. But after release, obligated still to function normally in a world that was painfully strange, no longer protected by the prison and its rules, I felt afraid. It was this nonspecific anxiety, never a component of the "me" I'd known all my life, that made me a stranger to myself now.

201

For as long as I could I hid my true feelings—from myself and from everyone I saw or spoke with—using the trick that had helped me before: if you act as if you're okay, you are okay—or at least, you will be in time. The glass structure inside me, like an armature beneath soft clay, kept me on my feet. Formed on the dock, enlarged under a threat of too-harsh justice, annealed in prison, it was all that prevented a collapse. Otherwise, the fiber was straw.

Before Hikmet brought me to the director's office we made two stops within the prison to satisfy bureaucracy's love of paper work. When we finally stood face-to-face, the director, whom I'd never met in spite of sharing two rides and a room in the court building, shook my hand. Hikmet kissed me good-bye in front of her boss before I was escorted from the building by Gant and Atilla.

They had a taxi waiting and the three of us, Gant in front with the driver, drove quietly away from Buja into town.

At the American consulate Gant left us, giving Atilla the name and address of a restaurant where tonight he was hosting a dinner—kind of a "you may not be free, but at least you're out of jail" party. The plan had been made without consulting me, and although I was tired, more tired than I'd ever been in my life, I made no protest. I remained silent as the taxi proceeded south on the road from downtown Izmir to Atilla's home.

Struggling under the load, Atilla helped me carry the bundles into a modern building and, by elevator, to her seventh-floor apartment. Quickly disposing of the parcels in a rear bedroom, which she said would be mine that night, we repaired to her comfortable living room where she made tea and we sat to talk.

I met Nena (Nine), Atilla's ancient housekeeper, considered a family member after twenty-five years of service. Old and religious, unable to speak my language, Nena gave me her hand and smiled with so much sweetness, I felt warmed by her touch. An hour later Atilla's beautiful daughter, Geuldal (Güldal), returned from the university where she was a graduate student and joined us. Although her second language was French rather than English, she added sparkle to the conversation.

Atilla was a perfect hostess, skilled at making me feel welcomed. It was comfortable in her home; all three women treated me like a cherished friend, yet I was unable mentally, at least, to leave the prison. My mind was beleaguered with images—women and beds, cement walls and floors—and the sounds of female voices speaking Turkish over the noise of a loudspeaker that scratched out throbbing, insistent Turkish music.

Atilla wanted to talk about the trial and the legal implications of the judges' order.

"They have not returned your passport," she said, wonderingly. "It is important that you have it since you will move into a hotel tomorrow and without it you may have difficulties."

"What can we do about that?" I asked.

"I shall return to the court tomorrow to request to have it."

"And if they don't give it? What does that mean?"

"Let us wait to see what they will say," she answered. "I have talked to the director before you joined us. He believes you should be put on a plane to return home."

At my questioning look, she went on, "This can mean it is expected you will go home. The director is also a prosecutor, that is, he is belonging to the prosecutor's office." She paused, thinking. "We must wait," she said, "The intention will be more clear if the passport is returned. If not, we shall see."

"I am very tired," I said.

"We have time before we must leave for dinner. You shall rest here for a while. Later we will change our dresses for tonight. You will wear the blue dress I have kept. Also," she remembered, standing, "I will return to you the ring and earrings I have promised to keep until you came from prison. I get them."

We spent two hours rehashing the trial, but the court order was what interested me. There was something about it I kept turning over in my mind.

"Atilla," I said, "I was very surprised by how low the bail was, fifteen hundred dollars."

"Yes," she agreed. "We have all expected it to be much more."

"Another thing, unless Makbule didn't translate everything, do you realize the order made no mention of travel?"

"Of course, you may travel anywhere you wish in Turkey while you wait for the trial next month."

"But they neglected to say anything about travel at all. They didn't even say I was not allowed to leave Turkey. The order said only that if I didn't appear in November the fifteen hundred dollars would be lost. It was as if they set the low bail and neglected to say anything about travel because they expect me to go home and forfeit it. Is that possible?"

"It is possible," she said, frowning. "I must have a copy of the order to study it."

Atilla thought I should buy clothing appropriate to the climate in Izmir, which was beginning to drop into the midsixties. Soon the yearly rains would start. As she had made a date to meet with Gant and me at the consulate on Friday at ten, after which she would move me into a hotel, we agreed to postpone shopping until Tuesday. By then I would have received money from the trust account and would also be more rested.

I changed into the blue dress and a pair of shoes I'd had in prison but never worn. At her insistence, I put on Atilla's navy topcoat. At 7:30, we left for the restaurant, which was on the far side of Izmir.

The ride north, with Atilla at the wheel of her car, had an aspect of déjà vu. The last time I'd driven through these streets at night was with Ludan, at the turning of the tide of my life. But where Ludan was skilled, Atilla was not a comfortable driver. Having delayed learning until two years earlier, she had mastered the techniques but was awkward in their use, tentative about which road to take, reactive to other drivers, clumsy at parking. When, after some minor difficulty, we arrived at our destination twenty minutes late, I was tense and ill at ease.

The restaurant, an open room bare of decoration, was empty except for two men seated at a front table. Gant was waiting and Nalle, whom I was surprised to see. After being seated at a table in a dark corner, Gant took over.

The conversation was superficial and, to me, revealing of Gant's insensitivity. In the presence of Atilla, a native and an attorney, and Nalle, an experienced hand in Turkey, Gant dominated the discussions whose topics he chose, trying to impress, for different reasons, all of us with his knowledge of Turkey, its cities, customs, and laws.

Atilla sought to divert him by turning the conversational topic away from her country.

"You are from New York, Mr. Gant. I have a sister living there. She is a doctor practicing at one of the hospitals of your city."

"Really," Gant replied, showing surprise. "Your sister is lucky to find work as a doctor in the United States, especially in New York. She must have been educated in the States."

"Not at all," Atilla said. "She received her education in Istanbul, as did all of my family. We are five sisters and one brother. Each is having advanced degrees from the university at Istanbul."

"Turks don't usually educate their women, I thought," he said, clumsily. "Your father must have been pretty rich as well as a man with unusual ideas for his time." He turned to me. "No wonder you and Atilla hit it off, Gene, both of you had the luck to have rich papas."

"That is not all we have in common," I said, and refused to say more. Gant offended me.

I had no desire to participate, anyway.

Feeling strangely disconnected from the room and my companions, I only half listened to the forced and foolish conversation, picking at the food Gant had insisted on ordering instead of allowing Atilla to choose. The rhythms and sounds of the cell block still reverberated in my head.

At the first chance I could politely do so, I asked to be taken home, excusing myself as being very tired.

In the car driving back to Güzelyali, the suburb where Atilla lived, I bluntly confided my opinion of Gant.

"I don't like him," I said. "He talks too much and says too little and I find his manner toward women more than a little condescending."

"He is rather strange," Atilla admitted, "but his personality is not important. Tomorrow when we speak together about your problems, I believe we will find out how he can be of use."

Before going to bed, though it was nearly midnight, Atilla and I changed into our nightclothes and sat in her living room together. Sharing cigarettes, the dark night enclosing us in protective silence, we shared confidences full of truth and feeling like schoolmates in a sleeping dorm.

I spoke about my childhood and the father whose public persona masked an indifference as a parent; of the pain caused by his three subsequent marriages after a divorce that occurred during our childhood, doing lasting harm to the potential talents and future fulfillment of his children's lives; of the material privileges that brought opportunity but could not make up for the loss of emotional security.

I told her about happy things—personal accomplishments, the love and loyalty I shared with my siblings, good friends, and Jimmy, who would turn the world upside down if he thought I needed or wanted it.

I learned from Atilla about her husband and the happiest of marriages that ended abruptly a year before when his heart had simply exploded without warning; of a bereavement that could not be assuaged except by forgetting herself in helping others; and about Geuldal, the bright, accomplished child of love who gave her mother companionship and joy.

At 1:00 we went to bed. I lay awake listening to the silence, then fell into a deep sleep from which I did not awaken until morning. It was the first time, in more days than I cared to remember, I had slept the night through. It was the first time in a month I'd felt safe.

Atilla shook me awake at 9:00, full of regret that because of our appointment at 10:00, I couldn't be allowed to sleep until I was finished. To that I replied it might have taken the whole day. Remembering my complaint that eggs were unavailable in prison, Atilla gave me a breakfast of toast, jam, tea, and boiled eggs, making me feel very cherished. It was something my mother would have done.

The protection of Atilla's home, so generously given, was available for only one night. It wouldn't be seemly, much as she may have liked, to give sanctuary to this accused criminal on a more permanent basis so, when I had eaten, I quickly dressed and packed. Offering to keep the bedding until we were sure it was no longer needed—she would then give it away—I had only my suitcase to carry to the consulate.

The meeting with Gant took place in Ludan's small, empty office, which Nalle kindly allowed us to use. Gant, having taken the seat behind the desk, did his best to manipulate the interview. I waited for him to tell me how he proposed to arrange my return to the United States and relied on Atilla to ask the questions to which I wanted answers. In fairness to Gant, faced

with the passive, dull-witted and oft-weeping woman I'd become, it took a perceptive person to see the intelligence and will
that lay behind this facade and a patient one to draw them out.
In Gant, those qualities seemed to be in short supply.

Gant handed me a letter prepared by the consulate, that
identified me as an American citizen without her passport—a
common, if not frequent, situation that occurs when passports
are lost, stolen, or destroyed. The letter was to protect me from
a soldier's challenge on the streets of Izmir and to satisfy the
requirements of the hotel where I would be staying.

Gant said to Atilla, as if I weren't there, "Before he left, this
fellow Ludan [Gant had never met Bob] suggested two places he
thought would be suitable for Gene to live when she got out.
You can check them out," he added, giving her a slip of paper
containing the details. Turning to me, he offered another envelope and, smiling in the manner of a grand signore, reached
across the big desk to give it to me with a flourish.

"There's thirty thousand lira in that envelope I got for you.
Use this to pay the hotel and meals. If you need more, ask me."

"Is this your money?" I asked, taking it.

"It's from the trust account," he replied.

"Then it's *my* money," I said.

"Of course," he agreed.

"I want more," I said.

"This should do you fine for today." he said, deciding for me.

"I would like to have more now," I repeated. There were
clothes to be bought and Atilla's bill to be paid. For some reason
that I didn't understand, the thousand dollars I'd arranged for
her to receive from my account in New York had never come
through. Thus far, Atilla had been working for me out of pocket
and good faith. I wanted to repair that omission.

"Well," he said, "I'll talk to them again tomorrow. The consulate doesn't keep a lot of money on hand, you know. That's
all they could spare today." And to avert further demands from
me, he shifted the conversation to discuss repatriation in a way
that implied criticism of me.

"We're going to get you home before you know it. I think
we should work on that, don't you?"

I nodded and Atilla moved into the breech.

She told Gant, who'd been present but had not understood

what was said, about the director's suggestion my passport be retrieved and I be sent home.

"That sounds good to me," he commented. "If I were you, Atilla, I'd get down to the court right away and work on getting it back."

"It is not possible I go today," she said, changing her plans of yesterday, "but I do this Monday morning. I shall also ask for a copy of the judges' order granting bail since Gene has noticed the wording may imply they will accept her to go home and the case continue in her absentia.

"If that's the case," Gant challenged, "why didn't they say so?"

Atilla smiled. "This is not so easy, Mr. Gant. How can the court openly suggest a person under detention for so serious a crime be released before the case has been fully heard? Anyway, we do not know if this is so."

"But you think the order suggests it?" he asked.

"Gene thinks it may be so," she answered. "I have no opinion until I have seen how the order has been worded."

"Personally," Gant dismissed this line of reasoning, "I am of the strong opinion that Gene should stay here until the next trial at least." He grew expansive. "This will demonstrate her good faith and give me a chance to use my influence with some important contacts to have the whole thing thrown out. I know a lot of highly placed people here, you know. I'd rather see her leave without any loose ends."

"Have you been encouraged to think this is possible?" I asked, upset to hear Gant suggest I remain in Izmir another month. Richard's voice sang a promise in my head. "If you get bail and your passport is returned—sayonara, Charlie." Wasn't Gant here to take care of that?

"I have every reason to believe we can get you out after November 29."

"But suppose they decide to revoke bail? Or worse. Since Atilla assures me I must eventually be found guilty, suppose on the 29th it is finished and . . ." I started to cry, contemplating reincarceration . . . "I am returned to serve three and a half years?"

"Not a chance," Gant assured. "Listen, I suggest you two get this gal checked into one of these hotels and maybe do some shopping. Take your mind off everything. Leave the worrying to me," he said, "and think about what I said about staying for the next trial."

I wasn't ready to leave the worrying or the decisions to Gant until I knew more about the man and his plans.

"I want to know exactly how you're going to go about getting me home," I said, "and when I can get more of my money."

"Gee," Gant replied, standing, "I wish I could spend more time with you, but I've got an appointment in . . ." he looked at his watch, ". . . fifteen minutes. What do you say we get together again here, Monday. I'm sure Nalle won't mind if we use this office. After all, it's our consulate; we pay the bills."

As we were rushed off, I remembered to ask Gant if my personal possessions, left aboard the ship, had been sent on to New York as requested, and who the man sitting between him and Nalle at the trial was. He knew nothing about the luggage and agreed to look into the matter. As for the stranger at the trial:

"Name's Emile, something Emile. From New Orleans, I believe. Has some sort of business interests in Turkey. You'll have to ask Nalle," he answered, leaving us outside Bob's office where Makbule sat at a desk.

"You are asking about Mr. Emile?" she interposed. "He is such a nice man. He has factories near Izmir and comes to the consulate often."

"Did you see him at the trial yesterday?" I asked her.

"He has been at your trial?" she said with surprise, "I did not see him."

Atilla interrupted, saying we ought to go since she had to be at her office but not before I was in the hotel. I was satisfied that the American I saw yesterday was definitely not Lasky, and saying good-bye to Makbule, we left the building.

The Kilim Oteli was one block from the consulate and I was sure this was why Bob had suggested it because there was little else to recommend it.

Izmir is Turkey's third largest city. By including its many outlying suburbs, it makes claim to a population of two million, but the city itself, by American standards, is a small town that straddles the magnificent crescent of the bay of Izmir and sweeps up a slow-rising plain to the crest of a low mountain chain ringing the shore some ten or more miles away.

From a northern point near the dock, south to the edge of the Konak, lies the most desirable inner-city real estate. In this area, called Alsanjak (Alsancak), on five roads running roughly parallel to the bay, can be found the newest apartment houses, the most stylish shops, the better class hotels, consulates, and NATO Headquarters for the Middle East. Centrally located within the district and overlooking the magnificent bay is a wide plaza commemorating the end of the debilitating war against the Greeks, when Atatürk, a general in 1921–1922, pushed the historic enemy from the shores of Smyrna (Izmir). On a marble base in the plaza, as if the Turkish people were still under his protection, is a heroic bronze of Atatürk astride a noble steed, looking out to sea.

The American consulate, on the fourth floor of the Citicorp building, is two blocks from the plaza. The building stretches the short block between the road that circles the bay, suitably named Atatürk Caddasi (road), and the street to the east, known as the First Kordon. Entrance to the lobby of Citicorp can be gained from either road, and there is a uniformed American employee with a walkie-talkie, who guards the lobby doors. In the recent past there have been threats against Americans at their embassy in Ankara and its two satellite consulates in Izmir and Istanbul.

Atilla and I walked north one block to the Kilim where I inspected a third-floor room. The accommodations were plain —twin beds, a rickety laminated-plastic dresser with desk and chair, a bare bulb that hung from the center of the room, as well as one standing lamp—but there were a phone, vintage 1940, two semi-upholstered chairs, and a bathroom with a tub! The floor was bare save for a small, thin, worn Turkish carpet but the room looked clean and the brochure promised hot water. What sold me was the two windows overlooking the side street entrance from which I had an excellent view of the southern half of the harbor and the gray-purple mountains in the distance.

Although one of the men on duty at the front desk (the designation is a glorification of the primitive) spoke English, Atilla handled the check in procedure in Turkish, identifying herself as my attorney. Lacking much in the way of identification, I offered to leave a deposit for my room but the suggestion was brushed away by the manager.

In the room, having assured herself I was okay, Atilla made some suggestions before leaving.

"You may go out of the hotel for your lunch," she said, "but it is not good that you should be on the street in the night. Therefore, you should eat your dinner downstairs. The restaurant is small and I don't know if the food is good, but it is better so."

I nodded my willingness to take her advice.

"Then," she said, looking around, "if there is nothing else, I will leave you. Tomorrow I will bring you to my house for a good dinner. I will come to get you at about two. Does this suit you?"

"I would like it very much," I said, reaching to hug her. "Thank you, Atilla, for everything. I could not manage without you."

"You have need of a friend," she commented, then said good-bye and left.

I was alone. I looked about the room. Alone. No one else. Only me. It was the first time I, who had spent so much of my life in privacy, had been alone in a month.

Oh, God. It was wonderful!

Always, the first thing I do when I check into a hotel room is unpack and turn down the bed. In this way I make the room mine, quickly feeling at home. This day, wanting to savor the silence, to bask in the privacy, to be in touch with my aloneness, I postponed the ritual.

In prison, except for three places, there was nowhere to sit; I had either lain on my bed, walked, or stood. When I sat it was to eat—on a hard bench without back support, to talk with Neshe—on warm cement when the sun was in the yard, or to write—on my bed where I could neither lean back nor hold my head erect: there was no headboard to support my back and the wood platform of the bed above mine was inches shorter than the distance from my "tush" to the top of my head.

Placed in front of the two windows, the wood-armed uphol-stered chairs had caught my eye during the inspection and I took one now. Sinking deeply against its slanting back, I lifted my legs and stretched them atop the nearest bed. Closing my eyes, I allowed myself to sink into the physical pleasure of such sitting, to experience it as fully as I could. Never, I vowed, would I take anything for granted again. The smallest things can be so delicious.

Eventually I got around to unpacking, after which I took the elevator to the dining room for a terrible lunch of broiled chicken, bread, and baklava.

I spent the whole of that day sitting by the window, writing in my journal, savoring the quiet, the privacy, luxuriating in the absence of stress. As the day darkened into dusk, I thought of Buja, my friends circling the courtyard in the evening count. Imagining Neshe, standing alone, looking sad, I felt guilty for having abandoned them.

Putting aside the writing, I watched the lights come on halfway around the crescent: dancing fireflies of light that made tent shapes out of the masts of ships lying at anchor and crossing the bay; pearl necklaces of light that marked the snaking highways; pinpricks of light that told me families had come together in their homes, way off and high up, in the mountains at the far side of the bay.

I watched the headlights of cars crawl, unbelievably slowly, along the road south of town that led to Atilla's house. The sky over the Bay of Izmir, washed the color of a coral shell, darkened and deepened until it was stained red, repeating the astonishing sunset I remembered from the bus. "If this incredibly beautiful spot were in a better-known part of the world," I said aloud, "it would be the most sought-after resort in the whole world."

Unable to face another meal in the hotel restaurant, I picked up the phone to ask that toast and tea be sent to the room. But the phone didn't work so I walked to the lobby.

"The telephone in my room is not working," I told the desk clerk. "How soon can it be repaired?"

The man looked at me as if I were crazy. "Not fix soon. Take time.* Tomorrow change room. One floor above. Same room."

---

*The wire connections, over forty years old, were frayed and needed to be replaced. It would be hard to prove, but I am certain this phone had been out of order for anywhere from three to ten years. Maybe longer. What I didn't know then was that the waiting time for new service was ten years. A bonus payment of (at that time) 15,000 Turkish lira entitled a new subscriber to receive service in five months. Maintenance and repair did not exist. No wonder the clerk thought I was crazy.

Move again? The notion alone exhausted me.

Before I left, the clerk, aggressively I thought, demanded a deposit, making me flush with anger and embarrassment. I tried that, I wanted to say, and my offer was refused. I wondered, as I went to my room to get money, what had caused the sudden change in the hotel's attitude? Within myself, cowering in humiliation, I was sure they must have learned I was a criminal out on bail.*

After eating the light dinner I'd ordered, it was time to enjoy what I'd been saving all day. Striding to the reasonably modern bathroom, I opened the hot water tap and began to draw a bath. I was going to soak in a good hot tub. Testing the water temperature frequently, the tub was half-full when I gave up and accepted the truth. There was no hot water. Not a dram.

Furious, a paid guest in good standing, I marched my indignation down two flights of stairs to confront the desk clerk again. "Yes," he said, nodding, "I am sorry. There will be hot water in half hour."

Three hours later—the water finally coming in tepid—sitting in two inches of water and incensed at my helplessness, I bathed and went to bed. The next morning, greeted by several cockroaches, I suddenly realized I was not so helpless as all that. I don't know if it was the phone, the food, the water, the bugs, or the attitude but, enough with the "hair shirt," I told myself, I'm moving!

Making several calls from a pay booth in the lobby, (whispering so the clerk three feet away wouldn't feel insulted I was dumping them for better accommodations), and with the help of Geuldal and Atilla who picked me up, I moved from the Kilim three blocks away to the Efes Hotel, the best and newest in Izmir. In a sixth floor room, attractively furnished in browns and burnt orange, I was comfortable at last. I'd lost the marvelous view of the bay but had my own balcony overlooking the garden, pool, and the Hamam, the Turkish bath, instead. And from the windows of the room, at night I could see what I thought was the spot where Sylvia had taken us the last day of

---

*My guess was correct. The morning paper had featured a flattering photo of me in the dress I was still wearing, beneath the headline "Smuggler Woman."

the tour—the citadel, high above Izmir, built by Alexander the Great. It looked very beautiful, lit up with spotlights—the only public electrification I can remember seeing in Turkey.

Though the summer season was over and the swimming pool closed, the Efes—one block from the Etap where I stayed before—did a good business with foreign travelers because of the sophisticated services it offered: a hair salon and barber shop, a coffee shop as well as formal dining room, and twenty-four-hour room service by waiters who spoke English (and German and French) from a menu of choices that sounded almost European. It even had a small news and sundries stand in the lobby. What a difference from the Kilim!

Offering a seasonal club membership to the officers of the American air force based in town, which gave them use of the health and sport facilities, not only added to the revenues during the otherwise slow winter months, it also kept the hotel from looking like a ghost town. Locals and foreigners could be found after 5:00, enjoying the plush couches and brass tables of the mezzanine lounge where a waitress in harem garb, looking bored and indifferent, served beverages. It surprised me, in this Muslim country where alcohol is anathema, to see Turks ordering mixed drinks, cocktails, and beer. Why couldn't they Westernize, I wondered, without picking up our bad habits, too?

I stayed with Atilla that day until 7:00, when she drove me home. It was a visit between loving friends.

She was wearing black—wool slacks and sweater that covered her completely—over which she wore a fire-engine-red wool-knit serapelike garment. Where I would have been overshadowed by such bold colors, in them she looked absolutely smashing! Atilla had style.

She'd prepared a delicious Turkish dinner, serving honey-sweet pastries for dessert with tea. Geuldal and Nena ate with us after which, while Nena entoned prayers in the next room, I was shown a photo album of Geuldal's engagement party.

The color pictures, including many of a beautiful, happy Atilla together with her handsome white-haired husband, were taken one year before—a month before his sudden death.

"I looked much younger at this time," Atilla, turning the pages, observed without self-pity. "You see how I have aged?"

"You looked beautiful then," I answered, "and you are still beautiful to me."

Geuldal and her fiancé, a handsome young Turk sporting a bold black mustache, wouldn't marry until both had completed their advanced studies—in two years time.

Out of a genuinely warm impulse, without considering the legal realities, Geuldal invited me to attend the wedding. I was touched and felt honored, accepting with pleasure and the provision I would be free. Atilla seemed like a new sister, her family an extension of mine. Geuldal was the age of the nieces and nephews I already had.

I learned Atilla was an active member of one of the three political parties whose candidates were competing in the upcoming election. In this capacity, she said, she was obligated to attend an increasing number of meetings as well as give performances as campaign orator. As a result, her time for me would be greatly diminished until after the election on November 6.

There was one date I insisted she make. Having been the beneficiary of so many personal kindnesses from both Atilla and Makbule, I'd decided a small dinner party was an appropriate way of acknowleging the debt. I planned to invite Makbule and her husband and now asked Atilla to come with Geuldal. Inviting Gant was an option I was not going to exercise. This party was for people who had touched me with their love and caring. Gant didn't belong in that category. I didn't know if he ever would.

As Atilla had no phone except in her office, we tentatively set the dinner for Tuesday night, which I would confirm after I'd spoken to Makbule from the hotel.

Throughout the afternoon, continuing on the drive to the hotel, we returned again and again to discuss the prosecution's intentions toward me. No new conclusions could be reached. Only after Monday, when Atilla requested my passport, would we learn more.

I realize now this weekend, beginning Friday afternoon, was a pause between struggles: a temporary cease-fire in the ongoing, unresolved war between a middle-aged American woman and Turkish justice. It was a phase in which I was putting the prison life behind me so that I could reset my bearings and direct myself toward home. Halfway between the two, I had not let go of Turkey nor had I really committed myself to getting home. It was my family, whose urgency reached across the miles, that began to pull me back.

In the hotel room, after Atilla had driven away, I reached for the phone to call Makbule. It rang before I picked up the receiver. "Yes?" I said, wondering who would know to call me here. It was Richard LePere, in Washington.

"Richard," I said, amazed, "how did you find me?"

"How difficult could it be, Gene? There are only three hotels in Izmir you could be staying at," he answered in his dry, no-nonsense voice. Richard made me laugh; more important, he made me feel stronger.

Not only had Lasky been on his way to Turkey, I learned, but Gordon had been coming with him. This was news and I was glad I'd aborted their plans. Richard asked the question uppermost in everyone's mind.

"Well, when should Jimmy pick you up at the airport?"

"They didn't return my passport," I told him. "Atilla's going to ask for it Monday."

"Will she get it?"

"I hope so. We don't know."

"And if you don't?"

"I'll ask the consulate for a new one."

"Do you believe you're really on your way?"

"Yes," I assured him, not certain at all, "I do. And there's always Gant, remember. He's implied he has some scheme up his sleeve to get me out." I didn't tell Richard that Gant wanted me to stay until after the next trial. If I got my passport Gant's plans might change.

We'd been skirting around the telegram that dismissed Yilset and Lasky. Richard tried to justify the decision I'd overruled.

"Richard," I said, confident on this, "I'm glad they didn't come. It was unnecessary. If that Yilset had come I bet I wouldn't have gotten bail."

"It's a crap shoot, Gene. Who knows? Anyway, as long as you're sure you'll be out of there fast, that's all that counts."

In the pleasure of talking I didn't realize that, though Richard had asked if I would get home, he had offered no plan for how everyone's oft-declared objective might be achieved.

When we had hung up, I drew the long-delayed hot bath and, soaking in the tub, thought of home. The conversation with Richard had been so leisurely and the line so clear, it was hard to believe home was far away.

Within the hour I had two more of what were to be long, daily calls from the United States. The first, which lasted a full hour, was from Naomi. Not very good at world geography, I grasped, for the first time, the miles that separated us when she said it was 9:30 A.M. in California. It had been dark for two hours in Izmir and was 8:30 P.M.

My heart turned over with tenderness at Naomi's controlled concern. Regardless of how much she may have wanted reassurance, she verbalized no anxieties, asking rather than demanding, to know how I was and when I would be home. Before she hung up, this woman who found it too oppressive to travel from Los Angeles to New York offered to come to Izmir if I had to stay in Turkey for an extended period of time.

I was already in bed when Jim's call came, though it was early afternoon in New York. I wept at the sound of his voice. Although our mutual history was fraught with disappointment and pain, our relationship was sustained by common interests and an unspoken but abiding concern for each other.

An intelligent and handsome man, basically good-natured and generous, Jim was, during the eleven years of our marriage, a progressively sick alcoholic. Four years after I had left him, friendless and destitute, he'd found the strength to halt the insidious illness that was slowly destroying him. Since that time, by his own wit and superhuman effort, he had fully recovered. My admiration for him was enormous. When, in the nadir of my depression, I despaired that my life was over, in the innermost secret places of my being the certainty that Jim was there and that he would never give up trying to get me out sustained me.

He, too, wanted to know when I'd be home and I heard in his voice he would have been happier with a more definite answer than I was able to give. We hung up on my promise to do everything I could to leave quickly and his, to call back Monday to find out if the passport was returned.

As the days passed and the calls continued, the realization

slowly dawned on me that, while I was waiting for—no, *expecting*—the family and the lawyers to get me out, they were waiting for—expecting *me* to get myself out!

Sunday, too timid to venture out of the hotel, I anticipated a quiet day in the room. But after calling Makbule, who was free to come Tuesday, I resolved to have a look at the dining room where the dinner party would be held and to check out the hair salon. Taking an elevator to the ground floor, I looked around.

By any standard, the Efes was a modern hotel, and the lobby, unlike the functional lobbies of the Etap or the Kilim, was built to impress: broad and deep, it had a ceiling that vaulted thirty feet above the marble floor. About fifteen feet from the street entrance, a wide, carpeted stair swept in a slow, graceful curve to the mezzanine, where the dining room, hidden by a crowded lounge, could be found. Right of the lounge, on this upper level overlooking the lobby, was a narrow balcony that led to the barber shop and beauty salon.

Deep in the rear of the lobby, tucked under the mezzanine's overhang, was the front desk, where two well-dressed managers were always in attendance. Midway between this rear post and the front door, somewhat to the right of center and shooting almost to the ceiling, was a mammoth statue of Artemis, a copy of the original in the museum at Ephesus, from which the Efes Hotel took its name.* This goddess of fertility, in an effusive but faithfully rendered display, had about thirty breasts thrusting from the front and sides of her naked chest. They hovered over the room like so many pale, pointed bean bags.

Hidden from view behind it was the lobby shop and a door that gave exit to the rear gardens I could see from my room. Satisfied with what I'd seen, I went into the shop, bought the most recent copies of *Newsweek* and *Time* and a June issue of *Good Housekeeping* magazine, then returned with them to my room and settled down to read. What I didn't know was that a whole new cast of characters was about to enter my life.

---

*Efes is the Turkish name for Ephesus.

I took three unexpected calls that day: one from the American chaplain, Father Nee, who had offended me during the brief prison visit from which I'd fled in tears, and a second from the English woman, Nancy Rust, who, representing the Catholic women of Izmir, had been so very gentle. The third came from a man who introduced himself as Aaron Emile. He was the American who demonstrated his concern by attending my trial. I wondered how all of them had found me.

Nancy invited me to join her and some of her friends on Wednesday. They were driving up the coast to a town called Ayvalik, where they wanted to shop at an outdoor market and have lunch. After some hesitation, upon her assurance I would be back in the hotel by three—I hadn't the stamina to be out the whole day—I accepted. She volunteered to pick me up before 9:00 Wednesday morning.

Mr. Emile, whose low, well-modulated, and kind voice matched his appearance, said he would enjoy meeting me. He apologized for being unable to manage it sooner, but he was flying to Istanbul Monday on business. As he wouldn't return until Wednesday, we agreed to meet in the Efes lounge Thursday at 5:00.

Father Nee's blustery brogue sounded over the phone, exactly as it had in the prison visitor's room.

"Gene," he bellowed, "ye made it, gel." When I made no reply, he added, "Eugene Nee. I'm in the lobby. How's about meetin' for a cuppa tea. I'll be waitin' in the lounge."

It was 8:00; I'd been alone in the room since morning. I was empty from too much reading and from a silence that had become oppressive.

The lounge, when I arrived, was humming with activity, but looking about, I spotted the priest without difficulty. Stocky at forty-five and sturdy as a short brown bear, Father Nee was a man vibrating with energy and good spirits. His broad face was wreathed in a grin as he rose to greet me and, ignoring the timidity of my approach, enfolded me in a rough embrace.

"Well, Gene," he said, pulling me to an empty seat on a leather sofa-for-two, "ye don't look any the worse for wear now, after all."

I took a seat, perching close to the edge, ready to spring to safety, while he ordered tea from the harem-clad waitress and kept up both ends of the conversation.

"The thing we got to do now, is get ye outta here. Yer people will get ye home. The Americans are wonderful! Best in the world, ye'll see. Ye'll be home before ye know it. But, what ye need while yer waitin' is good American food, ye know. I got somethin' here fer ye." He pulled an envelope from the inside pocket of his jacket and, handing it to me, continued, "Entitles ye to eat at the Kordon.* Good American food. This Turkish food's no good. Weakens ye. At the Kordon they got everythin' and ye'll be with yer own kind. Americans."

I took the letter without reading it and slipped it into my purse.

"Tryin' to work it out for ye to move inta the Kordon. Very hush hush, ye know. Don't say nothin' but ye need to be outta this expensive Efes.

"Had me a bit a trouble with the powers-that-be," he said, causing me to remember what a fuss I'd made to Ludan about never having to see him again, "but that don't matter a bit. I'm stickin' to ye like glue, Gene, ye can't get rid o'yer namesake so easy as that. We priests never give up. That's me middle name, 'never-give-up.' "

When he'd gotten the pep talk out of his system, the good Father and I talked about ourselves and I learned that, while he'd been born in the United States, Gene Nee's Irishness was come by honestly. His life, until fifteen years ago, had been spent in Ireland and he had been an air force chaplain for the past twelve.

Somewhere he'd gotten the idea I was short of funds, something I didn't refute, and because of this he kept coming back to the theme of my moving. He'd already checked out three other "less expensive, ye know" hotels and gave me a note with their names and the cost, in lira, of their accommodations. At that moment, moving was the last thing I wanted to do.

By the time we parted I had changed my mind about him. In my fragile condition it was hard not to shrink from so much

---

*One of two American air force officers' clubs that provided daily meals and interim housing for Americans transferred for a tour of duty before permanent housing had been secured.

heartiness, but I knew now that the bull-in-the-china-shop manner covered up a loving and sensitive heart. I confessed I'd never known any priest before and that he was nothing like what I'd expected one to be.

He laughed with delight, then went serious. "Ye got to be real, Gene," he said, solemnly. "Don't want all that formality and rituals to separate ye from people."

This time, when he hugged me good night, I accepted the embrace with more equanimity.

Arriving at the consulate Monday morning, Atilla and I learned Gant would not keep our appointment. Another, unexpected and too important to forgo, was forcing him to stand us up. He'd telephoned his apologies to Makbule and left instructions that I be given another 30,000 Turkish lira—if I wanted it. He'd meet with us tomorrow—same time, same place.

The inconvenience to Atilla angered me and his cavalier manner with my money was frustrating. Still, I needed him and hoped this "appointment of importance," which he had told Makbule was related to my affairs, would have an outcome worth the inconvenience.

Having decided a talk with Charnaud was in order, I took a *taksi* to see him, while Atilla went directly to the court to file the request for my passport. We agreed to meet afterward at her office when she would tell me her progress with the court and I'd report mine with Charnaud's memory.

Key Tours was located on two floors of a dirty building on the Atatürk Caddasi some ten blocks north of the consulate. Upstairs I found Charnaud in his shirt sleeves, gentle, courtly, and seeming happy when he congratulated me on being out on bail. I told him I had come "in the hope that by relating what I remember happening at the dock, it will refresh your memory."

I went over the story in exquisite detail; every word and sentence was clearly imprinted in my mind. When I was finished, he shrugged.

"I am sorry, Mrs. LePere. I believe you but I cannot remember."

"But you must," I insisted.

"Ah," he said, regretfully, "it is unfortunate I have a poor memory. I would like to help you, but . . ." His voice trailed to a halt, then recovered, "I have already said to my superior in England that I prefer not to testify. He has told me I must."

"Surely, Mr. Charnaud," I said, urgently, "there is *something* you can say about me in court that will be helpful. Anything."

"I do not speak Turkish very well," he answered, not meeting my eyes. "I am afraid," he went on, now fixing a hard look on me, "I will make a mistake and say something that may harm your case."

I wasn't too swift at the time, certainly not at my best, I admit. Notwithstanding, I know a threat when I hear one.

"Look here, Mr. Charnaud," I said in a flush of anger I strained to control, "I speak no Turkish at all. There will be someone present to act as my interpreter. I see no reason why you may not use the same translator as I."

But no logic was persuasive to this unctuously soft-spoken, stubborn man. He fell back once more on a poor memory. Nothing I had already said and, I saw, nothing I would ever say, would budge him from the determined position he had chosen to take.

For the life of me, I couldn't understand what motivated him to refuse me help. All I asked was that he tell the unvarnished truth.

Frustrated and furious, sitting in Atilla's office twenty minutes later, I poured out my bewilderment.

"I do not know the answer," she said. "If it will help, I will speak with him again."

As to the passport, she told me, "We shall have no answer until Wednesday."

So much for the results of a day's work.

I was alone a great deal during which time I had nothing constructive to which I could apply my slight, but growing, energies. Lack of purpose and the inability to make use of my hours in meaningful work or pleasurable play, combined with the frustrations I'd encountered with Gant and Charnaud, encouraged a sense of futility and kept me depressed.

This was the mood I took to the consulate on Tuesday morning. Determined to get enough money to pay Atilla, while we waited for her to arrive I approached Gant again for funds.

"In the first place," he answered with some impatience, "you've gotten what amounts to over two hundred dollars already. I can't imagine what you'd find in a crummy town like Izmir to spend that kind of money on. In the second place, I've already told you this is a small consulate and they don't keep large amounts of cash on hand."

"You might have asked them to get more. I need at least four thousand dollars in Turkish money."

"What do you need that much money for?" he demanded, like a critical parent to a difficult child.

"I want to pay Atilla, for one thing," I said, "and I need the rest for clothes and the hotel and meals."

"You don't need that much for Atilla," he said with the trace of a sneer, pontificating. "Let me give you some valuable advice, Gene. It isn't smart to pay a Turkish attorney until the job is done."

"It is my money," I said, controlling a rage that threatened to spill over as tears. "I don't see why I can't have it and spend it as I see fit."

Atilla came through the door, ending the argument before I lost my poise.

In minutes we were ushered into Nalle's office, a large one overlooking the bay, where Nalle greeted us without getting up from his impressive mahogany desk in the corner.

As the interview unfolded, I had a strong impression that the set had been chosen and the actors coached by Gant, for despite Nalle's presence, he participated minimally. It was Gant who directed the meeting.

The subject was my going home. No one argued that my departure from Turkey was important. The threat of a finding of guilt, looming like a thunderstorm over my head, was again confirmed by Atilla, whom even Gant now accepted as our expert in Turkish jurisprudence. The consulate, obliged to act in accordance with what the Turks deemed proper, was sympathetic, concerned, but helpless. Where I parted company from the others (Atilla was silent on this issue) was over the timing of my departure. I wanted to leave right away. Gant had made it clear that he wanted me to stay until after the hearing on November 29. In this he had Nalle's support.

"I have reason to believe that by then I will have been able to get the court to agree to allow you to go home. It will be done with their cooperation," he argued.

"But what if I agree to stay and nothing has changed?" I asked, feeling cornered, "I will have lost a whole month for nothing."

"You will be no worse off than you are now," Gant said, overlooking the point of my complaint.

"Suppose the judges learn I am planning to leave. They will put me back in prison. You remember the judge who was against me. If he thought I was even speculating about forfeiting bail, he'd have me back in Buja in no time."

"We can handle him," Gant said. "It is much better if you agree to stay."

I looked at Atilla, sitting quietly in a chair to my left. I couldn't ask her what to do. It seemed wrong to talk about leaving in front of her, even though, as my attorney—even in Turkey—our conversations were privileged.

"Have you had a chance to read the court order?" I asked her, hoping in this, at least, I would find support.

"I have asked that a copy be made," she said, "but I have not been given it."

I turned to Nalle. "Do you think I should wait for the 29th?" I asked, plaintively.

"I think it would be best," he said.

I was defeated. I couldn't justify what my "gut" told me was so. Who was I against these powerful men? Once I had trusted my own judgment, those gut feelings. Now, shaken by what had happened to me, I'd lost the courage to act on my own decisions.

"I give in," I said, crying softly in an agony of disappointment. "I will stay until the next hearing."

I used my concession to plead for the preparation for a new passport. As we still didn't know if the existing one would be returned, why wait until the last minute? Gant, now the gracious victor, supported me.

"Sure," he said to Nalle, "why not. Have one of your people get it started."

Gant remained with Nalle when I followed Atilla from the room.

"We will see Makbule," she said, "and ask her why your money has not been given."

"They don't have the cash on hand," I told her. "I asked Gant before you came."

"This does not sound right to me," she answered, and let the subject drop.

When, in her office, I asked Makbule to "start the new passport," she looked disconcerted. Excusing herself, she left the room, I supposed to get authorization from Nalle, and when she returned it was with a smiling Gant.

"Makbule's going to give you the application form for your new passport," Gant said. "You can take it to the hotel and fill it out there."

"I'll bring it in tomorrow," I told Makbule.

"You will need photos," she instructed, handing me the form. "I will give you the name of a photographer who makes them in twenty-four hours, if you wish."

"Wonderful," I said.

"I have other 'wonderful' news," Gant said, beaming. "Mr. Nalle tells me they've just gotten in some money. You can get all you want."

His work was done. "I'm off, now. Got to keep after some good things I'm stirring up for you."

"When will you have definite news?" I asked, hoping to pin him down.

"Soon, soon. I'm going to have something to tell you pretty soon."

"How can I reach you if I need to?"

"You can't," he said without apology. "I'm staying with friends and am on the go every minute."

Up to now, I'd never been alone with Gant, and it occurred to me his evasiveness might be due to the fact that Atilla was always along when we met.

"May I speak with you privately for a moment?" I asked.

"I'm in a big rush right now," he said, and paused, thinking. "Come out to the elevator. I'll give you two minutes."

Alone, I put it to him.

"Mr. Gant, I need some time for a real talk. When can we do that?"

"Some time." He mulled it over, "Well, how about tomorrow?"

"Tomorrow I'm driving to Ayvalik with some friends," I answered, "unless we meet in the evening."

"I'm busy from one o'clock on," he said, "and Thursday's no good either. It'll have to wait for Friday."

I nodded.

"Okay," he said, opening the door to the elevator, "Meet me here Friday at ten."

"Not here," I said.

"Not here?" he repeated, "Okay, you name the place."

"Do you know that statue of Atatürk in the plaza on the bay?" I asked. He did. As he stepped into the elevator, he called, "See you Friday at ten."

Sitting beside Atilla as we drove up the First Kordon to look at clothes, what worried me most was how my family would take the news I would not be home for Thanksgiving.

As far as Atilla was concerned, the shopping was a success. Listlessly I let her choose for me: a burgundy skirt and two blouse coordinates of a heavy material that made me uncomfortable but that, since Atilla pronounced them "very smart," I agreed to take. We found a lightweight, dressy raincoat of the same color in a water-repellent fabric that had a greasy texture. Atilla said it was becoming. The single garment of my choosing was a white, downy-soft orlon sweater. In less than an hour, in a store I thought overpriced, I acquired two parcels of poor-quality and shabbily manufactured clothing that I didn't like. They cost me over $200.

We drove next to the Konak, where Atilla had her office, and bought a pair of low-heeled walking shoes and a bag that matched the coat. Agreeing these items should hold me for a while, I was happy to be taken to her office.

While she made instant coffee, I sorted out my money and handed her a generous fee. It was more than she'd asked for that Saturday when we'd met, but Atilla had given way beyond the services either of us had anticipated.

If only I could say the same of Gant. His behavior disturbed me. Random pieces of a puzzle I had yet to solve skittered around my brain, prickling undeveloped thoughts.

"It seems odd to me," I said, "that before the meeting Gant insisted there was no money."

"It is difficult to like this man," Atilla said.

"Yes," I agreed, "he is not forthcoming."

"I do not know this word, forthcoming."

"He isn't straight. He doesn't say what he thinks. He's secretive and he's manipulative." This was a new thought.

"I believe the money has been there and he has asked your consulate to keep it from you," Atilla said.

"I believe you're right. But why?"

"This is a question. I believe he has some purpose in mind."

"Of course. No one does anything without a reason."

"Perhaps," Atilla suggested, "he is only trying to protect you."

"Then why can't he tell me what it is? I'm not a child. I can accept legitimate reasons. Just tell them to me."

"In any case," she commented, "you have gotten your money now."

"Yes, but only after the meeting—after I'd agreed to stay in Izmir for the next trial date. That's what he was waiting for."

"It is so," she agreed.

"It's as if he didn't want me to go home. Yet, I am told that's why he's here. To get me home quickly and safely."

"Perhaps you must ask him this, yourself."

"I plan to," I said, and told Atilla about the meeting with Gant set for Friday.

"That is good," she said. "It is possible he has not wished to give the true plans with the consulate and myself present."

The more I thought about this conundrum in the days before we were to meet, the more anxious I became. Leaning on Gant's promise to rescue me, I was making little effort to help myself. His presence in Turkey was costing me dearly, not only in terms of money. While I waited for him to move, the hours and days of my life were spilling into a room in the Efes Hotel and trickling onto the streets of Izmir.

His perplexing character and suspect motives had raised doubts so serious, I was edging close to disbelief in his trustworthiness. If Gant was to overcome my misgivings, he would have to be "forthcoming." Anxiously I waited for Friday.

I chose to walk back to the hotel, a trip of about two miles, wearing blisters on both heels from the new shoes. Ducking into the hair salon for women, which was empty of customers and managed by a woman who spoke English well, I was given an immediate appointment. Selecting from a chart, I allowed the male beautician to dye my hair to match the color of my eyebrows—a change for me—and to exercise his own taste in creating a new styling. For the passport photos I would take tomorrow afternoon, I wanted to look unlike the woman whose departure from Turkey might be restricted.

A stranger stared at me from the mirror and I wondered what Bonnie Boyle, my beautician back home, would say when she saw this head.

Afterward, feeling like a stranger to myself, I barely had the time to bathe and dress in the new skirt and matching blouse before Atilla and Geuldal arrived. They acknowledged my hair with faint comment, but my "elegant" appearance drew raves from both.

The evening was a success. Makbule's husband was as attractive and easy to be with as she, and although we had no single common language in which to converse, because we were nice people meeting as friends, it didn't seem to make a difference. It was obvious my guests were enjoying themselves since they lingered at the table until well past eleven, a time when I was just barely awake and starting to feel ill.

I woke in the morning with a throat that scratched, a nose that ran, and a raspy voice, but unwilling to miss the trip, I dressed and waited to be picked up, carrying a good supply of tissues.

The morning was overcast and cool. A day to match my mood, I thought, climbing into Nancy's green Renault.

A tall, slender woman, she was totally at ease in traffic at the wheel of her Turkish-built car. Because her husband was a NATO officer, Nancy had lived most of her married life in exotic countries where she had learned to adapt. Three of her four children had been born far from home. To me she was courageous, charming, and had an easy, unassuming manner. Living in

Izmir for almost five years had given her time to explore the
countryside. She was gracious in sharing what she knew, pointing out many sights of interest along the way.

Her children were away at boarding schools in England.

"We 'Brits' haven't the resources your American air force
families have here, no base exchange nor English schools, but we
get along. I've come to enjoy Turkey. The people are grand,"
she said.

There were two other women driving with us: another British NATO wife and her American friend on a visit. Following
behind Nancy, in a large Chevrolet driven by an air force
officer's wife, were four more.

The drive took nearly two hours, during which the women
expressed an interest in my "dreadful" experience. I was shy
and too embarrassed to talk about it so their concern expressed
itself in tales about the problems other tourists had encountered
in Turkey. It was frightening but at the same time it was good
to learn that my arrest was not unique.

They told of an Italian who, on a tour of Ephesus two
months before, picked up a small piece of brick from the ground.
Hearing the hapless man was still in Buja waiting for a trial, I
wondered if he was the reason Ludan had called the Italian
consular officer the day after I was detained.

There were other stories: of two American sailors, both of
whom, Nancy said, had been "a bit tiddly, you know." One,
climbing the statue in the plaza, took a seat on the horse behind
Atatürk, inadvertently breaking a bit of the stirrup. The other
had "pissed" on the Turkish flag. Both thrown into prison for
insulting the Turkish state, they were in time set free when
their lawyer claimed the first "had admired Atatürk so much he
wanted to be near him," and the second "thought he was pissing
on the Russian flag—they do look a lot alike."*

Nancy related two incidents that couldn't be laughed off.
During the time I was in Buja a man was arrested for smuggling
a full crate of antiquities, and I saw there was good reason for

*Both flags have a white crescent on a red field. But the persuasive part of
the argument rests upon the Turks' intense dislike for Russia.

the Turks' anger. The smuggler, in this instance, was a professor of archeology at a German university.

It was the last story they told that chilled my blood. Fishing in a rented boat, a German tourist strayed into restricted waters. A Turkish gunboat approached and, calling over a bullhorn, ordered him away. When the man failed to respond, the gun crew fired on him before learning that, not knowing Turkish, he had not understood the command. It was too late when they uncovered this fact. The German was dead.

And my family wanted me to flee Turkey—alone in a rented boat!

I must have seemed strange to the women with whom I walked the outdoor market and lunched that day. Preoccupied with an irrational fear of being recognized and arrested, nursing the start of a cold, I was silent and unresponsive, a quiet ghost wanting to seem invisible.

We lunched by the sea, although it was too cold to eat outdoors, and afterward drove back to town. Arriving there at 2:30, Nancy dropped me at the photographer where I sat for the photo and, after agreeing to pick the prints up the next day, walked back to the hotel.

Alone, I thought about something Nancy told me that shed light on Charnaud and his puzzling attitude.

"Poor Charnaud," she had said after I complained of his reluctance to testify, "he's a Levantine, you know. The government just confiscated half of his garden to widen the road."

I was ignorant about Levantines and about how the Turks dealt with "aliens" in their midst. But Nancy explained.

The Levantines were merchant families that left Europe to live as traders around the Mediterranean. Charnaud's family came from England two hundred years ago, planting roots deep in Izmir where they flourished and acquired wealth but never gave up their British citizenship. Over eight generations, every pregnant wife was sent back home so her child could be born on British soil. Charnaud, who had never lived in England, carried a British passport.

The present government of Turkey was tougher than the last and, resenting this tangible lack of commitment to the land in which they were flourishing, it was starting to turn the screws on its Levantine residents.

While I sympathized with Charnaud, I still didn't see, if justice in Turkey was as enlightened as Atilla said, how testifying for me could hurt him.

I was reading in my room when Atilla, tired by her day and obligated to give a speech later that night, knocked at the door. The passport had been returned!

After ordering sandwiches for our dinner and inviting Atilla to rest on my bed, I examined the document I would never again take for granted.

Turning the pages, there was nothing I was looking for. This was a symbolic stroking designed to make me know it was mine. Just holding it enflamed my belief that the court would sanction my departure from Turkey.

When I came to the page that contained the official stamp of entry, marked clearly "Alanya," there was another symbol saying "Izmir," which had been overstamped with a red bar. Carefully printed in ink beneath it were Turkish words I didn't understand. Eager to know what they said, I gave the passport to Atilla.

Her face, which I had learned to read, tightened as she studied it. Before she spoke I was tensed for a blow.

"It says, 'The bearer has been detained and is to be held for trial,'" she said. "I am sorry, Gene, it is not a help to you that your passport has been returned."

My disappointment was like acid corroding my spirit. I was back to square one. No meaning was to be inferred by the court's accession: the passport was useless, and to have returned it held the suggestion of a sneer.

Now I was glad I'd not waited to start the process for another. In the morning I would take the completed application to the consulate; at three I would pick up the photos. I wanted a valid passport. By Friday I'd have it.

After Atilla left I got into bed. My cold had spread from my nose to my chest; my head and my body ached. It had been foolish of me to leave the hotel today, and I hoped for a good night's sleep that would set me right. But a series of what I can only entitle "controlled-panic calls" from the family made things worse.

It was Jim, keeping his promise to find out about the passport, who spread the alarm and brought me to tears. When I told him I'd agreed to stay until after the next hearing, his impatience flared. "Maybe you just don't want to come home," he barked. What answer was there to so irrational an accusation? There was nothing I wanted more.

Richard and Naomi were unhappy. Each handled it a different way. Richard asked questions, evaluating the facts I gave him, and bolstered my resolves with ideas and optimism. Naomi commiserated.

After she hung up, I realized that as much as Richard gave me strength, Naomi's warm-water acceptance bath wasn't good for me. As much as I loved her and appreciated the daily calls, they were excessive and debilitating, most often leaving me weak, in tears, and feeling sorry for myself. It was with mixed feelings I remembered her offer to keep me company in Izmir.

My troubled sleep didn't refresh me. Tossing about, restlessly, throughout the night, I awoke in the morning feverish, achy, and feeling very ill.

I have always been unwilling to give in to sickness or pain, even at home where I am safe and everything can be put off to another day. Feelings of anxiety and fear about my circumstances created a terrible urgency, propelling me to grasp at every straw and hold tight, not daring to let go.

Taking the papers to the consulate according to plan, I came straight back to bed where I fretted, depressed by my isolation. I had to pretend I was well so I could be with people. By acting as if I were well, I told myself, I will be well—but it wouldn't hurt if I had something with which I could dose myself.

I called Nancy at home. She came with a bottle of English cough syrup and a dose of TLC.

At three she drove me to the photographer and brought me back to rest, staying with me until it was time to dress for the meeting with Aaron Emile.

I was red-nosed and coughing, but ready when he called from the lobby promptly at 5:00. We met in the lounge a few minutes later.

Close up, Emile looked less like Gary Cooper, although he had the same lanky build. His Semitic features, framed by a lush growth of coarse, gray hair, reminded me of a well-groomed, older Barry Manilow. It was the cocktail hour but we ordered tea, sharing a mutual dislike for alcohol that gave us a common ground. Venturing slowly into discovery, he asked about my life at home and told me about his.

Makbule had been right. Aaron, as he asked to be called, made his home in New Orleans but he had business interests that took him to many parts of the United States and Europe. He was in the "shmatte business," he said, using the insiders' term for clothing manufacture. His garments, I surmised, were far from "shmattes," a word in Yiddish meaning rags: they were made from the finest grades of leather.

"The Turks," he explained, "tan wonderful quality leathers and the cost of labor is favorable. I provide the designs, ship in the patterns and dyes, and make a nuisance of myself by poking my nose into everybody's business."

I liked his light touch—A successful businessman who didn't take himself seriously.

"Are you a designer?" I asked, fascinated by the combination of financial acumen and creative talent.

"Alas, no. I have only a business head. Your father, on the other hand, seems to have had the abilities of both. I have seen the museum in Washington and admire him very much."

Talk of my father made me uneasy. I didn't want to be given friendship based on that association alone.

"Do you contract the name designers to create your styles?" I asked, shifting the conversation back to Emile.

"No. I employ a number of fine designers who work for my company exclusively. Three, in fact, are in Turkey right now. You see," he explained, "although I make as many as six trips to Turkey a year—we have three plants making our designs—twice a year I bring the designers to work the bugs out of the production before we turn out too many coats with wrinkles and sagging pockets."

"How wonderful to be in a business that allows you to travel," I said with envy.

"Not so wonderful if you do it all the time," he answered with a smile, "One becomes tired of hotels and restaurants and would be happier to stay home and enjoy family life."

"So," I asked, "how long must you be away from home this time?"

"Nearly a month in all," he said sadly, "We go from Turkey

on the fifteenth to Frankfurt for an important show on the seventeenth. When the staff is with me, we spend the better part of a week in each plant. Istanbul, we are done with. When we leave Izmir we fly to Ankara and from there to Germany. In fact," he said, taking a pocket calendar from the inside of his suit jacket, "it has been on my mind to ask you to dinner while I am still in Izmir."

"I would like that very much," I said.

"So, how's Wednesday? I leave the following morning."

Believing I would be feeling myself again by then, I accepted.

"I keep a car in Izmir," he said. "I'll call the hotel before I pick you up."

"Thank you so much for your interest," I said when we parted. "It's good to be with someone from home."

Aaron was so normal, his concerns so familiarly American, because of his visit I felt less depressed. And he satisfied my curiosity as to how he had come to attend my trial by saying he'd heard about my plight during a routine visit to the consulate and wanted to show some support for an American, alone and beleaguered, in a country he knew so well. Nee was right. Americans *are* wonderful!

Friday morning I dragged myself out of bed drained of real energy, motivated solely by tensions. The two goals I'd set for myself induced opposite kinds of stress. My brief business at the consulate stimulated positive excitement, but distrusting Gant, the anticipation of seeing him made me anxious.

Somewhere, hidden by a weakness that enshrouded me in a cloak of invalidism, I knew no matter the number of people who offered help—free of charge or for a fee—it was I who had the basic responsibility for my life. *I* had to assess the options available. *I* had to choose whom to believe and whom to follow. Having invested all of my hope in Gant, what I feared was that he would let me down.

After going to the consulate I waited for him in the plaza beneath the hooves of Atatürk's horse. The photos were now safely in Makbule's hands, and though she was vague about when the passport would be ready, I felt relieved just knowing I'd completed my part.

Gant came striding toward me, and studying his lumbering

walk, I decided he was either a powerful man or a man pretending to be powerful. His kiss on the cheek was perfunctory, lacking affection. I felt none for him. At my suggestion, we set off on a walk up the Atatürk Caddasi beside the gray, white-capped waters of the bay. We'd spent some minutes in small talk, when Gant fired the first shot.

"By the way, Gene," he announced, "I'm flying to New York tomorrow morning."

"Back to the States?"

"Yes. Something's come up in the office. No one else can take care of it."

"Where does that leave me?" I asked.

"Just where you've been," he said. "You're not going anywhere and I'll be back in time for the trial at the end of the month."

"I see," I said. "Then your plans for me have progressed no further. . . ."

"My plans are exactly as I've told you they were," he interrupted. "Nothing's changed."

"Your plans are still a secret from me."

"No one's keeping secrets from you, my dear. I have my people considering alternatives whether I'm here or not."

"What are these 'alternatives'?" I asked, quietly.

"We want to get you home safe and sound and I'm working damned hard to see that you do, with the help of some of the top people in Turkey."

"I want to go home now," I said in a voice that was tight with tears.

"My friends don't think that's a good idea."

"But my family who hired you . . ."

"I don't care what your family has told you," he said. "What these Turks think is more important than what your family thinks, believe me. Sure they want you home, we all want to see you get home, but what can your family do for you in Turkey? Who do they have pull with?"

I had no answer for that and looked at the bay, remembering a time when its importance relied solely on being the place from which the *Sea Princess* was to sail to the next port.

"I have everything together for the new passport," I volunteered.

"Yes," he said, "I know. You brought the photos in this morning."

"How do you know?"

"I was there, myself." He waited before continuing, "I'm afraid your expectation isn't going to work out."

"What do you mean?"

"They say they can't give you a passport without Ludan. You're going to have to wait until he gets back. Something about . . . procedure . . . legality. Ludan's the expert. He's the only one who knows."

"I can't get my passport," I said, close to tears.

"That's what they say."

He stopped walking and gave me a hard look.

"Now I don't want you pulling any stupid stunts while I'm gone."

I was openly crying now.

"I'm not as brave as you think," I said.

My tears gave him confidence.

"Listen, little lady," he said with more sympathy than he had previously shown, "why don't you just relax and enjoy your stay since you're going to be here awhile. Maybe one of your sisters can come down and keep you company. See the sights. Have you been to Ephesus?"

"I saw it," I said, and with a low moan, added, "what your 'contacts' want is more important to you than what I want."

"Of course," he said. "You're not in a position to evaluate the relative importance of these issues. All you know is that you want to go home."

In the silence that followed, I turned and began walking, slowly, back to the plaza. I was beaten. He was right. What did I know?

Walking beside me, Gant sighed.

"This damned case of yours is the most difficult I've had to deal with in a long time."

"Why?" I asked, "because my family's well known?"

"Because . . ." he hesitated, ". . . you're not the easiest woman to get along with, you know."

I was defenseless, weeping again with hurt, believing the accusation unfair. Should the doctor blame his patient for not getting well? I said nothing.

Gant walked with me to the hotel steps and said good-by.

"Well, I wish you luck, Gene. Try to relax," he said, stooping to kiss me on the cheek. "Everything's going to be okay. So you won't be home for Thanksgiving. Think about it, Christmas is only two months away. You're sure to be home by then."

Gant wouldn't be missing Thanksgiving with his family, I told myself, resentfully. "Good-by Mr. Gant," I said aloud, "have a safe trip home."

Agonizing in my room, I needed someone to talk to, but Atilla was not available. She had excused herself between now and Tuesday as the pace of campaigning stepped up in the last days before the election. I respected her right to have a life other than the part she shared with me.

Gene Nee had been faithful in calling and dropping by. Failing in his mission to move me into the Kordon, he hadn't given up suggesting cheaper hotels and imaginative escape plots. He'd been kindness itself, bringing me a book called *When Bad Things Happen to Good People* and discussing with me, after I'd read it, how its meaning could be used to accept the trauma I'd suffered.*

But I didn't know how to reach Gene and felt too fragile to be bruted about by his vigor.

The truth was I was too depressed and too ill to reach out to anyone. No one, I believed, not Nancy—not even a priest—wants to listen to someone complain all the time. They would reject me for whining, abandon me; I would be more alone than I already was.

Repressing my feelings, I spent two and a half days in the hotel room reading. Except for telephone calls, I spoke to no one

---

*Rabbi Harold S. Kushner, New York: Schocken Books, 1981. Nee's inscription inside, written in a bold, erratic hand, said:

To Jean LePere

FROM

Fr. Nee

4 Nov. 1983

The Choice is Yours =

You FIGHT *OR*

ROT in this Life

Courage versus Cynicism

FAITH versus FEAR

except the maid who came every day and the waiters who brought the trays.

There were two significant developments in the condition of my health over that weekend although, with my usual "it's not there if I don't acknowledge it" attitude, I didn't recognize their meaning until later. At the time I attributed both to my terrible cold and tried to be grateful my body had waited until I was out of prison to break down. Food, for one, had become a problem.

Meals eaten in the room—there had been many since living at the Efes—had become ritualized once I learned what the kitchen prepared well. For breakfast I ordered *börek* (the flaky triangular cakes) and toast, served with good Turkish butter and marmalade. I drank black coffee—American style—made from powder. Lunch was the main meal of the day when I had a sandwich that wasn't very good but better than the hotel's pretentious attempts at broiled meat. Turkish food, made well, would have been my preference but was seldom available. Typically, dinner consisted of baklava and another pot of coffee.

The thought of these foods made me, literally, gag, but belonging to the school that says "eat, you need your strength to get better," I wracked my brain thinking of something I could swallow and keep down. This from the woman with the cast-iron stomach!

Boiled eggs were the solution. I had them for breakfast and lunch. Boiled potatoes (the kitchen knew nothing of baked) became standard dinner fare. No bread, no butter, not even tea. Water, eggs, and dry potatoes. Over that weekend and for days afterward, eggs and potatoes were all I could swallow. So much for food.

The second symptom was a manifestation of tears.

The best Turkish hotel room lacks amenities we, at home, take for granted. Don't expect TV; you'll be disappointed. There *was* a radio with three stations, two of which broadcast in Turkish. The third played continuous music from a tape that repeated itself, like Muzak, every two hours or so. Reading was my major distraction, and that weekend I began a new paperback of *At Dawn We Slept*, which exposed the Japanese planning to bomb Pearl Harbor while the American navy looked the other way. The radio was tuned to "Muzak," playing a low and hard-to-hear accompaniment of contemporary background music.

The story held me. I was barely fifteen when the events detailed took place, when I learned of the bombing on December 7, 1941, in the company of my friends at an afternoon dance at a temple in Great Neck and, shocked as only the innocent can be, wept in anticipation of the blood to be shed.

No longer an innocent or afraid of the Japanese "threat," I could not explain to myself why, as I was reading, I was crying as well.

My thoughts, which I believed were in Hawaii, circa 1941, didn't prevent the pain, repressed in 1983, from oozing out of my unconscious and dripping onto the pages.

Monday, frantic and feeling desperate, I called the consulate and, crying uncontrollably, begged Nalle for an appointment. Alarmed, he offered to come to the hotel, but the angst that drove me couldn't wait. Dressed and waiting two hours until the consulate opened, without any idea of what I wanted to tell him, I said I'd come right over.

In his office, blind to my surroundings, deafened by raw pain, I exposed my grief without reserve, naked and alone in front of Nalle. Only by hearing my voice and the torrent of words that spilled into the room, did I get in touch with the feelings I'd been pushing down.

"I don't know what's wrong with me," I began in a flood of tears. "I'm crying all the time and can't stop . . . can't eat . . . no Turkish food . . . been living on eggs . . . not sleeping . . . can't concentrate . . . try to read . . . crying. . . . Can't wear the Turkish clothes . . . make me sick. . . . It's not like me, this crying . . . food . . . and Friday, Gant tells me you can't give me a passport. . . ."

"That's not true," Nalle interrupted, "we can give you a new passport," thereby telling me Gant had lied.

Sobbing afresh, all the resentments poured out.

"How could he treat me that way? I could understand the Turks treating me like a criminal, a nonperson. I could handle that. But Gant, my own countryman, to treat me as if—as if I had no feelings—like an object, a *thing!* He said I couldn't get money; you had none. When I said I'd stay 'til the trial, suddenly there was money. I'm a *person,* I have *feelings.* I've tried to cooperate but I can't be brave *all* the time. I need to go home, I need thyroid. I can't stay in Turkey *forever.*

For many minutes—a very long time it seemed to me—the
pain spilled itself into the room: hurt, anger, despair, humiliation, and an unwillingness to suffer any more. The glass armature, so strong yet so fragile, had shattered under the blows of
Gant's contempt and treachery. Without it I collapsed, empty
of will, bleeding from the shards.

Nalle sat quietly listening to the crying and repetition until
the stream slowed to a trickle, then took charge.

"I don't know why Ed told you we couldn't prepare a new
passport," he said, "but we can and we will. About the thyroid,
I'll make an appointment for you at the [air force] clinic and call
you at the hotel to let you know when it is."

He reached for a pad and wrote something down.

"This is the name of a friend of mine I'd like you to see," he
said, handing it to me. "She's a neurologist, a Turk who speaks
English."

I looked at the name, Ture Tuncbay, and grimaced.

"Her name is pronounced Turay Tunchbye," he said, helpfully. "I think you should see her. I'll call her now for an appointment."

"I will see her," I said. "I will see anyone. I can't stand
feeling like this."

Everything was arranged quickly, and I walked back to the
hotel wearing sunglasses, embarrassed to be seen with red, puffy
eyes. The outpouring had brought some relief although the
depression had not lifted. My appointment with Nalle's doctor
was for tomorrow morning.

Calling her a neurologist didn't fool me. Dr. Tunchbye was
a "shrink" but that was okay with me. I had no hang-ups about
psychology or psychiatry, and realizing Nalle's genuine alarm
over my condition, I wondered if he was afraid I might commit
suicide.

Suicide was not anywhere in my mind.

How often we can be of two minds at the same time. One,
an emotional self, in my case, grieving and depressed; the second, an observer who sees and assesses from a rational, emotion-
less position outside. My second self was germinating an idea:
suppose the Turkish doctor believed that it was dangerous to my
health to remain in Turkey? Then, might not the Turks join in

an effort to send me home? But that was only a tangential thought in progress. Getting home was the main theme.

The time was past when I would depend on anyone or anything but myself to get me home. I was taking charge of my own case. This decision, made at a time when to others I appeared weakest, was a turning point, giving me hope and renewing my inner strength.

My mood hadn't lifted. People who visited or called that Monday were treated to more of the emotional purging. Nancy was sympathetic over the phone but was too busy to see me until Wednesday. There was a new pizza place she thought was not bad. We made a date for lunch.

Gene Nee perceived my mood as one of defeat and stepped up his pep talks accordingly. The third time he said, "Ye can't give up, Gene, it's fightin' back you gotta do," I answered sharply, "What do you think I'm doing? I *am* fighting back."

Nalle called to say a Doctor Knox would see me on Wednesday at the clinic at two, but I thought Wednesday too crowded already—lunch with Nancy, dinner with Emile. It was postponed until Thursday afternoon. An American doctor, it occurred to me, if I were still in the same mood then, might add his weight to Tunchbye's in arguing for my release. But these were things I couldn't count on. I had to find a more certain way.

Dr. Tunchbye's office was in a modern building on the Atatürk Caddasi. The lobby beyond the dusty-glassed front entrance was decorated with four potted trees. Makbule, whom Nalle had sent to help, directed me up a few marble stairs to an upper hall and through a door to the right into a waiting room filled with patients and their families. It was good Makbule was there, since the receptionist, a young Turkish woman, spoke no English, and I had company during the half-hour delay until the doctor saw me.

Having heard some frightening stories about harsh penalties accruing from insults against the Turkish State, I worried that I couldn't be frank. Makbule assured me that communications with doctors in Turkey were permissibly confidential, just as they were at home.

Turay Tunchbye was a beautiful woman, professionally

cool but kind. She had been trained in the United States, she said in good English. A few questions later I was sobbing the story I'd given Nalle. After testing my hearing with a tuning fork and my reflexes with a hammer, she pronounced me in good neurological health—if a bit jumpy—and my condition a severe depression of psychological origin. Gently she probed around the question of self-harm, and though I assured her I was not suicidal, I saw Dr. Tunchbye wasn't convinced.

Making no attempt to treat the cause, she wrote two prescriptions for tranquilizers to alleviate the symptoms, dismissing the Valium I already had as "too strong." I was to call her Wednesday, after taking the medication as directed for one day, to report how I was feeling, and see her again Friday morning. Her fee for a forty-five-minute session, which I paid on the spot, was 7,000 Turkish lira—$28.

Stopping only to have the prescriptions filled at a pharmacy ($1.50 for two vials of 100 tablets each!), I went directly to the hotel, bewildered by a mentality that gives potent drugs to a patient thought to be suicidal.

That afternoon I took the drug prescribed. It made me less tense, if not less depressed. Before going to bed I took a different pill, which put me into a nightmarish sleep from which I awoke stupified. When I checked in with her before meeting Nancy for lunch, I'd already decided to forgo Dr. Tunchbye's drugs and lied to her over the phone.

She was writing a letter, she said, to the court, telling them that I had to be sent home. This declaration did more for relieving my depression than a whole arsenal of tranquilizers.

In my exploration of possible escapes, there was something I remembered Nancy talking about in the car on the way to Ayvalik. Eagerly anticipating the chance to approach her on the walk to the restaurant, I was also fretful about how British Catholic Nancy might view such unorthodoxy. I went about it as carefully as I could.

"There's something I have to ask you," I said, "which I hope you won't find offensive."

"Ask away," she invited.

"It's a bit irregular. I don't want to compromise you in any way." I hesitated. "All I ask is that if you can't help me on this, please don't tell anyone what I've said."

"I can promise that," she said.

"Well." I stalled, "in the car last week you mentioned a man who had a boat. Something about him bringing electronic equipment in from Greece."

"Yes," she interrupted, "I know who you're talking about."

"Do you think he might be willing to take me to Greece?" I blurted. "Or maybe if he won't do it, might he know someone who would?"

"That's a tough one," she said, not the least bit shocked. "I can ask him for you, if you like."

I knew I could trust her not to expose me but never had I anticipated she would join in the conspiracy.

"Oh, God, Nancy, it's such a relief to be able to talk to someone about this."

"I wouldn't count on it, you know."

"Oh, I'm not," I quickly denied. "It's the least favorite of possibilities. The story about the German tourist getting shot was a real turnoff, but I'm not sure what else I could do. The problem is whether my name is on some list at the ports and borders."

"You could cross one of the small, remote border posts by car," she said, getting into the spirit of things. "They are rather lax, you know. I've driven through myself, many times."

"Do you think I could?"

"Well, it's always risky, I suppose, but that would be your best chance."

"I guess I could rent a car." I said, thinking aloud.

"Do you know if your name is at the ports?" she asked.

"I don't, but I assume it must be."

"I think you should try to find out."

"Yes," I said, wondering how to go about it.

We were approaching the restaurant, where it wasn't safe to continue the conversation.

"Then you'll check on the boat?" I asked.

"I happen to know the man's away at the moment," she answered.

"Well, maybe you'd better wait a bit anyway. As I said, the boat is a last resort. If I can find a safer way I prefer it."

"Then I won't say anything until you say I should."

"Good," I said, "good."

We entered a small, square, crowded-to-the-rafters room filled with talking diners. Still unable to swallow Turkish food, I'd agreed to try the pizza place, hoping, if skeptical, that the Turks could prepare Italian food resembling the real thing better than they did American.

Nancy, with her wonderful vocabulary of Turkish words, helped me to order from a menu that listed thirty combinations, and when they came, the pizzas—small round portions served on small round individual boards—were good.

Afterward, hearing I was due at the American clinic the next day, Nancy walked with me to the hotel taking a roundabout route, pointing out the hospital building and a bookstore that carried American magazines and paperbacks.

We reentered the Efes from the rear gardens, giving me a chance to see close up, the Hamam, the Turkish bath. Now I understood why the tub at the Caravanserie in Kusadasi was square and deep with a seat, instead of like the ones we have in America. Turks, like many other people around the world, very sensibly have no wish to lie in a tubful of water where dirt scrubbed off the body stays afloat. After washing, they rinse the soap and dirt down the drain. Sensible or not, I preferred my tub at the Efes and longed to use my own at home.

The rest of the afternoon I set my mind to the task of preparing for an authorized departure. There were many things I needed to know before I chose the actual route to take.

First, of course, was learning more about border lists and where my name might be known. Second, whatever route I chose—excepting escape by water to Greece—my passport had to be valid in every particular. The old one had an entry stamp but couldn't be used. A new one, I assumed, would also need an entry stamp. How else did I represent my being in Turkey as legal?

By what means checks of the lists were made at the border was a fine point, but not to be overlooked. If I could fly out of Turkey in an international carrier, how much safer I'd feel. Where would I get the strength—or the courage—to drive myself out? I was scared every time I stepped into the streets of Izmir. Anyway, I didn't have an international driver's license. My God, I didn't even have my New York State license! It was still on the boat.

No, unless I could get someone to drive me—I'd never ask Nancy—a departure from a remote border post wasn't feasible —unless I traveled by bus.

Carrying an American Express card gave me the means to pay air fare and hotel bills without using cash, but I'd have to get some dollars from the consulate. I wouldn't feel right without them. Now, what excuse could I use to ask for them? I'd find one. Maybe the consulate wouldn't care, now that Gant—that bastard who cut me off from my money—was gone, how much money I asked for or why.

Thinking of Gant, I hoped Richard would call. Only to Richard would I vent my fury. Gant was going to be fired and the conniving prick didn't even know it. Jim was too hot-tempered for this assignment. Richard would fire him with style.

Aaron called, as promised, and picked me up at 7:00 driving a navy blue Renault. The only one assembled in Turkey, it was the foreign car most often seen on the roads.

"I have a place in mind," he said, as we drove away from the hotel, "that prepares chicken very well. If you like chicken, that's where I'll take you."

"Chicken's my favorite food," I answered. "You couldn't have made a better choice."

We took the road south from Izmir, passing Atilla's apartment, which I tried to identify in the dark without success. The election was over but I had no way of knowing which party had succeeded in garnering most votes. I hoped, for the sake of her hard work, Atilla's party had won.

"Do you know the results of the election?" I asked Aaron, believing his interests in Turkey would have motivated him to find out.

Giving a low chuckle, he answered, "The results haven't pleased the government in power. Their party—I believe your attorney is a member—has made a poor showing, and the party which won, the most liberal of the three that ran, has done so by a large majority."

"I don't know the name of Mrs. Akat's party," I said, but I'm happy to learn there will be changes."

"She wears a button in her lapel," he said. "I saw it not long ago when we met at the courthouse. In any case, I don't look for a lot of quick changes but in time this will be good for my business. The new president is a man interested in economic growth and I believe he will encourage international trade and investment."

"I'm surprised the electorate had the courage to voice opposition to the military men in power," I said.

"There is an irony here that I find humorous. You know the people were forced to vote or be penalized by a fine of 2,500 lira."

"Ten dollars doesn't seem much to us, but I know from being in prison, ten dollars is a small fortune to most Turks."

"Absolutely," Aaron agreed, changing the subject to my imprisonment, which neither he nor I had mentioned in our first meeting.

"Are you discovering a resolution to your difficulties with the Turks?" he asked, couching his curiosity in the language of diplomats.

"No resolution," I said, grimly, "and there's a lot I need to know before I can make any decisions about what to do."

"If you feel like asking me some questions, perhaps I can help you think it through," he offered, opening the door to confidences I was reluctant to burden him with.

"Perhaps you could give me answers to some of the technical questions," I said carefully. As with Nancy, caution guided me. I didn't want to get anyone in trouble.

"I hope I will have the answers," he replied, "but, perhaps we should wait until we are seated. The restaurant is just ahead."

The road was covered by low-hanging branches, but through the trees a clear night and full moon gave light to the highway ahead.

"There," he pointed, "do you see the neon sign?"

I looked through the windshield, following his finger. To the left in the distance, growing clearer as we covered the remaining fifty yards, I saw a chicken, brightly outlined in yellow. In glowing red beneath it, was some Turkish writing.

"The sign says," Aaron translated with a laugh, " 'Finger-lickin' Good' "

"The Americans have left their imprint on the world," I commented, joining my laughter with his.

The restaurant was large: a good place to hold a barn dance. And such an event, I thought, wouldn't be out of place here. The decor was rustic: checkered tablecloths covered comfortably large, square tables placed far enough from each other to ensure privacy. We were the only patrons in this dining room in a seaside village abandoned in winter.

Aaron ordered for both of us, now comfortable on high-backed, rush-seated chairs, a salad and broiled chicken, which came with crisp, hand-cut, golden-brown, beautiful French fries. The food, as predicted, was delicious.

"Now," Aaron said, returning to unfinished business, "what can I help you with?"

"What do you know about passports?" I asked.

"Only that we must have them," he smiled.

"The passport with which I entered Turkey bears an entry stamp but cannot be used for departure from Turkey since the Turks have written a memo that says I am being detained for a trial."

"I see. That is too bad."

"Yes," I said, "but the consulate will issue me a new passport. The problem is, how do I get a valid entry stamp to prove I'm not a spy who sneaked in over the border?"

"You are in luck," he said, smiling again. "This question I can answer since I lost mine three years ago and had to go through the process of obtaining a new one."

He paused to take a bite of chicken.

"First you must have a letter prepared, of course, in Turkish, which says you are an American who has received a replacement passport and so on, that you have entered Turkey on such-and-such a date, at so-and-so port."

"And this letter? What do I do with it?"

"This you take to the port where you entered—Alanya, correct?"

I nodded.

"The letter goes first to the chief of police and then the mayor of the town. These officials verify that the date of entry and name coincide in their records. They then validate the letter which is given, together with the new passport, to the control at the border when you leave."

"That seems doable," I said, relieved.

"Yes," he agreed, "it is easy, except that Alanya is a long way off—a drive, perhaps, of ten or more hours."

"Could I mail it to Alanya?" I asked, having no timetable for a departure.

"Oh, yes," he said, "that you may do."

"Good," I said, thinking how to use this important information.

"Is that all?" Aaron asked, enjoying his role as answer man.

"No," I said, slowly. "There are other questions about the border posts—the control."

"Okay, shoot."

"Can I assume a list is maintained at each port containing names of people restrained from leaving Turkey?"

"You may assume that."

"May I also assume my name is already on this list, at least in Izmir, both at the dock and the airport."

"That," he said, "should be a given, although there are no flights from Izmir directly out of the country. All flights to Europe, and elsewhere, leave from Istanbul or Ankara."

"Well," I said, "there is no restriction against my travel anywhere in Turkey."

"No," he said, "I heard the judge's order, myself, at the trial."

"So, should I wish to fly home, I must leave either from Istanbul or Ankara, is that right?"

"I would think so," he agreed.

"So the proper question is: how long can it take an order of the Izmir court, restricting my travel outside of Turkey, to get to these cities?"

"This," he said, gravely, "I don't know, but you *must* find it out. I can tell you though," he said, volunteering helpfully, "Istanbul airport is now equipped with computers. The chances are they already have your name."

"And Ankara?" I asked.

"They have no computers, but whether they have your name, I don't know."

"Can you find out?" I asked, holding his eyes.

He looked away before answering. "Perhaps," he said. "I will try."

"I would be so grateful."

"When I am in Ankara, I will ask a friend. If I am able to learn what you want to know, I'll call you."

"Oh, Aaron, it won't cause you any trouble, will it?"

"No. It will cause no 'trouble.' "

We ate without speaking for several minutes; then Aaron returned to the same subject.

"Have we exhausted your questions?" he asked.

"Only one more," I said.

"I hope this is an easy one."

"I think you'll think it is," I said, smiling. "A travel agent in Izmir. Can you recommend one I can rely on?"

"You are right. That is the easiest of questions. On the First Kordon you can find the Pan Am office and next door to the Efes is a reliable travel agent. I use both."

"Then, I release you," I said. "The questions are finished—until I think of another."

The remainder of the evening was devoted to talk about New York, a city Aaron knew well, and our respective families. Aaron's wife was asthmatic and lonely, his children grown and married. There were five grandchildren, whom he obviously adored, and another on the way. A comfortable man to be with, Aaron Emile had given me an enjoyable evening.

A refined gentleman, he brought me into the lobby of the hotel and before leaving restated his promise to call if he was able to learn anything about my status in Ankara.

"I shall speak with you again, in any case," he said, "before flying to Germany. Think about any messages you'd like me to bring back to your worried family."

The long-silent Atilla called the next morning, asking, in a worried voice, if I wanted to speak with her.

"Of course," I exclaimed, "Why not?"

"I have heard of your illness from Mr. Nalle," she said. "I have studied psychology and understand what it is you are going though."

"I always want to talk with you, Atilla," I assured her. "When can we get together?"

"I am very tired," she said, "We are, of course, disappointed in the elections, and now I have learned my mother is ill in Istanbul. I must go there."

"When are you leaving? Will I see you before you go?"

"I cannot get away until next Monday," she replied, "and I

must talk to you now since I cannot leave my cases at the moment.

"I believe you should go home," she continued, "and I would like to have a letter from this Turkish doctor, Tunchbye, to bring to the court asking for permission you shall go home."

"Oh, Atilla," I said, excited, "that would be wonderful."

"Please," she cautioned, "I do not know how the court will think about such things. Today I shall drop in on the prosecutor and see what he believes about it."

"I am to see a doctor at the American clinic today," I volunteered. "I can ask him if he will write a letter to the court also."

"This may help," she said, "but from a Turkish doctor it is more important."

"She told me yesterday on the phone she plans to write a letter."

"It is good. You shall bring it to me on Sunday. If you are well by then and will like to go with me, I like to take you to a very pretty resort not far from Izmir where you will be my guest for dinner."

"Yes, I am well enough. I've missed you, Atilla, and," I said, "since I am to see Dr. Tunchbye Friday morning, I'll ask for the letter and bring it with me."

"Good," Atilla concluded. "I shall pick you up Sunday at one o'clock."

Things seemed to be starting to fall into place, and sensing it, I was in a much better mood when I met Dr. Knox that afternoon.

My experience before this, with the American military establishment, had been restricted to movies, and I assumed this encounter would be formal, but I was wrong. Housed in an old, three-story building on a back street in Alsanjak painted inside a clean white, the clinic was carpeted and quiet. After I gave a corpsman sufficient personal data with which to open a file I hoped would immediately go to dead storage, he took my blood pressure—slightly elevated—and Kirby Knox came out to get me.

We sat, informally, in his small office while he asked a great many questions about my general health and how I'd fared in prison. Without a physical examination he went on to the state of my mind and emotions.

"I'm feeling better, now," I said, "You should have seen me a few days ago. I was a mess."

But Knox, a very young doctor, slender as a piece of spaghetti, wasn't taking my word for it. Getting out a mimeographed form, he asked me to identify which of four answers to each question best reflected my mood of the past several days. "Not just how you feel today," he said, "but how you were feeling since Monday."

Reading the first few questions before I began, I smiled. "I have a good appetite," it said, "1) Always, 2) Most of the time, 3) Not very often, 4) Never; I believe I am attractive, 1) All of the time, 2) Most of . . ."

There were about thirty items in all, most of which were measures of self-esteem, energy, and self-preoccupation. The last question threw me a curve.

"I think about sex . . . ." it asked.

Giving it the first "4" answer I'd been challenged to use, I laughed aloud. If there was one thing I hadn't thought about since arriving in Turkey, it was sex!

"I'm afraid I'm not going to look very depressed today," I apologized, and Knox agreed.

But, after totaling all of the numbers, he told me with mild surprise, "Well, it adds up to twenty-two. You still are somewhat depressed."

"For which I have exellent reason," I said, bitterly.

"For which you have excellent cause," he agreed.

There was nothing more to be done. Amenable to giving me a letter for the court, he went to prepare it while I filled my prescription for thyroid at the clinic pharmacy and waited for him to return.

"I hope you'll come back any time you're depressed," Dr. Kirby said, handing me an envelope. "I honestly feel you are still in danger and should go home if possible."

Promising to return if it seemed necessary, I walked back to the hotel where Nancy, whom I'd called and asked to meet there at 4:00, was waiting.

"I need a letter typed," I said, without preliminaries, "in Turkish."

"Why not in longhand?"

"Not official-looking enough."

"You have it there?"

"No," I said, "I've got to write it first in English."

"Oh," she said, "if you need a Turkish translator, you might try the notaries at the courthouse."

"Not a chance," I said with a meaningful look.

"I see," she said, quietly thinking.

"Don't you know someone less official?"

"I think I can help you," she said at last, and looked at her watch. "Can we go now? It's not far."

"Do we have time to write it out before we go?"

"If we hurry," she said. "Let's go to your room."

With Nancy's help it took only a few minutes to compose a brief letter. Immediately upon finishing, we went out and I was back in the hotel by 5:30 with a good result. Typed on quality bond Nancy thought would pass inspection in Alanya, I had a usable document and was ready to work on the next step—getting it there.

Nancy, my expert on all things Turkish, had made three suggestions: to hire a willing Turk who would ride the bus to Alanya, take care of my business, and return; to allow her to drive the two of us to Alanya; or to hire a car and driver from a tour agency with instructions to the driver to secure the validation.

Unwilling to take advantage of Nancy—two days was a long time for her to leave her husband—I was also uneasy at the thought of being away from my telephone for the same period of time. Thus, one suggestion was eliminated. Of the two that remained, by Nancy's estimate, a bus trip should cost about 3,000 Turkish lira, including fare, a night's lodgings for the messenger, and his fee. A hired car would certainly be more.

Due at the consulate Friday morning to pick up the passport and some money, I decided some time that morning, after the appointment with Dr. Tunchbye (in whom I'd lost all interest excepting the letter she would write for the court), I'd just pop downstairs to the travel agent and see what a car and driver might cost.

Anticipation was beginning to grip me: my mind raced with details that should be arranged. Did I dare have my luggage inspected with the journal in it? How could all the clothes I now owned fit into the small suitcase? When should I go and from which airport? The last I answered without hesitation. There would be no departure without Aaron's information. When could I reasonably expect him to call? Not before tonight, or tomorrow, I thought.

But Gene Nee's calls came frequently. The next time he asked me for breakfast or coffee, I'd give him the journal and the useless passport—also dangerous to have in my possession when fleeing Turkey—to mail home via the APO. I could hardly wait for Friday.

The regular calls from home continued but with the family I dissembled. I did it partly to relieve them of false hopes and myself of the pressure such hopes would place on me. But mostly I kept my plans secret out of a fear of saying over the phone anything that I didn't want a Turkish agent to overhear. Without being "bugged," my phone calls may have been listened to by the English-speaking staff of the hotel under instructions to report suspect conversations to the government that opposed my leaving.

The more I plotted, the more anxious I became. The more anxious I was, the more cautious I grew. As the moment for action grew closer, the fear of alerting the Turks, with their penchant for punitive retaliation, charged me with an energy born of danger.

It was 7:30 Friday morning when Aaron called.

"The weather's clear in Ankara," he said. "Do you understand?"

"I'm glad it's clear," I answered. "I understand."

"Have you thought of anything you want me to tell your family?" he asked.

"Just say you've seen me and I'm well."

"I'll call your sister Naomi from California. I'll be there in two weeks."

"You have the number?"

"I put it in my wallet with my money," he laughed, "where I'm sure not to lose it."

"Thanks for the weather report, Aaron," I said, and trying to fool the spies, added, "I plan to make a visit to Ankara since it's the one city in Turkey I've never seen."

"Got to run, Gene," he replied. "See you in New York soon, I hope."

"I hope so and thanks, for everything."

So the weather was clear in Ankara, I said to myself after replacing the receiver. Good, then I shan't postpone my trip. Who knows, the weather is so changeable in Turkey, it could cloud up if I don't hurry.

I stopped at the agency before going to the consulate, speaking with an unsmiling young woman whose English lacked finesse but whose grasp of bilking tourists had been honed to a fine edge.

"For a car and driver to take you to Alanya will be 100,000 Turkish lira," she said, as if $400 was chopped liver.

Anxious to the point of hand wringing, my indignation gave me courage.

"That's too much," I said, firmly. "Much too much."

"Large car, two day, hotel . . ."

"A large car is not necessary," I said, "nor a hotel for me. I'm not going."

"Small car, 80,000."

"I will think about it," I said, and changed the subject. "I want to make a short trip to Ankara. What can you tell me about flights?"

"Ankara? What day you go?"

I'd given the matter some thought since Aaron's call two hours before. With the weekend ahead, government offices would be closed until Monday morning. The trip to Alanya required two full days, the second being Monday to take care of business and return. I wanted to go as soon after as possible.

"Tuesday morning," I answered.

"Morning?" she repeated, looking at a schedule, "Tuesday morning. Eight o'clock."

"How long is the flight?" I asked.

"How long? It means time?"

"Evet," I said.

Holding up one digit, she answered, "One hour."

I nodded and, trembling with guilty fear, waited ten minutes while she prepared the ticket. Paying in Turkish lira, about twenty dollars, I hesitated before leaving. I would have liked to ask if there were connecting flights the same day to New York but thought better of it. Separating my business made sense: Pan Am could arrange the rest of the trip.

Everything was ready at the consulate when I arrived. All I had to do was sign the passport before Makbule stamped it and put my signature on a receipt for the money. About $5,000 remained in the trust account, which, if I got home safely, I'd ask to be returned. Failing that, I would need the money here in Izmir whether I remained at the Efes or was returned to prison. Pushing visions of failure from my mind, I concentrated on trying to plan for every contingency to improve the chance for success.

When I left, snuggled against the ticket to Ankara inside my purse were $1,000 in American "green" and a beautiful, blue-covered, almost-valid passport. Clutching the bag tightly, I walked to the doctor's office.

Thursday at the clinic my blood pressure had been 127/70. Friday morning, by Dr. Tunchbye's reading, it was 100/60, normal for me. Was it possible that renewed hope, by itself, could compensate for heightened fears and excitement?

Answering her questions, I told Turay Tunchbye what she wanted to hear—that taking her pills resulted in a reduction of all symptoms previously observed—and came away with a handwritten letter to the court containing her diagnosis and recommendation. In the end, if I got out Tuesday, perhaps Atilla could use them to explain my absence.

Concerning the hoped-for escape, it troubled me—the lady who hated giving up control—that I might have to rely on some Turk I'd never met to execute so delicate a mission in Alanya. I was torn between a desire to handle the crucial assignment myself and a preference for hiding in my room at the Efes safely ignorant of the details.

The cost of a driver was outrageous. A man going by bus, someone known to Nancy and chosen for his reliability, seemed safer as well as less expensive. Though she was trying to locate such a man, if I was to leave Tuesday, the messenger must start from Izmir Sunday morning. The decision of whom to send had to be made by Saturday morning.

Impatient to have it settled, I kept myself busy by sorting

through papers and books, removing those I considered too dangerous to carry with me. Gene Nee and I were meeting for breakfast Sunday, when I planned to give him the things to be mailed. There were clothes to be discarded too, but I couldn't part with anything from home; it was the Turkish clothes that meant nothing to me. Filling a plastic sack with sweaters from prison, the blouses and skirt, I decided Nancy should have them to keep or give away.

Saturday morning Nancy called. Unable to find someone she again volunteered to drive but, knowing Sunday and Monday would be my last days in Izmir, I declined. It was decided. I would pay whatever it cost.

Returning to the agency next door, I negotiated with a woman who spoke better English. After explaining precisely what was to be done, we successfully concluded an agreement.

"The driver must be reliable," I demanded.

"We have such a man," I was assured.

"He must leave Sunday morning, sleep overnight, and take care of the business as soon as the offices open. It is absolutely necessary he return Monday night with the letter."

"If he has no difficulties, it will be done."

"He must bring the document to the hotel," I said, "no matter how late he gets back."

"It may be very late," she said. "It is a trip of at least ten hours. If he has some problems . . ."

"He will be driving a reliable car?"

"Yes, madam."

"He should be back by ten or eleven," I said, allowing the morning for the mayor and chief of police.

"Perhaps," she said, "perhaps later."

"I don't care how late it is, even if it's two in the morning. He is to come to the hotel desk. I will leave a message; they will expect him. I will be waiting in the room. They will call me. I will come down."

"If you wish."

"Yes," I said, "this is what I wish."

"You will pay now the 80,000 lira," she said.

"I will pay 70,000 lira only and I will give 40,000 now. The remaining 30,000 I will give the driver when he has brought me the letter."

There was a long, calculating pause before she replied.

"It is agreed," she said, "40,000 now, the balance to the driver.

"Good," I said. Removing Turkish bills from my bag, I gave her four 10,000 lira notes. "I must have this letter before Tuesday morning. It is important. Very important, you understand. Monday night, no matter how late."

The tension I was under must have shown in my face, for the woman volunteered, with some kindness, "I will ask the driver to make a call when he is ready to leave Alanya on Monday."

"Yes," I said, "that is very good. Will you call me when you have heard from him?"

"I will call," she said. "You are at the Efes?"

"The Efes, room 620."

"I will call."

The transaction was completed but still I lingered. Nothing remained to be said, yet I was reluctant to go. Did she understand? Did she know how important this was? I wanted to repeat the instructions one more time.

Recognizing in myself a compulsion, generated by an anxiety that would be assuaged only when I held the validated letter in my hand, I quelled this impulse. It was done. *I* had done everything I knew to do. Somehow I'd live with the doubts and anxieties until Monday night.

Don't think about it.

From the Efes to the Pan Am office was a walk of six blocks up the First Kordon. In a heightened state of awareness, I observed the film of dust that blanketed the city, dimming the color of cars and the leaves on trees. Stepping carefully as I trod the cracked and uneven cement sidewalks, I studied the tense, unsmiling faces of the people I passed in their dark, somber clothing and watched them looking down at their feet, as I looked at mine, taking care not to trip.

Everywhere were the soldiers; khaki trouser bottoms tucked neatly into brown leather boot tops, they wore hand guns at the hip and rifles slung over the shoulder.

Where in this city, I wondered, was gaiety? If it was here, I hadn't seen it.

Almost afraid to enter, I lingered a long moment at a door

with the Pan Am logo affixed to the glass. Then, taking a deep breath, I stepped inside. In a room off the street no larger than a shoe-repair shop in the United States, I saw before me five empty plastic chairs to serve waiting customers. To my right stood an unused desk beyond which, at another, sat a man in a black coat talking to the Pan Am agent across from him. I took a seat to wait my turn.

It wasn't long before the man stood, giving me a look at his face. A shock of recognition made me draw back in fright, I knew him! But, terrified, I couldn't remember how. All I feared in that horrified moment was that I'd been unmasked as a woman trying to escape from the law.

That he recognized me too was plain to read by the surprise in his face.

"Madam," he said, seeming bewildered, "you are still in Izmir?"

"I am," I answered. My God, who was he?

"Well, I am sorry," he commented, looking grim, not sorry. "It is our law. It cannot be helped."

If I could remember who he was—surely some official from the dock or the court!—I might have understood what he was trying to tell me. But paralyzed with fright, I was unable to think of anything but, would he report my presence in the Pan Am office to the police?

He, himself, had no plans to arrest me for, touching his hat in a gesture of dismissal, he walked past me to the exit and out into the street.

Shakily I walked to his vacated chair, my heart beating a rapid tattoo, and sat down before the ticket agent.

"That man," I said, "I recognized him but can't remember his name. Who is he?"

Before she answered, she gave me a penetrating look.

"His name is Mr. Atkan," she said, and waited.

But the name meant nothing to me.

"How may I help you," she asked in the silence, bringing me back to the purpose of the visit.

"I would like to fly to New York," I said, quietly.

"Yes? On which day?"

"Tuesday," I answered, numbly.

"You are leaving from Izmir?"

"I will be in Ankara," I said. "I want to leave some time in the early afternoon."

"There is a flight from Ankara to Munich which you may take at forty-five minutes past five o'clock."

"Not earlier?"

"Lufthansa is the only flight on Tuesday."

"It goes all the way to New York?"

"To Munich. You may take a Pan American flight from Munich to New York.

"It will do," I said, placing my American Express card on the desk. "Please make a reservation. I will wait for the ticket."

Returning to the hotel by 3:00, I checked at the desk for messages just as if I had no guilty secret. There were two: from Atilla and Nancy.

In my room, this odd place that had been my home for two weeks, before returning the calls I took out the tickets and the passport, examining each in turn. Their existence alone made freedom seem real, and before returning them to my purse, I kissed each one lovingly, thinking, What a surprise I have in store for my family!

The image of Mr. Aktan's face lingered: if only I could remember where I'd met him before. Was he a real or imagined threat? Where else could I have seen him but the dock, the prison, or the courtroom? He couldn't be a friend; if he were I'd know him. If only Nancy could tell me.

When I called her back I learned she wanted me to have dinner at her home Monday night. Since her husband was on a trip, we'd be alone. Thanking her for providing a distraction during the anxious wait for the driver's return, I gladly accepted.

Then I told her about seeing Mr. Atkan, knowing it was doubtful she'd know who he was. Just airing my concern brought relief. My brother calls it "discomfort-shifting," which described very well my feeling that Nancy, now that she knew, could do some of my worrying for me.*

---

*It is a good indication of the state of my mind that to this day I cannot remember who Mr. Atkan was.

Atilla's news was not only disappointing, it was alarming. When she'd presented the prosecutor with her idea that the letters should induce the court to "order" me home, he brushed the suggestion aside.

"We have the finest medical treatment in Turkey as is available all over the world," Atilla quoted him. "It is not necessary Mrs. LePere return to the United States for treatment."

"Let's put off this discussion until tomorrow," I told Atilla, "when we have more time to go into detail. I'll bring the two letters in any case." Privately, I thought afterward, I was glad I'd decided to rely only on myself to get home. What I didn't need now was to find myself locked up in a Turkish "nut house." Buja, I was sure, was a paradise compared to one of their psychiatric wards.

Although he wasn't to know it, I said good-bye to Father Nee the next morning over a pleasant breakfast. Asking no questions, he said he'd be happy to mail the parcel I gave him containing letters from home and one defunct passport.

While it's true someone else might have destroyed these dangerous materials, I am unable to throw away anything. I eat leftovers and in restaurants frequently ask for a "doggy bag." The Great Depression of the 1930s, which, in our comfortable home, was experienced second hand and without discomfort, had nothing to do with it. The reason for this thrift is better understood by knowing I was a child of the poorest kind of immigrants, who trained me to believe that waste is sinful and recycling, God's work. At the time, while I had no plans for making use of them, without faith that I'd ever board Lufthansa's flight, I clung desperately to everything that connected me to home.

"So," Nee said, "yer cleanin' house. Thinkin' o' movin' to a cheaper hotel?"

"I'm thinking about it," I answered.

"Seems to me yer feelin' a bit better these days," he commented. "Gettin' used to old Izmir. Not a bad place at that."

"I've been less lonely since Nancy befriended me," I said. "I have you to thank for it."

"Nancy's a grand woman," he said, enthusiastically. "I'm glad you and her hit it off."

"And I want to apologize for the trouble I caused you that time at the prison. . . ."

"That's over and done with," he interrupted.

"You've been a wonderful friend to me, Gene. You've never deserted me, always trying to help. I just got a bit scared off by . . . I was overwhelmed by your energy at a time when I had none."

"Yer comin' along fine, now. I'm glad if I've been some help. Say," he asked, changing the subject, "Have ye been takin' any o' yer meals over at the Kordon? Their breakfasts are grand. Eggs and bacon . . . pancakes . . ."

"I haven't been getting up early enough to make breakfast at the Kordon," I said, smiling sheepishly, "and I just haven't had a chance to try the lunch."

"One of these days we'll go there together," he said. "I'll give ye a call."

Gene handed me a photocopy of an article that he said would interest me. Printed in England from excerpts of letters written by an English prisoner in Buja, I wondered if it would be safe for me to carry. Glancing quickly at the first page, I saw an indistinct photo of the author, bearded and emaciated. I recognized his face, although I'd seen him only twice: the day I first met Nee and another time when I was walking to the visitor's room.

"I would prefer," I said, "to look at this now, and if you wish, you may mail it to the States with the rest of my things."

With his permission I read the article while Gene sipped his tea. It held my interest. Daniel de Souza, my fellow prisoner and veteran of the Turkish penal system, was a gifted writer. In clear, precise, and often poetic language, he brought to life the pain and ugliness of his experience. Sentenced to thirty years for smuggling a few kilos of hashish into Turkey, Danny had already served nine and, with "good time," would be required to survive another seven. From this hasty examination, I perceived that male prisoners were treated worse than the women, and I searched for reasons by which to explain what was, to me, an odd distinction.

"Can it be," I asked the priest, "that women prisoners in Turkey are treated better—certainly less harshly—just because they are women?"

"It's the way of the Turks," he said, "It's a hard time those boys are havin'."

"I think women in Turkey are too inconsequential to be treated badly. The men constitute a threat. There is some awful kind of respect implicit in the degree of punishment they attract."

"That's possible," he said, "I've not met any women prisoners except yerself. Ye think the Turks are chivalrous toward women, do ye?"

"It's condescension, not chivalry. But maybe that's what chivalry really is. Tell me, Gene, why is de Souza still in prison after so many years? Can't he go home on a prisoner exchange the way our people do?"

"It's a pity to say it but the British haven't gotten around to makin' an exchange treaty with the Turks. Most of the European countries have them now, but I'm wonderin' if the British know what a hardship they're puttin' on their citizens rottin' away in them Turkish jails, seein' the Germans and Swedes, even the Yugoslavs go home."

"I think it's terrible."

"It is. Poor Danny's hopin' for an amnesty."

"Atilla Akat, my lawyer, told me there might be one. Do you think there will?"

"Yer guess is as good as mine. The prison scuttlebutt says there will but ye can't judge by that. Those poor devils have got to have somethin' to be hopin' for."

"I wish there were some way to help him."

"We're doin' our best."

Learning about Danny de Souza made me feel not only sorrow but guilt. I was out on bail, hopefully on my way home. Even if my plans fell through, I had the prisoner exchange to rely on. Now, in addition to being angry at the English for abandoning me to the Turks, I was furious at their indifference to their own people.

Embracing before we parted, Gene hugged me, kissed my cheek, and whispered in my ear.

"Listen, Gene, whatever yer up to, be careful," he said, "I wish ye all the luck in the world. I'll be sayin' yer name in me prayers."

That wily old fox! I hadn't fooled him at all.

I did better with Atilla. She never caught on.

Since early November the climate in Izmir had grown cool and rainy, but Sunday, the 13th, the sun was shining. I, who was accustomed to frequent long drives at home, enjoyed what was for me a treat. Hugging the convoluted coast on a broad, four-lane highway, the ride afforded me the chance to see parts of Izmir I'd never seen before, including an industrial area north of town and an enclave of workmen's shacks.

Atilla, nervously reacting to the other drivers on the road, asked to postpone conversation until we had reached our destination, a large and expansive, mostly deserted, stretch of beach, restaurants, shops, and hotels that must have been beyond the purse of the average Turk. Thirty-five minutes from the Efes we pulled into a parking lot and walked to a café Atilla said Geuldal recommended.

The place was deserted, and though it was cool, we took seats under the edge of an outdoor canopy where the sun reached us. Asking first if I was willing to eat local food, Atilla ordered a dish made of lamb called *döner kabap*, which she said was representative of good Turkish cooking. Waiting for the meal to be served, we spoke of the elections, of Geuldal, and, finally, of my court case, when I gave her the letters submitted by doctors Tunchbye and Knox.

"I will make a translation of Dr. Kirby's letter at the notary," she said, "and will give it to the court a few days before the trial to be held this month."

"I don't want them sending me to a psychiatric clinic," I said. "If I am returned to an institution, Atilla, I prefer to go back to Buja."

"Yes," she said, trying to hide her concern, "we must use these letters with care. I believe the court will have no wish to withdraw your bail when they have seen you will have remained in Izmir and are coming to the trial. Perhaps it will be wise not to give them the letters just at this time. We must find a way to have you go home with their approval. If this can be

264

accomplished, I will bring to the court these letters explaining your condition has worsened, therefore the consulate has sent you home."

"Should you implicate the consulate?" I asked. "There has been no suggestion that they would involve themselves in helping me leave Turkey."

"I must give it more thought," she said.

The food was served on large oval dishes with a finely chopped salad reminding me of the ones Neshe prepared.

"I've been thinking a lot about my friends in prison," I told her. "Do you think it would be alright if I wrote to them?"

"Of course," she said. "Why should you not write them? By all means, you may do it."

"And the blankets and sheets," I said. "If the court does not revoke my bail, it may be many months before the trials are over. Perhaps I will be home."

"Let us hope this is the case."

"If I have no need of them," I said, "will you bring them to the prison for the poor women to use?"

"Perhaps," she reminded me, "you will prefer that the victims of the recent earthquake in eastern Turkey shall make use of them. I think these people will have more need than even the poorest prisoners."

"You are right. Give them to the earthquake relief," I said, glad they would be used for a good purpose.

"We have time before making this decision."

"Of course," I agreed. "I may need them yet."

Knowing it might be a long time before I saw Atilla again, I allowed myself the luxury of enjoying her company: watching the expressions of her face as they changed with her thoughts; memorizing the rhythms of her formal, sometimes awkward, always lilting, English; feeling the genuineness of her affection and concern; loving this strong woman who would always be my deeply cherished friend.

It was almost dark when she left me at the hotel. Wanting to hug her close and to let her know the depth of my gratitude, my need to protect her held me back.

"Will you be gone long?" I asked.

"Not long. Perhaps a week, perhaps less. Not longer."

"I hope you find your mother in better health."

"She is old, but she is strong. I believe she will be all right."

"Send my love to Geuldal."

"I forgot. She has asked I give you hers."

"And Nena."

"Also Nena says hello."

"I love you, Atilla. I will miss you."

"It is only a week. I will telephone when I return."

I stood at the curb watching as she steered her car to the corner; watching as she made a cautious turn going south; watching until the little blue auto drove out of sight down the tree-lined First Kordon.

I will call her from New York, I promised myself, when I am home.

I spent the evening writing letters to Neshe and the others in care of Eminay, who would be able to read them. "I have not forgotten you," I told them. "I will never forget you. And I will pray that your lives will soon be better." As I prayed mine would soon be.

The driver was in Alanya. I visualized him there: in his hotel room, at dinner, tired from the long drive, and going to sleep. Sleep well, I told him, be up early in the morning. I will be with you in the offices of the police chief and the mayor. I will think you back into the car and all the way back to Izmir. I will thank you tomorrow night with money in the lobby of the Efes Hotel.

Before I slept, I promised myself to find Neshe's brother-in-law, to leave a special message for my lovely, lonely friend.

Monday morning, after the maid had tidied the room, I began packing. Only the clothes I would wear tomorrow, the gown and robe for tonight, and a few toilet articles remained. In less than a half hour this room, which had seemed friendly and warm, had reverted to the impersonal place it had been when I'd first arrived.

Going to the lobby, I told the desk clerk on duty I'd be leaving for Ankara the next day on a trip of short, but as yet, undetermined length. I asked if space would be available when I returned and volunteered to call ahead for a reservation. Then, anticipating an early-morning rush, I paid my bill at the cashier's cage through the 15th. Every morning at seven, a bus left the TAL office next door for the airport. Tomorrow morning I would be on it.

Only one more preparation was required: an instruction for the desk manager on duty tonight. I stood watching as it was written and placed in my mailbox. The note said sometime after 10:00 tonight, a man would come to the hotel asking for me. No matter how late he arrived, I was to be called. I'd be waiting in my room. It was very important.

Then I walked from the hotel into the back streets of Alsanjak where I'd never before ventured alone. I was determined to find William Washington, an air force corporal of the United States and Neshe's brother-in-law, whose address I had kept.

Like a miracle, everything looked familiar and I had no trouble finding my way. Izmir had suddenly become a friendly place where I was no longer ill at ease, no more a stranger. Now, just when I was leaving, I felt at home.

It pleased me to recognize the names of two hotels Father Nee had suggested I see and, two blocks away, to find by myself the store behind the hospital that Nancy had pointed out. Remembering the long wait between planes in Ankara, I went in and bought the latest editions of *Newsweek* and *Time*, and a paperback that looked like it would be good airplane reading.

In front of the BX, the American Air Force Base Exchange, I ran into two of the women I'd met in Ayvalik, greeting them as casually as I would a friend at home. One of them apologized for not calling me sooner, "could we have lunch?" Not wanting to reveal my plans, I postponed making a date, believing she would understand when Nancy told her I'd gone home.

When I found Bill, he was at work. But after explaining who I was, he took a few minutes to talk about Neshe. Since time was short, Bill suggested we get together again, "for a drink." For the second time in less than an hour, I put a nice person off with a promise I hoped not to be able to keep.

My errands were done. Leaving Bill I hurried to the hotel: it was 1:00 and long past the time when the driver should have left Alanya. When there was no message at the desk I became apprehensive and rushed into the travel agency next door where I found the agent who'd promised to to call.

"Have you heard from the driver?" I asked, anxiously.

"Yes, Mrs. LePere," she said, calmly. "I have tried to reach you but you were not in your room. He has called at 11:30 to say he was starting back."

"Thank you," I said, greatly relieved, "Thank you very much."

Containing my elation, I took the elevator to the sixth floor and entered the room, closing the door. Then, spinning wildly, I sang aloud, "He's on his way back! He's on his way! He has the validation." He must, mustn't he?

Nothing may be taken for granted, I reminded myself. Nothing. But no admonishment could subdue the excitement that was growing inside me.

I was going home. I would leave tomorrow.

Sitting at the desk table where I ate my meals, I began a detailed list for U.S. Customs of the many articles—mostly gifts —I'd bought since landing in England on August 27. How was it possible, I wondered, it had been nearly three months since I'd left home. So much had happened; so many new people had come into my life.

Nancy was to pick me up at 6:00, and before leaving the hotel I made sure the message left for the night clerk was still in its place in the mail cubicle. It was hard to leave my post even for a few hours, knowing very well the driver couldn't arrive before 9:30. To relieve my anxiety I left word I'd return no later than 9:30 and wrote Nancy's number on a piece of paper for the clerk. Only then could I step to the curb and wait for Nancy's car.

This was the first time I'd been allowed to see the inside of an Izmir apartment other than Atilla's. Except for the oddly laid out rooms, it seemed much like any apartment one might find in most modern cities of the world. The main door opened into a small hallway, beyond which lay the living room, overlooking Izmir's bay. Large, but cozy, it was furnished with overstuffed chairs and sofas upholstered in flowered patterns of cheerful chintz that were placed in a seating group around an oval coffee table. In an adjoining room, a round, sturdy table of a size sufficient to seat the members of Nancy's family was laid with placemats for two.

"I hope you like liver," Nancy said, taking me on a tour that included the kitchen. "The butcher had fresh beef liver today that looked awfully good."

"I love liver," I told her. "That was a really good choice."

After asking my preference in music and putting a cassette into a player, Nancy joined me on a sofa, carrying wine and two glasses.

"This seems rather a special occasion," she said, smiling. "One which I thought required a bottle of good Turkish wine."

"What a good idea," I said, delighted.

"I don't want to make too much of this," she went on. "I'm sure you must be quite nervous and excited already, but I would like to toast the success of tomorrow's venture."

"I'll drink to that," I said, lifting my glass, and added, "To a smooth flight tomorrow; and you can take that any way you choose."

"To a smooth flight," she repeated, "and I mean it in all possible ways."

For a long moment we sat in silence. Then, because I wanted to remember Nancy in this place, her home, surrounded by a family it was unlikely I'd ever meet, she brought an album to the table, and together we pored over her memories recorded in snapshots.

Her children were strong and handsome, her husband, slender like Nancy, had a gay smile. Midway through the photographs and explanations, the telephone rang and Nancy went to answer it.

"It's for you," she said a moment later.

"For me?" Yes, I'd left the number, but I hardly expected to be called.

It was Aaron. He was in Ankara.

"Gene," he said, "I thought I'd better call you as soon as possible. There's been a change—a couple of changes since we last spoke."

"What changes?" I asked.

"I'm sorry to give you bad news, but there's been a change of climate in Ankara."

"A change in . . ." My hand tightened on the phone.

"The weather's no longer favorable. Thursday it was clear. Friday that was no longer true." He waited a moment before going on. "I've had a call from the Izmir plant so I won't be leaving for Frankfurt just yet. We can talk in Izmir."

"It can't be." I said, refusing to accept a disappointment that had the taste of gall. Tears, not seen for days, flushed my eyes.

"Listen, I can't talk any longer. I'll leave for Izmir an hour after I've put the staff on the 5:45 flight to Germany. I'll call you as soon as I get in."

"Yes, Aaron," I said, forcing myself to speak, "I'll talk to you tomorrow. Thanks for letting me know."

Putting down the receiver, I turned to Nancy, who had come to stand at my side.

"What's wrong?" she asked, her eyes full of concern.

"My name has appeared on the list at the airport in Ankara."

"What bad timing," she commented in a sympathetic but steady voice. Taking my elbow, she led me back to the sofa. Without will, I moved with her.

"There must be some solution," she said, when we were again seated. "You can always stay on here, of course, and attend the trial. Or, you might want to go on to Ankara any-way . . . ." her voice trailed to a halt. Nancy didn't have an answer. Neither did I. Weeping softly, I felt a despair deeper than any I'd known before.

"What will you do?" Nancy asked gently.

"I don't know."

"Perhaps we ought to get dinner started," she said, getting to her feet. "You'll feel better once you've got a bit of food in you. Sit with me in the kitchen while I finish it up. It won't take but fifteen minutes, I'm sure."

I was empty of words but Nancy kept up a smooth-running chatter that filled the room with well-modulated noise.

Unable to concentrate on what she was saying, I didn't try. Inside a struggle was being waged. On the one side I was full of self-pity, fueled by a burning rage against Edwin Gant, whose tactics to delay my departure from Turkey were the real reason for this crisis. If I'd been helped instead of hindered, I'd have been home before my name reached Ankara. It was his fault.

Doing battle against surrender was the fighter, looking for a way to rob Gant of his long-delayed and horribly unexpected victory. Yet, the least of my feelings revolved around Gant. I was dizzy from trying to reverse directions.

In my head I'd already made the transition from Turkey to the United States. I'd said good-bye to friends and experienced a nostalgia for the small city I'd grown to like. Psychologically, I had turned my head toward home and, being ready, couldn't wait.

But the risk of going through passport control at the Ankara airport—frightening before—had become almost foolhardy. Unless I could mitigate the danger, it no longer seemed a sane thing to do.

I ate the dinner Nancy prepared but said little. Afterward she drove me to the hotel. It was a tearful parting with neither of us knowing what was to become of tomorrow. If Nancy called my room would I be there or gone? The next time Nancy had word of me, might she learn it from a story in a Turkish paper relating how the "smuggler woman," free on bail, had been apprehended at the Ankara airport trying to escape?

I'd taken a mighty blow and felt beaten. The fall from hope was too abrupt a descent. Why did God let me get so far with my plan, then snatch it from my hands at the last instant? If I hadn't held the tickets . . . paid my bill. If only . . . The decision was mine and I didn't know how to make it.

There was time, yet. If the driver never arrived from Alanya, if he failed to obtain or deliver the verification, there would be no decision to make. It would be another fait accompli.

At 10:30 I was still waiting: there had been no call from the desk. I assumed the man had not appeared but would arrive any time now. Every detail had been planned ahead: I would remain in my street clothes until he came—all night if necessary. If I was tired (in fact, the day had become so distressing and the evening so filled with anxiety, I was yawning with exhaustion) I would lie down on my bed in the dark, perhaps even sleep.

By 11:15 I'd begun to doubt, not the driver, but the hotel clerk. He hadn't seen the note. The driver had come but been refused. My imagination drove me to the telephone, but the clerk was not at fault. He had memorized his part; the driver had not come.

Fifteen minutes later the telephone gave its accustomed two short rings and I leapt to answer. It was Nancy.

"Gene," she said, "if it's any help, I've gone over every departure from Turkey I've ever made and I can't remember a time when my passport was checked against a list."

"Maybe you just didn't see them do it," I said, disbelieving even the Turks could be so careless.

"Has the driver arrived?" she asked.

"Not yet."

"Well, I shan't tie up your line. Good luck, Gene. Give me a call if you're still here tomorrow."

"I will," I said, "and thank you."

"Well," she said before closing, "remember what I said—for whatever it's worth. Maybe everything will work out, yet, *Inshallah*."

Inshallah, God willing, indeed.

"I'll remember," I said, hanging up.

Lying on the bed in the darkened room, I tried not to imagine the worst while visions of flat tires and car collisions tormented my thoughts. Where was he?

Maybe he stopped for lunch . . . or dinner . . . or both. My God, what's the difference, Gene, he's got all night. You can sleep in your clothes. So they call you at 2:00. You told them they could call you at 2:00.

Sleep was impossible. Relighting a lamp I tried to read, but that was impossible, too. I'd turned only a few pages when the phone rang again. Jumping a foot off the bed, I grabbed the receiver.

"This is the desk, Madam," a calm voice announced. "A man has arrived asking for you."

"Yes," I gasped, breathlessly, "tell him I'll be right down."

Hours ago I'd placed three 10,000 lira notes in the left hand pocket of my cotton jacket. Before racing to the door, I made sure they were still there. Then, grabbing my room key, I ran through the corridor to the elevator. During the descent, I composed myself to seem calm, as if this meeting were of negligible importance.

The driver, a thin young man, was waiting.

He doesn't look tired though he must be, I thought irrelevantly, closing the distance between us.

Seeing the desk clerk motion the man that I was the woman

he was waiting for made me realize the driver spoke no English.

Without a word he handed me a small brown envelope and I was instantly alarmed. This was not the same envelope I'd given the agent.

Is that all? I gestured. That was all.

Stepping aside to open it, I took out a small sheet of paper and panicked. This wasn't what I'd been expecting. I'd been waiting for my own letter to be returned with some official stamp on it. Where was my letter? I didn't dare ask.

My heart was racing as I tried to read what it said. I was so afraid.

I tried to think, to focus on the Turkish writing, to get some sense out of it. The desk clerk interrupted, "This man says you must give him something in return."

"Yes, yes," I said, impatiently, "in a minute."

Frantically I wondered if I could ask the clerk to tell me what the letter said and hesitated. Suppose it said, "This woman is trying to escape from her trial as a smuggler in Turkey and she cannot be allowed to leave."

I stood paralyzed and indecisive: unwilling to pay unless it was what I'd asked for, terrified to reveal myself as a fugitive. The driver was impatient; there was no time. It was a risk I had to take.

Handing the letter to the clerk, I held my breath in the ominous silence before he began a halting translation.

" 'Gene H. LePere has legally entered Turkey on the 28th day of September, 1983, at the port of Alanya,' " he read, commenting, "There is an official stamp."

Relief washed over me, and now the danger was past, I wondered, self-consciously, what these two men might think was going on.

It was done. I held in my hand what I had so desperately wanted. Giving the driver his lira, I watched as he counted them, saw him nod in satisfaction, and followed his progress toward the exit.

My spirits soared with the elevator as I rode back to the sixth floor. I couldn't believe it! Everything I needed to leave Turkey was mine—except a safe way out.

One problem down. Face tomorrow, tomorrow. It was time to sleep.

I would leave for Ankara in the morning. A wake-up call for
5:30 would rouse me in time to catch the bus to the plane.

Undressing, I packed the clothes I'd removed, got into my
gown and into bed, turned off the light, and willed myself to
relax and to sleep. Tomorrow was going to be a very difficult
day.

The operator's ring at 5:30 brought me to my feet, instantly
awake but close to a dream I'd been having. Lying abed for a
long minute I tried to recall it clearly.

Yes. In my dream I was at the airport, going through customs, a complicated process that involved many desks and people and places. There were corridors, walls, barriers, all painted
a clean shining white—and there had been no problems. I'd
gotten through.

I am not given to remembering dreams and, though I am
sensitive to their hidden messages, don't confer to them the
power of prescience: dreams do not predict the future. Yet,
somehow, this dream strengthened my resolve and infused me
with energy. I was feeling high.

This day, I promised myself, I am going home. Somehow I
will work it out. I'm leaving and that's all there is to it.

At 6:30 I was ready and called for a bellboy. Though I knew
I'd be toting my suitcase all day at the airports, it gave me grim
satisfaction to let someone else do it now.

In the lobby I noted the long line in front of the cashier and
congratulated myself on being so clever as to have checked out
a day early.

The street was quiet and the sky just beginning to lighten
outside the hotel entrance when I was escorted to the bus
standing in front of the Turkish airline office. My bag, taken
by the driver, was placed inside the luggage compartment
while I stepped into the empty vehicle and took a seat near the
front.

I felt overdressed wearing a skirt, two sweaters, and the
burgundy raincoat, but Nancy had warned me Ankara, far to
the north and high in the mountains, would be very cold. In fact,
she'd been so concerned that I would catch a chill, I had to fight
her insistence to give me her own winter coat.

Slowly the bus filled with passengers, and promptly at 7:00, with a grinding of gears, it pulled away from the curb on a rocking drive through the awakening streets of Izmir.

Watching from the window, I was filled with a sense of the finality of my departure: I would never again see this colorless, dust-covered city with its broad, tree-lined avenues and narrow, crowded side streets. Leaving Alsanjak, I closed my eyes, resting before the hurdles ahead.

When, twenty minutes later, I felt the bus slow and come to a halt, I looked out to find we'd arrived at a small shack and, with a shock of fear, saw the sign painted in bold black letters that said, "KONTROL." Now what?

The driver passed through the aisle collecting all the airline tickets. With trepidation, my heart pounding and stomach tense, I gave mine up. I was relieved ten minutes later to have it returned and to feel the bus resume its journey toward the terminal, a single-story building that served both arrivals and departures.

Together with the other passengers, I stepped from the bus and through the entrance doors to a low counter where we were to be checked in while the luggage, hand-carried by the driver, obstructed our progress to the desk. Anxious, I stared at my feet, feeling like a criminal about to be caught.

After a time-consuming procedure I received a boarding pass and a claim check for the bag, which, having been warned by Nancy under no circumstance to lose, I put away carefully. There was another warning Nancy had given.

"They will have your baggage on the tarmak and before boarding you must point it out. If you don't, it won't get on the plane. It happened to me once," she said.

I hugged this bit of intelligence like a miser, waiting for the notice to board.

The passenger lounge was large, dirty, and bare of beauty or amenities. Because I'd been near the front of the line, I was lucky to find a chair, observing in relative comfort the growing number of travelers forced to stand. My seat faced a glass wall beyond which the airfield stretched like a prairie plain beneath the lightening eastern sky. Transfixed, I contemplated the dawn of day in a blood-red world bleaching salmon and pink: a reverse equation of the sunsets I had witnessed with so much awe.

Huddled in my discomfort I was afraid to meet the eyes of the other passengers: turned in on myself, alone and vulnerable, I clasped my hands to hide their trembling. Time inched forward in interminably slow increments. But at last, when there was a stirring, I stood, wondering where to go.

Two lines were forming in front of the wide exit door: a long, ragged line of men to the left, a short, bunched trickle of women to the right. Tentatively I took my place behind an enfeebled woman whose husband was aiding her slow progress to the door. The line crawled and every minute seemed an hour. When, finally, I stood at the head of the line, I showed my passport to and allowed my handbag to be searched by a female soldier screening passengers. Without warning, I felt her pass her hands over my body, touching my breasts and belly, digging rudely into my crotch. Shocked and feeling violated, it took all my control not to protest or back away. But the search was over in seconds and I was allowed to pass through.

Outside, I remembered to point out my bag and waited to see it lifted and carried ahead of me. Then I walked across the black tarmak to board the plane by a rolling stair.

The flight itself was uneventful, taking less than an hour. Except that the announcements were in Turkish and that the breakfast snack consisted of tea and a horrid-tasting sweet cake, it could have been a short flight between cities anywhere in the world.

Debarking at Ankara, the modern capital of Turkey, I discovered a two-story terminal with no more conveniences than I'd found in Izmir. Baggage claim was a crude, drafty affair where, in a twenty-minute wait for the luggage, I was assaulted by the chilling cold of winter blown in by a wind off the airfield outside.

It was only minutes after 9:00 when I was done, yet, aware I still faced eight interminable hours of waiting, I hoped to find a quiet corner in which to hide. At least, I told myself, in Ankara there was no chance of running into anyone who would know me.

Now, to find the departure lounge.

A broad, marble-stepped stairway led to the upper floor where I found some hard seats arranged in a single row and the

Lufthansa counter. Made of wood varnished to a dark brown mahogany finish, it was dulled with grime and scarred by years of abuse.

No one was about, but the wooden floor was littered with paper, debris, and cigarette butts, as if a herd of smoking Turks had recently departed. In my search through the terminal I had seen no cafés or vendors where food, coffee, or even tea could be purchased, where the waiting could be done in comfort. As this was the only seating I had discovered, placing my suitcase at my feet, I began an impatient vigil and set my mind to the task of preparing for the terrors ahead. Somehow I had to find a means of reducing the risk of rearrest—if the list checkers turned out to be competent at their job. One idea had already occurred to me.

If, I reasoned, I could demonstrate my intention to return for the trial, perhaps I would not be imprisoned but merely be turned back.

My idea was to exchange the one-way ticket to New York for a round trip that would put me back in Izmir two days before the trial. What I needed was a reason, an excuse, some explanation for this alteration in plans.

Where else did this plane stop besides Munich? I didn't know.

Anxiously, I opened *Time* magazine and, starting on page one, began to read. Startled by each sound and movement, I looked up frequently as people came and went.

At 11:30 a large group of passengers entered, led by a woman who seemed to be their guide. Judging by their clothing I decided they were Europeans but was unable to identify their country of origin from the language they spoke.

Had it been summer I'd have thought them to be tourists on their way home, but why vacationers would come to Ankara at so inhospitable a time of year was beyond my understanding. Not that it mattered. They were a diversion and, more important, they provided a dress rehearsal for my own departure. I watched everything that happened with great care.

After some minutes, when the Lufthansa clerk appeared, the guide collected the tickets, presenting them en masse at the counter. Knowing the act I was preparing to commit, I envied each of them his anonimity: being a part of a group allowed them all to hide. No one stood out. Everything that had to be processed was handled together. And therefore, I thought, with less care.

That was it. I needed to be part of a group.

Ah, but where was a group that would have me?

My hopes grew wildly when I observed the sequence of steps that followed. As the guide returned the tickets, she gave each passenger a green card, the same as I remembered from my own almost-departure in Izmir, and when the card was completed, it was returned to the guide with a passport—just as our tour group had given them to Mr. Jackson on the bus.

The passengers stood about in groups, chattering idly—some serious, some with humor—unaware and uncaring as the guide did her work. But I watched her intently.

Clasping more than twenty-five in both hands, she carried the passports to a booth at the farthest right corner of the room where, under a sign that said "KONTROL," they were handed through a window slot to the soldiers whom I could barely glimpse inside.

That in itself wasn't remarkable. But what arrested my attention was her attitude during the time when the soldiers were checking names against a list and authorizing exits with their official stamp.

Laughing and behaving in a familiar manner, it was obvious this guide been here thousands of times before. She knew the soldiers. They knew her. Not only were they on the best of terms, familiarity had bred carelessness. It was clear she was distracting them from their work!

There was no doubt in my mind that if I could make myself a part of a group, the odds for a successful, if unauthorized, departure would greatly increase.

No longer interested in the departing group, I tried to still my excitement and a rising panic.

Think. Think. How can this be accomplished? Would there be a group boarding my Lufthansa flight? How could I insinuate myself into their midst? I knew the idea was a good one, but unless I could create the perfect situation, I might as well accept the vulnerability of a lone exit.

The more I concentrated, the more the solution eluded me.

Disheartened, I gave up the conscious effort, allowing my sub-conscious mind to make its own connections without interfer-ence. I was far from relaxed. As the time grew nearer when I would have to face the terrible risks ahead without a solution, I was close to tears, thinking not only of my disappointment but that of my family and friends back home, of Nancy's concern and Gene Nee's, even of Aaron Emile, who would be back in Izmir tonight, expecting to see me—Aaron Emile!

He would be back in Izmir tonight. After he'd put his de-signers on the plane for Frankfurt—this afternoon! My God, was it possible we were booked on the same flight? What time had he said they were leaving?

I was sure it was some time after 5:00.

It had to be the same flight. Didn't the Pan Am agent say only Lufthansa had a flight out this afternoon? Hadn't I asked for an earlier flight and she said this was the only afternoon flight. It must be. It *must* be.

The clerk was still at her post although the tour had disap-peared through a door beyond the passport control booth.

Timidly, I stood. It was time to rewrite my flight. Steeling myself to pretend a casualness and a calm I did not feel, I ap-proached the Lufthansa desk and laid my ticket on the counter.

The clerk looked up, questioningly.

"Do you speak English?" I asked.

"Yes, Madam," she answered in an accent I couldn't place. Her coloring was dark, her hair black; I only hoped she was a German and not a Turk.

"I am holding a ticket for this afternoon's flight to Munich," I said, searching for the right approach. "I have friends in Frankfurt; I would have time to visit them. Does this flight also go to Frankfurt?"

"Yes, Madam," she repeated. "Would you like to change your ticket to debark at Frankfurt?"

"Yes, please, and rebook me to connect with a Pan American flight to New York." Then, as if it were an afterthought, "Oh, yes, since you're writing a new ticket anyway, you may as well book the return flight, since I now know exactly when I'd like to be back in Izmir."

"That is possible," she said, taking my ticket from the counter. "When do you wish to return?"

"On whatever date I must leave New York to arrive in Izmir on the 27th of November. I must be back by then."

"Yes, Madam," she said, pulling a ticket blank from under the counter.

Looking about while I waited, I wondered how she would determine which flights were still open. There was no computer in sight. Having grown accoustomed to computers, taking them for granted, I'd chosen to forget it was not many years ago when we had done without them, too. If only the Turks would screen passengers electronically as we did, I thought resentfully, it wouldn't be necessary to suffer the indignity of being "felt up" every time you boarded a plane.

"How will you make payment for your fare?" the woman asked, intruding on my thoughts.

I gave her my American Express card and waited several more minutes until she was done.

"I have canceled your ticket to Munich and will arrange credit," she said, placing some papers before me. "Please sign for both."

"Thank you," I said, and complied. After putting away the new ticket, I asked what time boarding would commence.

"An hour before flight time," she informed me.

Three more hours to wait.

"Thank you," I said, again, and, feeling the momentary relief of another hurdle successfully cleared, returned to my seat.

Opening the paperback, I tried for some minutes to read. But the problems that still lay before me commanded my thoughts and I couldn't follow the story.

Survival under peril makes one a narcissist. It requires total self-concern. My world had narrowed to the immediate: to myself, to the room in which I sat, to the single, small but critical, fascinating, horribly compelling steps yet to be faced. All parts were essential to reaching my objective; I disciplined myself to look only to the next and not beyond.

Aaron's arrival gave me grave concern.

Surely when he saw me, he would know right away what I was trying to do. But I doubted he'd guess what I wanted of him or be the one to offer assistance in making my escape.

No. What I needed from him would have to be requested; it was not for the taking. It required his agreement and would put him in jeopardy. Nothing but the desperation of my need would have induced me to ask so much of anyone, let alone a friend of such new and tentative bonding.

His complicity, if he agreed to it, must be made to appear accidental: he must seem innocent of any intent, to have been a victim of my manipulation. Aaron had to be protected—somehow.

Oh, I wouldn't blame him if he refused me but, my God, how badly I needed his help.

I had no plan for approaching him. I had to have one.

By 3:00 prolongued tension and lack of sleep began to show and tears began to ooze from my eyes. Although I was fully rational and in good control otherwise, my body, clenched like a fist for hours, was so tense that I could feel my heart thumping irregularly. Could stress like I'd experienced for the past seven weeks, I wondered, cause a heart attack? Exhausted, I longed for the relief of safety that lay beyond the two dimensions of time and luck: two hours until Aaron arrived; how many before I faced the monstrous barrier of the KONTROL booth?

Some of my weakness, I knew, was the result of having no food all day. Yet I knew if a feast were set before me I couldn't force down a single bite.

I waited.

The book remained open on my lap. I turned pages reading every word. To this day I have no memory of the characters or the plot. I have even forgotten its name.

As the hour for boarding drew near I found myself incessantly checking the watch on my wrist and stopped all pretense of reading. Putting the book away, I stared at the large entrance door from which passengers were beginning to trickle into the room. Aaron would arrive soon, I was sure.

It never occurred to me he might not come. As his plans had already undergone a change, they might have again been altered. But I didn't think of it. I was spared that terror.

What did come to mind, thankfully, in those final minutes of waiting, was that because Aaron was staying in Turkey, if I were arrested, he could notify the consulate and Atilla. On a bit of paper torn from a wrinkled cigarette pack, I wrote her phone number and Nancy's, placed the note in my pocket, and looked up just as Aaron, graceful and elegant in a black leather topcoat, strode into the room.

Unable to move, I remained in my seat watching. My heart was beating wildly: I could feel the pulse in my neck and a flush of blood that heated my cheeks. A dozen feet away Aaron stood talking to two men and a woman. Facing the Lufthansa desk, his back was toward me. I waited.

Slowly turning, with a sweep of his head he took in the scene about him and I watched his eyes slide smoothly past me sitting small in my chair. Then, with an abrupt motion of his head, his eyes returned and fixed me with a stare of surprise that I saw turn into alarm.

Turning to his companions, the designers I assumed, I watched as he excused himself before he began to move solidly in my direction, coming to a stop two feet away.

"Gene," he said, in a voice that reflected a mild question, "I am surprised to find you here." The look in his eyes was one of deep concern.

"I'm surprised, myself," I said, in the moment realizing it was true. God, what was I doing here?

"You have come to meet someone?"

"Not exactly," I said, "but in a way."

"I certainly didn't expect to see you today in the Ankara airport," he stated the obvious, too polite, I thought, to be more direct.

"I was all set to leave," I said, blurting out everything. "I had my passport and reservations . . . and my courage. I was leaving, I'd said goodbye . . . and then your call came. I couldn't turn back."

It was a long minute before he spoke again.

"What you are trying to do is extremely dangerous. I advise you to give it up."

"I cannot."

"If they catch you . . . who knows, you may find yourself back in prison."

"I know."

"Are you willing to take such a risk?"

"I must try," I said. "I've done everything I can think of to minimize the risk."

"What have you done? What *can* you do?"

I stood to face him more squarely, looking up from my five-foot, three-inch height into his kind, worried face a head above mine.

"I have a round-trip ticket with a return to Izmir on November 27th. If I am stopped, I shall say, 'Don't you see, I plan to be back for my trial on the 29th.'"

"There is only the slimmest chance anyone will be fooled by that ploy."

"Yes," I agreed, at the same time arguing, "but the ticket is the proof and their guess is only conjecture. You cannot be punished for something you might do in the future when you have proof that is not your intention."

He shrugged.

"What else?"

"For the rest," I said, calmly, "I need your help."

"What do you imagine I can do. You must realize that if you are caught I can do nothing to help you."

"No," I said, "I know there is nothing you can do if I am caught. I don't expect it. The help I ask for is now, not after, although I would appreciate your contacting a few people . . . if I am arrested."

"That, I can certainly do," he said, "but I would prefer to talk you out of going. I understand how badly you want to get home, but if you would wait a bit longer, something will surely break in your favor. It could make the difference between going home and going to prison."

"I have already waited too long," I said. "I should have left last week, before my name was on the list."

"What are you afraid of?"

"I am afraid of being found guilty. I am afraid of being asked to serve a three-and-a-half-year sentence for something I didn't do. Atilla . . . Akat, my lawyer, says I will certainly be found guilty . . . that possession, not motive, is the deciding factor, that because of the museum director's attitude she is finding it difficult to prove the single head that was ancient was not rare, not important. Everything is stacked against me. Even a prisoner exchange would take months to effect."

I drew a deep breath before going on.

"I am going now," I said, "with or without your help. And

I wouldn't blame you if you refused it. But let me at least tell you what I would want you to do."

"Of course," he said with compassion. "Since you are determined to go, I want to help you in any way you think would be useful."

"Wait until you hear it before you decide," I said.

He smiled. "I will wait," he said with great kindness, "Now, tell me."

"If you would allow me to pretend to be one of your designers . . ." His face shut down and I realized I'd put the request badly.

"No, I don't mean you have to tell them I am one of your designers. Just take my passport and give it to the Kontrol together with theirs. Say nothing."

His silence forced me to go on.

"You know the people here. You've been through this airport with designers and alone many, many times. Isn't it so?"

"Yes," he answered.

"I am safer in a group. You need say nothing. If they catch me you can say you had done me a courtesy; that we were acquaintances from the States; that you had no idea there were problems about my departure. I will tell them the same, that I took advantage of our meeting. You knew nothing."

Still he didn't respond.

"Aaron, it is more than presumptuous of me to ask this of you. I am desperate and will protect you in every way possible."

"I am not afraid for myself," he said. "It is your safety that concerns me."

"It is what I wish. It is my decision. The consequences are my responsibility and mine alone. I will try it anyway. All you will have done is improve my chances for success by a fraction."

"All right," he said, at last, and held out his hand.

I turned over to Aaron the passport with the authorized-entry letter and the short list of names to be called.

"Thank you," I said, inadequately.

"One last thing," he said.

"Anything."

"My staff is not to know. I will introduce you as a friend from the States. That is all."

"I promise," I said, meaning it. There would be no "discomfort-shifting" this trip. I would keep my terrors to myself.

Together, Aaron carrying my suitcase, we rejoined his employees, who met me politely. There was no indication from their manner that they'd ever heard my name before. And mine, casual and easy I hoped, gave no sign of the turmoil I was really feeling.

I had arrived at a state of fear that lacked outward expression. My terror was now absorbed into every cell of my body, and now that the moment had arrived, my external self was calm.

Back at the Lufthansa desk, that poor, shabby, wooden affair, Aaron collected all four airline tickets and the passports of the other three, presenting them in a group to the agent, the woman who'd written my ticket. While waiting, I stood near the woman designer, engaged in an exchange of superficial pleasantries.

When the passports were returned, they were accompanied by the green exit cards. Now Aaron waited while I and the others, standing at the counter, filled them in and returned them to him.

Now the moment of truth was upon me.

They were the worst minutes I'd ever known, minutes that burned out for all time my willingness, my ability, to tolerate stress of such magnitude.

Dizzy with fear, I pretended to be carefree. Laughing, smiling, seeming at ease, I stumbled through short answers, comments, meaningless words—replies to a woman chattering at my side—to sentences I barely heard and didn't comprehend, all the while surreptitiously watching Aaron.

Taking the passports, he carried them to the booth and presented them through the window slot to KONTROL.

Now he was waiting, conversing easily at the window.

God, if I could only see what was going on beyond my vision, inside the booth.

If a heart can be said to stop beating, mine had.

Then, suddenly we'd passed the most crucial mark. Aaron was on his way back. He was returning the passports; he was giving me mine.

Quickly, but without seeming to be in haste, we were ush-

ered toward two small booths to the right of Passport Kontrol
and Aaron was shaking hands and saying good-bye. He could
not go farther with us.

He had no special words for me. Only a deep look before
leaving. Then he was gone.

I moved like an automaton, not looking back. I did not realize until I was well into the booth and saw the woman soldier
standing there, that I was passing through "weapons control."

As she probed my purse, digging into every corner, I was
fiercely glad Father Nee had taken all the incriminating documents. With the return of my purse, I braced for the frisk.
With a sure, swift passage of hands down the front of my body
—not so personal as the woman at Izmir—and a nod, I was
passed to the other side where I faced a broad flight of marble
steps that led to the departure lounge at ground level, a floor
below.

Is that all? I asked myself. Am I really in the waiting room?
Have I actually gotten through the worst threats? Is it possible?

I was far from relief. Vibrating with alertness, my senses
acute with tension, I asked myself, When will you feel safe? And
the answer came, Not in this dismal waiting room. That's for
sure.

On the plane? I asked. Will you feel safe on the plane? No.
Not on the plane.

When we take off? I doubted it. They could make the plane
turn around and come back.

Then, perhaps when we were out of Turkish airspace?

Maybe. That sounded better. Maybe then.

The lady designer, finding a seat, was having a smoke. Her
companions, the men, stood together on the far side of the door.
Walking to her side, I took an adjacent seat and began a new
conversation.

Having turned her on I let her do all the talking. I was
incapable of stringing one coherent sentence together, so busy
was my mind with protecting me. My lips smiled, my head
nodded at appropriate pauses. I prodded her on with two-word
questions. ". . . then what?" ". . . oh, no!"

My eyes darted to every corner of the room.

Uniformed men and women. Why so many? Were they soldiers? Or airline personnel?

One carried a walkie-talkie, and I kept a good eye on him for
a sudden look in my direction: a surprise arrest.

When would we be boarded, for God's sake!

Forty-five minutes and five cigarettes went by.

At last we were called to board. Lolling casually, I waited for
my new "friend," as if I hadn't the least concern or urgency.
What lay outside, what threats awaited, I didn't know and
couldn't imagine. Would there be another offensive "frisk" at
the door? Terrors and humiliations were what I now expected
to be in store for me.

Show your ticket and your boarding pass.

We were outside.

Where was the plane? My God, it couldn't be one quarter of
a mile away! It was.

A soldier passed as we were walking and chatting. I
managed a disarming smile.

We were at the tarmack, at the stair, on the plane.

As it was half empty, we obtained permission from the German stewardess to take seats together. Or was she German? Her
hair was dark, not fair. Perhaps she was a Turk.

I could no longer tell the difference.

My companion and I went through the motions of getting
comfortable: placing coats in the overhead rack, purses on the
seat between us, fastening safety belts. My mind was outside the
plane.

Have they discovered their mistake? Will the soldiers rush
aboard and grab me? Will I be escorted off in front of all these
people? My God, when are they going to close the door?

The delays seemed interminable. Panic lay, barely controlled, at the base of my throat.

I willed the door to be sealed. Shut the danger out!

The stewardess closed the door, turned the handle, and the
plane began its taxi to the take-off position at the end of the
runway.

They had radio contact. I knew it could still be called back.
I watched, listened, felt for any strange, abrupt movements.

As the plane began to build momentum I watched the landmarks beyond the window being swiftly left behind, then felt the wheels leave the ground.

We were airborne!

I was *almost* relieved. I could not relax.

Perhaps, I thought, terror has become a way of life. You can relax when the plane is out of Turkish airspace, I promised myself. But, how will I know?

My friend maintained a harmless monologue that I began to find interesting as she described her work and her life. Anyone's life was more interesting than mine. Mine exhausted me. But I couldn't let go.

Listening carefully to the pilot announcements, I learned the route we would take to Munich, our first stop outside Turkey, and how many hours it would take. But it was an hour before I heard we'd just flown over Istanbul and, remembering the map of Turkey, knew we'd just crossed into the airspace over Europe.

I felt better. Not relaxed, but better.

They cannot really call us back now, I thought. But I didn't feel safe.

I remembered Aaron, wondering if he had called Nancy to say I'd gotten off the ground and was on my way home. She would tell Gene Nee. The consulate would soon know. If Bob Ludan had returned, I thought he'd be happy for me. They all would, I wanted to believe.

Only Atilla worried me. I hoped this wouldn't cause her any problems in the defense of my case, in her efforts to exonerate me.

The inability to believe in my freedom left me anxious, and when my seat partner excused herself to go to the restroom and I was alone, I ventilated the confusion of emotions that battered me. Hugging myself, I rocked in the seat, chanting aloud, "I don't believe it, I don't believe it," over and over again. "I don't believe I'm on the plane. I don't believe I've escaped."

I looked in my handbag for the passport, wanting to see the exit stamp. If it was there, maybe it was true.

Was it really there? Yes, there it was. I had proof. I was really out.

Then a new panic hit.

Where was the little letter from Alanya?

Hunting all over, I couldn't find it. It was gone and I was frightened, again, panicked. What had happened to it?

I had to remind myself, Who cares? I don't need it anymore. The passport control people must have taken it.

Everything is a mystery, I said. Everything has been a mystery, I corrected myself. Disbelief had accompanied detention, arrest, imprisonment. It was associated with bail. Unprepared for so much that had happened, how could I believe I was really out?

A few hours later a pilot announcement informed us the plane had begun its descent into Munich. Believing and not believing at the same time, I got ready, as if it were true. Everyone was obliged to debark for customs, and the stewardess tagged our seats, reserving them for the short continuing flight to Frankfurt.

When the plane had halted, engines stopped, and door opened, I was very excited but at the same time, very apprehensive. I had the most terrible feeling I'd been tricked: that this was not Munich at all, that I would get off the plane only to find myself back on Turkish soil.

But the exit from the door led onto one of those moving corridor sleeves, which Turkey seemed to lack, and when I reached the end of it, what I saw reassured me. There it was, spick-and-span, clean spaces, and a sign in German—*Ausgang*—perhaps the most beautiful word I'd seen in my life.

Now, for the first time in almost two months, I *did* feel safe.

I wanted to get down and kiss the damned floor, to kiss the clean and shining walls. Self-consciousness alone prevented it.

And the irony of these feelings didn't escape me. To feel such peace, such security and absolute safety in Germany, seemed a cruel joke on a Jew.

Going through customs was mindless and instantaneous: we passed through a gate saying "NOTHING TO DECLARE" and took seats in a clean corridor awaiting the call to reboard. Full of elation, I was empty of energy. Out of peril, ready to lay down the burdens of too long and too hard a vigil, I listened to announcements flowing from a crystal-clear-sounding loudspeaker, thinking that German, guttural and heavy, was the most beautiful language in the world.

An hour later I was in Frankfurt, and the flight crew, standing at the door when I debarked, smiled and said they hoped we'd had a good flight. Bursting with exaltation, I responded,

"It's been the most wonderful flight I've ever taken," and didn't give a damn what they thought may have prompted so effusive a farewell.

Retrieving my suitcase, I took care of the only important thing that remained undone. I phoned home. Collect. To Jim.

"Gene," he said in a voice as awed and excited as mine, "where *are* you? The operator said the call was collect from Frankfurt."

"I'm in Germany," I wept, "in Germany! In Frankfurt! I'm on my way home! I'm safe! I'm free!"

"My God, how'd you get out?"

"My God, for sure. I'll tell you everything when you pick me up at the airport. *Inshallah*," I said.

God had helped me this far. I thought it was fair to assume He'd see me the rest of the way home.

ACKNOWLEDGMENTS

Most of the people in my story are presented exactly as I knew them. Where it seemed necessary, I've changed some names and otherwise altered identifying information to shield those who need protection. Only a few characters are fictional constructs based upon real people who said the words, performed the acts, and collectively participated in the events described.

In Turkey
Atilla Akat, my attorney and friend, whose energy, skill, and love supported me throughout the ordeal.

Makbule Sevil, secretary, U.S. consulate, Izmir, whose interest in my plight far exceeded her duties.

Lutfi, Neshe, Sara, and Eminay, whose understanding and help sustained me during the bewildering imprisonment.

Nancy Rust, to whom I am deeply in debt.

Bob Ludan, whose knowledge, efforts, and gentle strength guided me in my darkest hours.

Aaron Emile, a man of compassion and courage.

Fr. Eugene O. Nec, then major, now lieutenant colonel, who kept my backbone ramrod straight and never gave up on me even when I was ready to give up on myself.

Many others, who know who they are and have been acknowledged in more direct ways.

In the United States
James W. Schroeder, attorney-at-law, without whose help I might still be in Buja Prison.

Sylvan Marshall, attorney-at-law, for his counsel, advice, and warm understanding.

Paul Attaguile, my personal attorney and friend, and his associate, Constantine Falardi, who together "didn't practice any law for the month of October," 1983, because they were working to rescue me.

Dr. Patricia Singleton, who, by helping me work through the aftereffects of the trauma, restored me to my former self.

The members of my immediate family, the Hirshhorns, and my extended family, the LePeres, who believed in me and put aside their own lives until I was safely home.

All the many friends and friends of friends who not only worried while I was away but who twisted every available arm to obtain help for my release, who remained patient during my recovery, and put up with my distractions during the writing of this book.

EPILOGUE

The events affecting my life that have taken place since November 16, 1983, have been numerous and so convoluted as to constitute material for another book. One which will never be written.

Yet, among my readers there should be many who would like to know something about my friends in Turkey and at home who stood by, agonized over my plight, and tried their best to help. And it would be less than fair not to report the resolution of the charges against me, without which there would have been no book at all.

June 11, 1984, after seven additional trials that occurred in November and December, 1983, and January, March, April, and May, 1984, the Izmir court adjudged me innocent of all charges.

Double jeopardy is not possible under the American judicial system: appeal in the United States is reserved for those who have been found guilty. In Turkey, it is possible to have been adjudged innocent but live under the threat of an appeal for a period of seven days following the verdict.

Within three days of the June verdict, the Turkish Ministry of Tourism and Cultural Affairs filed a pro forma appeal to the supreme court in Ankara seeking a reversal of the Izmir court's decision.

Eight months later, I received the following letter from Atilla Akat, which I quote in its entirety:

Dear Gene,
    Today I am writing you this letter to give you the

good news. The file has returned from the Supreme
Court and the decision of the Court has been
approved for what you call, maybe the correct word
is upheld.

On Monday I'll go to the Court and get the papers
informing the entrances to Turkey that the decision
about you can be changed and that you may enter
and go out of Turkey whenever you want.

So the whole story has ended. You are free as a
bird and can fly to Turkey whenever you want.

Dear Gene, I hope our friendship will continue and
hope to see you again.

I am writing the letter in a hurry so please excuse
me for the mistakes I make.

Güldal and Nine will also be happy when I'll give
the news to them in the evening. I also made a call to
Makbule, American Consulate. She was happy too.

Nine, Güldal and I send you our congratulations
and kisses and regards to all your family.

With love,
A. Akat

After arriving home, I went through a long and difficult
period of recovery from post-traumatic shock disorder. The
symptoms from which I suffered were chronic sleeplessness,
nightmares, severe depression, memory interference, frequent
and too-easy crying, and a constant daytime reliving of the
events that had shocked and humiliated me in Turkey, preventing me from reentering a normal life. Unable to socialize or to
work, I was described by my friends and family as remote and
fearful. Nearly eight months passed before I had fully recovered
both physical strength and inner confidence.

Because my thoughts were still focused in Turkey, through
letters I kept in close touch with many of the characters the
reader has come to know through the book. As of the time of this
writing:

Nancy Rust is still living in the same apartment in Izmir
with her husband. She writes that she looks forward to remaining there for another five years, making yearly trips to England.
She loves her life in Turkey.

Bob Ludan, together with his wife, Sharon, also in the foreign service, completed his duty in Izmir in the summer of 1984. The Ludans are living in the Washington, D.C., area, preparing for their next assignment.

Gene Nee, after completing a one-year assignment at an air force base in Texas, retired from military service with the rank of lieutenant colonel and has accepted an assignment for the Catholic Church in England.

Aaron Emile, unharmed by his generous act in my behalf, still lives in New Orleans and commutes to Turkey, Europe, and New York. He never failed to call when he was in New York but our contacts have diminished since I moved to Los Angeles in May 1987.

Daniel de Souza, my gaunt, courageous fellow prisoner, after serving thirteen years in the Turkish penal system, was released from Buca prison in May 1987, not as a result of England's long-delayed but much welcomed entry into a treaty agreement with Turkey for the exchange of prisoners, but as a result of a general amnesty granted by the Turkish government for prisoners. He is living with his father in the German Democratic Republic in East Berlin.

Neshe has completed her sentence and returned to her family in Izmir. It grieves me that I've had no word of the other women who befriended me in prison, most of whom are able to write neither Turkish nor English and, by now, may have been released home or transferred to other prisons in Turkey.

Atilla Akat is a modern success story. In early 1985 she ran for and was elected to a two-year term as district chairman (Izmir) of one of the leading political parties of Turkey. In the thousand or more year history of her country, Atilla is the first woman to have attained this position by election. This now-famous woman has recently completed her first visit to the United States, where she was my guest for five weeks.

Richard LePere remains a successful magazine consultant living in Washington, D.C., with his wife, Carol, and their (now) two children, Alex and Dana.

Jim LePere is managing his real estate interests and remains my best friend and adviser. We are talking about traveling to Turkey to attend the oft-delayed wedding of Attilla's daughter, Guldal.

My sister Naomi and brother Gordon are well; Robin and her husband returned to their home in a suburb of Boston from Germany in September 1984, where they continue to reside.

Edwin Gant practices law in New York City.

A final note: In early November 1986, the U.S. State Department issued an advisory statement relevant to the subject of this book, entitled, TRAVEL ADVISORY—TURKEY—CAUTION, in which travelers to that country are advised "to cooperate with travel restrictions or other security measures imposed by Turkish authorities" with respect to certain southeastern provinces of the country where martial law remains in effect due to "sporadic attacks by separatists."

In a long-overdue caution that also suggests a change in the legal availability of antiquities for export, the bulletin goes on to say:

UNAUTHORIZED PURCHASE OR REMOVAL FROM TURKEY OF ANTIQUITIES OR OTHER IMPORTANT CULTURAL ARTIFACTS IS STRICTLY FORBIDDEN. VIOLATION OF THIS LAW MAY RESULT IN IMPRISONMENT.

TRAVELERS WHO WISH TO PURCHASE SUCH ITEMS SHOULD ALWAYS OBTAIN FROM THE SELLER A RECEIPT AND THE OFFICIAL MUSEUM EXPORT CERTIFICATE REQUIRED BY LAW.

November 1987

ABOUT THE MAKING OF THIS BOOK

The text of *Never Pass This Way
Again* was set in Janson by
ComCom, a division of The
Haddon Craftsmen, of Allentown,
Pennsylvania. The book was
printed and bound by R.R.
Donnelley, Harrisonburg,
Virginia division. The typography
and binding were designed by
Tom Suzuki of Falls Church,
Virginia.